Teaching Music with Technology

G-5275

Teaching Music with Technology

2nd Edition

Thomas E. Rudolph

GIA Publications, Inc.

Chicago

For Tiiu, Liia, Gusten, and Kalev

G-5275
Copyright © 2004
GIA Publications, Inc.
7404 S. Mason Ave., Chicago, IL 60638
www.giamusic.com

Book design and layout: Robert Sacha
Cover design: Yolanda Durán

ISBN: 1-57999-313-3

Table of Contents

Foreword by Don Muro

The first edition of *Teaching Music with Technology* was published eight years ago. Since then technology has become an integral part of the educational process at every level. Computer literacy, once considered an enrichment option, is now part of virtually every school curriculum; it is also a required skill in an ever-increasing number of occupations.

The impact of technology on music and music education in the past 15 years is without precedent. Never in the history of music education have there been such powerful and interactive tools for classroom teaching and performance. The selection and the appropriate use of these tools, however, can be overwhelming—unless one has this book.

Tom Rudolph once again has managed to break down a complex subject into a series of chapters covering virtually every aspect of technology and its application to music education. *Teaching Music with Technology* is a resource book, a method book, and a how-to book all in one. The second edition has been expanded and updated to include the most recent developments in hardware, software, and pedagogy. New material has been added to every chapter, and a new chapter on digital audio has been included. In addition, the book has been re-organized for easier reading and comprehension.

The most notable addition to the book is the inclusion of a CD-ROM that features activities, student assignments and projects, lesson plans, and an extensive list of links to web sites for free software, demo programs, and up-to-date technical information. These features, combined with an expanded list of review questions for every chapter, should guarantee the book's status as a required text for undergraduate or graduate courses dealing with technology in music education.

Tom Rudolph's gifts as a technologist and master teacher have continued to develop during the past six years. He brings the fruits of his most recent classroom experience and research to this edition. I hope that everyone involved in music education, from seasoned administrators to music education majors, has the opportunity to read and to benefit from this important book.

Acknowledgments

The writing of the 2nd edition of *Teaching Music With Technology* was greatly enhanced by the collaboration and efforts of many people.

First and foremost, I thank my copy editor, Tiiu Lutter, for helping me to focus my thoughts and for her uncanny ability to re-write my sometimes awkward sentences and paragraphs into ones that make sense.

To Stefani Langol for the countless consultations about the 2nd edition and for creating the graphics and layout for the CD-ROM. She did a terrific job putting the CD-ROM materials into a sleek, neat package. The many conferences and phone conversations about the book and CD-ROM had a huge positive impact.

To Ken Peters for contributing many comments and suggestions for the chapters and for assisting with the entering of initial edits. His many suggestions helped tremendously, especially with the new chapters for the 2nd edition.

To Dr. Sam Reese for improving the end-of-chapter questions, activities, lesson plans, and tutorials. I appreciate his many suggestions for improving this valuable section of the book and for sharing your own activities and web sites.

To Justyn Harkin, my editor at GIA. You helped the production of the book in many ways. Your attention to detail really made a difference.

To Alec Harris, President at GIA, I am grateful to you for your patience and unconditional support as I had the unnerving tendency to continually miss my projected deadlines for the 2nd edition. Your support of me and this project is most appreciated.

Additional thanks to my friends and colleagues who contributed ideas, comments, and inspiration including Debra Barbre, John Dunphy, Steven Estrella, Michael Fein, Tim Lautzenheiser, Vince Leonard, Lorry Lutter,

David Mash, Dennis Mauricio, Mike Moniz, Don Muro, Barton Polot, Ken Raessler, Rocky Reuter, Floyd Richmond, and Lee Whitmore.

I would also like to thank the companies who contributed materials for the CD-ROM including SoundTree, Roland Corporation, Yamaha Corporation, Carl-Fisher, Inc., J.D. Wall Publishing, MENC The National Association for Music Education, and TI:ME, Technology Institute for Music Educators.

—Thomas E. Rudolph
Email: terudolph@aol.com

Introduction

In the great words of Victor Hugo, *"An invasion of armies can be resisted but not an idea whose time has come."* Even though these words were written over 185 years ago, they accurately describe the impact that technology has had on music in general and music education in particular.

This book has been written with two audiences in mind: music teachers and college music education majors. The text can be used as a resource for ideas and to better understand today's technology. The concepts and strategies presented have come about as part of my experience using technology with my students since 1982 (when MIDI was just a women's dress!) and training several thousand music teachers in week-long summer workshops at colleges and universities throughout the country.

It is not my intention to present technology as a panacea for music education. However, technology provides valuable tools or "musical crayons" for both students and teachers. You will find 199 teaching strategies for integrating technology in music education addressing every level, elementary through college. Each strategy is numbered and displayed in a box, and then detailed in the text. In as many places as possible, graphic examples are also included. I have also cited products and publishers. This was done at the request of many teachers with whom I have worked as they almost always request specific recommendations of software and hardware. However, this is not to say that if a product is not listed in this text it is not a good one. On the contrary, space would not permit an exhaustive list of products and since technology is changing rapidly, new products come to market all the time. Try to read the book with an eye for applications and how technology can be used to improve your music education curriculum.

I also recognize that music educators have a wide range of experiences with technology. If you have very little experience using technology, I recommend reading the chapters in order, since concepts and technical terms are presented in a sequential manner. However, if you have experience with technology, peruse the book reading each boxed teaching strategy. When you come to one that is not familiar to you, read that section.

The 2nd Edition

In the second edition of *Teaching Music With Technology*, every chapter has been completely rewritten and updated to reflect the advancements in software and hardware since the book's first printing in 1996. The significant new changes of this edition include a chapter on digital audio, multimedia and Internet applications, and frequent reference to on-line materials. In addition, you will find a CD-ROM on the back cover of the book. On this CD-ROM are the expanded and updated end-of-chapter questions, activities, lesson plans, web activities, and tutorials. So after you read about a particular concept or application, you can go to the CD-ROM to further explore it.

It is my hope that this book and companion CD-ROM will help you better understand technology and its role in music education and how it can be used to motivate and educate your students. Please contact me with your reactions and suggestions. You can email me at terudolph@aol.com.

Chapter 1

Technology in Music Education: An Overview

Technology is everywhere in our culture. The word technology applies to and describes a wide variety of devices and applications in music and music education. By general definition, technology is anything that uses science to achieve a desired result. Technology has assisted performers and music educators for centuries. The organ, harpsichord, piano, and phonograph are all examples of technologies that were as amazing to those who originally used them as computers are to us today. The trumpet was played without valves throughout the Baroque era. In the Romantic period, the valve was incorporated into the design of the trumpet and this technology revolutionized the instrument. Likewise, the invention of the silicon chip and computer microprocessor in the late twentieth century have had as great of an impact on music and music education.

Technology

The term technology, as it will be used throughout this text, refers to the most recently invented state-of-the-art devices such as computers, electronic keyboards, CDs, CD-ROMs, and DVDs. Other devices such as the overhead projector, phonograph record player, cassette recorder, and filmstrip projector are no longer considered cutting edge. In the last 20 years many tools have become available to music educators that can significantly enhance student learning. These devices include computers and electronic keyboards plus all the high-tech equipment listed above. It is important for music educators to be aware of the full capabilities of these tools that can help students to better perform, create, and understand music.

Types of Technological Devices

Technological devices are either passive or interactive. A passive device merely plays music or displays information. Passive devices include the phonograph record player, cassette tape deck, television, video cassette player, DVD player, and overhead projector. With passive devices, the student perceives the material but there is no interaction with the device or medium. For example, a class listening to a recording of a musical composition is taking part in a passive exercise. Tape and CD players are passive devices—they merely play an audio recording of a piece of music. If the goal is simply to play a musical recording, then a CD player is a fine choice. Certainly, music lessons and classes can be enhanced with the use of passive devices such as videos of performances, instrument demonstrations, and the like.

Devices that engage the user directly are referred to as interactive. Playing a video game and using a computer are interactive activities. We know from experience and years of educational research that interactive learning is much more effective than passive learning.[1] Technology offers many forms of interactive learning. When the term technology is used in this text, it will be in reference to devices such as the computer and other computer controlled interactive instruments.

Implications of Technology

In the past 100 years, technology has had a huge impact on music in general and music education in particular. Neil Gershenfeld, in his book *When Things Start to Think*, states:

> It used to be that people played music, because that was the only way to hear it. When mass media came along, society split into a small number of people paid to be artistically creative and a much larger number that passively consumes their output. Reducing the effort to learn to play an

instrument… points to the possibility that far more people will be able to creatively express themselves. Improving the technology for making music can help engage instead of insulate people.[2]

This suggests that new technology has the potential to engage students in making music in more and varied ways. Therefore, technology, when used appropriately, can be used to enhance the musical experience.

Technology in Education

Since the time of John Dewey, educational researchers have been advocating active participation as a key ingredient of effective learning. Music teachers have embraced the philosophy of "learning by doing" for decades. Students can use technology to compose, perform, and learn music. Technology provides ideal media for music education.

Technology is having a broad impact on education. In 1983 the Carnegie Foundation published *A Nation at Risk*. This publication cited that changes must be made in our approach to education. One of the suggestions the Carnegie Foundation offered was to embrace technology.[3] Then, in 1994, music became part of the Government sponsored Goals 2000: Educate America Act. As part of this act the National Standards for the Arts were developed.[4] With the development of national standards, a high priority was placed on using technology in all subject areas.

> ### Teaching Strategy 1
> Use technology to implement the National Standards for the Arts as defined by MENC. Technology can be used to enhance all nine music standards.

Technology can be used to enhance the national standards. This is supported by a study that found that the majority of all American teenagers are comfortable using a range of technological devices, including computers, compact disc players, fax machines, and cell phones.[5]

One thing has been constant over the past ten years: technology continues to improve and gain popularity at all levels. School districts have been integrating computers into the curriculum beginning at the elementary level and technology is being supported in many subject areas.[6] If used appropriately technology can "...extend the reach of both the art form and that of the learner."[7]

Technology and Music Education

The place and purpose of technology in music education must be found before beginning to properly apply the technology. Simply making technology available is not enough.

> For the arts, technology thus offers means to accomplish artistic, scholarly, production, and performance goals. But the mere availability of technology cannot ensure a specific artistic result: the pencil in a student's hand ensures neither drawing or competency nor a competent drawing. [8]

David Mash, Vice President for Information Technology at Berklee College of Music, states that technology has created new opportunities in the field of music and that we, as music educators, must prepare students to interact with and utilize these tools.[9] Chamberlin, Clark, and Svengalis, in their article, "Success with Keyboards in the Middle School" state that if "music is to stay a viable part of the school curriculum and meet the needs of students, it must combine technology with traditional skills as other subjects are doing."[10] Teachers have found that technology can enhance cross curriculum teaching, hands-on learning, cooperative learning, independent study, and higher level thinking skills as well as provide an excellent assessment tool.

Research has been conducted on the effects of technology on music learning. Yamaha Corporation conducted research relating to music education and the use of technology. The result of the study included several key findings resulting from successful use of the technology in music education. These include:

- Student attitudes toward classroom music are not only positively enhanced, but levels of interest and motivation are sustained across multiple academic years.
- Long and short term music achievement, as evidenced in standardized tests, is significantly increased when compared to existing approaches of classroom music.
- Students who received hands-on instruction had greater comprehension of musical concepts compared with students taught with traditional approaches and methods.
- Music instruction provided through a technology assisted program contributes to a sense of professional development and personal growth on the part of the music educators.
- Additional outcomes of the study showed that technology improved student concentration, maximized time on-task, developed and enhanced cooperative learning, and fostered higher level thinking skills. Classroom teachers and building administrators noted that these aspects carried over to learning in non-music classrooms.[11]

I have found similar results to those stated above with the integration of technology both through my teaching and my interactions with many music educators over the past 15 years. At Haverford Middle School we use a lab of electronic keyboards for general music and our middle school students have shown a significant increase in their motivation and enthusiasm toward general music class. Furthermore, electronic instruments and computers provide a tool for creativity at all levels. Music teachers throughout the country report similar findings.[12]

Technology Applications: Tutor, Tool, Tutee

There are three ways to use interactive technology in education: tutor, tool, and tutee.[13] Each of the three modes offers a wide range of possibilities. Incorporating technology into the music curriculum can create exciting and productive classes, lessons, and outcomes.

Education experts feel that technology can be used to support the theories of "Dewey, Montessori, and Piaget that children learn by doing and by thinking about what they do."[14] A combination of the tutor, tool, and tutee applications of technology can be tremendous teaching and administrative tools for music education.

In the tutor mode, the device (usually a computer) presents information to the student in an interactive manner. First, the software is programmed by an expert. The lesson or information is then delivered by the computer. The difference between a computer and a video tape is that the computer can interact with the user. The student enters a correct or incorrect answer and the computer gives appropriate feedback. The majority of music education applications lie in this area.

Technology also has many functions as a music education **tool**. The tool role includes a computer using technology to record, play back, and/or print music and as an electronic typewriter to assist with administrative duties.

The tutee, or learner, mode offers powerful capabilities. Here the user programs a computer with an authoring language. Applications in the tutee mode include designing new computer software and creating multimedia presentations and projects.

The Crayons of Music Education

There are essentially two types of students in our music programs: performers and consumers. The performers are students who choose to participate in chorus, band, orchestra, and other related performing organizations. They perform and are active participants in the music program. We also have the consumers—our general music students.[15] Technology can be used to benefit every music student, both the performers and consumers. Computers and electronic instruments can be used to enhance performance and classroom music experiences for every age student.

Music technology can be compared to the art supplies used in art education. Undoubtedly, art education was enhanced when materials such as crayons, proper papers, and modeling clay became available. Computers and electronic keyboards can be viewed as modeling clay, construction paper, and crayons for music. Technology allows students of all abilities and ages to compose, perform, and create music in new and exciting ways.

Computers and computer-controlled instruments are crayons for music class. Just as art students create successfully using crayons and other creative tools, so, too, all can music students create, compose, and perform music with the aid of technology.

Technology and the Music Curriculum

The best way to select the ideal use for technology is to first focus on the curricular goals and desired educational outcomes and then select the materials or devices that will best accomplish the stated goals. There are two general categories of goals for music curricula at all levels: skills and knowledge. Skills refers to the ability to play musical instruments, sing, create, and perform music. Knowledge refers to understanding and comprehending information about music such as a composer's biographical information, music theory concepts, and so forth.

Teaching Strategy 2

Establish the goals of the music curriculum. Then ask how technology can best serve the desired outcomes.

The National Standards for the Arts as developed by MENC contain nine distinct areas. These are:

1. Singing, alone and with others, a varied repertoire of music.
2. Performing on instruments, alone and with others, a varied repertoire of music.
3. Improvising melodies, harmonies, and accompaniments.
4. Composing and arranging music within specified guidelines.
5. Reading and notating music.
6. Listening to, analyzing, and describing music.
7. Evaluating music and music performances.
8. Understanding relationships between music, the other arts, and disciplines outside the arts.
9. Understanding music in relation to history and culture.

Technology can serve virtually all of the above areas to enhance learning. Specific applications will be addressed throughout the chapters that follow. State of the art technology is a complex subject and has many different levels of application. It is helpful to organize the various applications into seven distinct areas.

The Seven Areas of Music Technology

The Technology Institute for Music Educators, or TI:ME, has divided technology into seven areas. They are:

1. Electronic instruments
2. Music notation software
3. MIDI/digital audio sequencing
4. Instructional software
5. Telecommunications and the Internet
6. Multimedia and digital media
7. Information processing and lab management

> **Teaching Strategy 3**
> Review the seven areas of music technology when searching for ways to find unique applications of music technology.

Each of the seven areas above have been grouped into either teacher or student applications. For example, with regard to electronic instruments, the text states:

> Music teachers need to know how MIDI connections are made among instruments, how to use MIDI in the classroom, and how to connect MIDI instruments with computers. They need to understand how to create layered and split keyboard sounds for performances. They also need to be able to choose and edit sounds from stored libraries and create sounds using an electronic instrument.
>
> Students can use electronic instruments as musical crayons creating simple to complex musical pieces while gaming dexterity and technique. They can learn musical processes with electronic keyboards and have fun at the same time.

Electronic instruments can also be used in performance to enhance traditional and electronic-acoustic ensembles."[16]

Thinking of technology in reference to student and teacher needs can help in identifying the most appropriate applications. In the chapters that follow, many applications of technology will be visited with specific reference to student and teacher application

NETS Standards
(National Education Technology Standards)

In addition to the MENC National Standards for Music Education, there are also the National Education Technology Standards (NETS). These standards were developed by the International Society for Technology in Education (ISTE, www.iste.org) and can be applied to any and all subject areas. The ISTE organization states that our educational system has a responsibility to produce technology-capable students. Six areas of technology standards (NETS) were created to address this goal.

The NETS standards for students are divided across these six broad categories. Standards within each category are to be introduced, reinforced, and mastered by students. Teachers can use these standards and profiles as guidelines for planning technology-based activities in which students achieve success in learning, communication, and life skills. The six NETS standards are:

1. Basic operations and concepts
   a. Students demonstrate a sound understanding of the nature and operation of technology systems.
   b. Students are proficient in the use of technology.

2. Social, ethical, and human issues
   a. Students understand the ethical, cultural, and societal issues related to technology.
   b. Students practice responsible use of technology systems, information, and software.

   c. Students develop positive attitudes toward technology use that support lifelong learning, collaboration, personal pursuits, and productivity.

3. Technology productivity tools
   a. Students use technology tools to enhance learning, increase productivity, and promote creativity.
   b. Students use productivity tools to collaborate in constructing technology-enhanced models, prepare publications, and produce other creative works.

4. Technology communications tools
   a. Students use telecommunications to collaborate, publish, and interact with peers, experts, and other audiences.
   b. Students use a variety of media and formats to communicate information and ideas effectively to multiple audiences.

5. Technology research tools
   a. Students use technology to locate, evaluate, and collect information from a variety of sources.
   b. Students use technology tools to process data and report results.
   c. Students evaluate and select new information resources and technological innovations based on the appropriateness for specific tasks.

6. Technology problem-solving and decision-making tools
   a. Students use technology resources for solving problems and making informed decisions.
   b. Students employ technology in the development of strategies for solving problems in the real world.

For more information, visit the NETS web site at http://cnets.iste.org/.

Music educators can make connections between the use of technology in the music curriculum and the National Education Technology Standards. By showing the connection to the NETS standards, music teachers can build support with administrators to support the use and purchase of technology in the music classroom. In the chapters that follow, many of the music technology activities support the NETS standards.

Integrating Technology into the Curriculum

A sound approach to integrating technology into the curriculum is by first identifying an educational goal or selecting one of the National Standards. Then choose the appropriate technology to accomplish the goal. After reading the chapters that follow, this process will become simple. Technology must not be the end in itself, but rather a means to an end. Teachers can use technology to enhance the national standards in many ways.[17]

Although there is some crossover in each of the nine areas, they are basically standards of skills or knowledge areas. Technology can be used to enhance all the skills and knowledge areas of the nine standards. For example, electronic keyboards make exceptional classroom and ensemble instruments, and computers can be used to create, compose, and perform music—making them excellent tools to enhance the skills/performance areas of music education.

Once the skills and knowledge based goals are in place using the National Standards as a guideline, technological applications can be selected to help students to achieve these goals. For example, if the music curriculum identifies specific knowledge areas as presented in Standards 6-9, technology can be used to help present, reinforce, and test this information. If, perhaps, it is determined that students will be able to perform, create, and improvise music, as mentioned in Standards 1-5, technology can be incorporated to help realize these goals as well. Specific examples of how to accomplish this end will be introduced in the chapters that follow.

Not a Panacea

Technology is not a panacea for music education. It will not solve all of the existing problems, and, as with any new educational tool, it will introduce some problems of its own. Technology works best when it is perceived as an enhancement or teaching device rather than the driving force of an entire music curriculum.

The emphasis of music education is not changing with technology. A teacher who attended one of my summer workshops asked if now she had to write a computer curriculum. My response was an emphatic, "No!" Rather, use technology to enhance the existing performance and classroom curriculum and to provide new technology-based programs that will advance curricular goals. Some subject areas that were not practical using traditional means, such as composition, can be now offered with the aid of technology.

The main benefit of using technology is that it offers an enticement to attract students to engage in the arts. "In the end, however, the use of technology in the arts instruction is meaningful only to the degree that it contributes to competence, and the contribution comes through instruction and study"[18] Music teachers must find ways to integrate technology so that it is not the end in itself.

Dr. Peter Webster has researched the current state of music technology and in his summary of research on music education states:

> So, is music technology effective and is it worth the trouble? On balance and on a very basic level, the answer to this question is yes. Does music technology hold the key for solving all our music teaching problems? Of course not. Are there abuses in its use? Absolutely. Does it always improve learning? No, much depends on the context—especially the teacher and its use instructionally. Is it worth the trouble to keep studying its role in music teaching and learning? Unconditionally, yes.[19]

Charles Argersinger agrees that technology can be a fantastic asset in the creation of music. However, he also warns that technology can create the illusion of sophistication without nuance. Argersinger feels we must emphasize the use of technology towards the creation of better work.[20] This is good advice. We, as music educators, must embrace technology and constantly strive to tie it to the outcomes or goals of our curriculum.

Summary

Technology is an effective and exciting way to augment and supplement the music curriculum. Music teachers are compelled to find ways to include technology in the classroom, instrumental, and choral curricula. The chapters that follow will explore many ideas and ways to include technology in the music curriculum in a positive, productive manner.

Review Questions

1. Define technology and give several historical examples of technology making a positive impact on music.

2. Give two or more examples of passive and interactive learning devices that may be useful for learning activities. Examples include computers, MP3 players, portable word processors, metronomes, tuners, and other similar devices. List the advantages of using an interactive device over a passive oneand give one example of how each device can be used for learning.

3. Research has been conducted investigating the benefits technology offers to music education. What benefits have been found?

4. Technology is not a panacea for music education. What does the research say about the effect of technology in music education?

5. What problems might teachers and students face when trying to use technology?

6. List all technology items that are found in the current music classroom: anything that at one time was considered state-of the-art technology, for example, the piano was high technology at one time.

7. List one or more personal experiences where you have benefited from using technology.

8. What are the nine National Standards for Music Education?

9. What are the seven areas of music technology as defined by TI:ME?

10. What are the six National Educational Technology Standards (NETS) for students?

11. What are the three ways that technology can be used in music education? Give one or more examples of each.

12. Describe the two categories of students in music education: consumers and performers. Give one example of how technology can be used for learning by each category.

13. Technology can be thought of as the crayons for music education. Explain this concept.

14. How has technology affected the majority of people over the years?

CD-ROM Activities

- Project 1.1 Explore the Chapter 1 web links: Write a short review of each site you visit.
- Project 1.2 Conduct an email interview of a music educator who uses technology in their teaching. Write a summary of the interview and how technology is used to enhance student learning.
- Project 1.2 Review the MENC National Standards and list ways where technology could be used to enhance the standards.
- Project 1.3 Reflect on the concerns that musicians have with contemporary technologies, such as performers losing work due of electronic instruments or the ease with which people can make and distribute illegal copies of musicians' recordings.

Reference

Argersinger, Charles. (1993). Side-Effects of Technology on Music and Musicians. *Jazz Educators Journal*. October.

Bauer, William (2002). *Research in Music Technology: Take Action*. The TI:MES, Newsletter. Technology Institute for Music Educators. October. Vol. 4. No. 1.

Booty, Charles, G. ed. (1990). *TIPS Technology for Music Educators*. Music Educators National Conference. Reston, VA.

Chamberlin, et al (1993) Success with keyboards in middle school. *Music Educators Journal*. May. Pp. 31-35.

Colwell, R. and Richardson, C. (2002). The New Handbook of Research on Music Teaching and Learning. Oxford University Press. New York, N.Y.

Dunn, R. (1979). Learning - A Matter of Style. *Educational Leadership*. 36(6). 430-432.

Facts About Technology Users (1994). *New Ways in Music Education*, Spring, 1994. Yamaha Corporation of America, Grand Rapids, MI.

Gershenfeld, Neil. (1999). *When Things Start to Think*. Henry Holt and Company, Inc. New York, N.Y.

Hasenstab and Flaherty (1991). *Teaching Through Learning Channels*. Performance Learning Systems, Inc. Nevada City, California.

Hess, G. (1999). The computer literacy of prospective music students: A survey. In S. Lipscomb (Ed.), *Sixth International Conference on Technological Directions in Music Learning* (pp. 96-99). San Antonio, TX: IMR Press.

Idea Bank (1986). Idea Bank: Does CAI really work?. *Music Educators Journal*, December.

Lockard, James et al. (1990). *Microcomputers for Educators*. Harper Collins Publishers.

Mash, David (1991). *Computers and The Music Educator*. Digidesign, Inc. Menlo Park, CA.

MENC (1999). *Opportunity to learn standards for music technology*. Reston, VA: Author.

Moore, Brian. (1991) Technology - A Resource Providing New Ways for Music Educators. *New Ways in Music Education*, Fall, 1991. Yamaha Corporation of America, Grand Rapids, MI.

National Standards for Arts Education. (1994) *Music Educators National Conference*, Reston, VA.

Nemiroff, J. (1988), Integrating computer into a reading readiness curriculum for preschoolers through teacher training and computer-based instruction. (ERIC Document Reproduction Service No. ED 295 593).

Raessler, Kenneth (2003). *Aspiring to Excel*. GIA Publications, Inc. Chicago, Il.

Reese, S., & Davis, A. (1998). The systems approach to music technology. *Music Educators Journal*, 85(1), 24-28.

Reese, S. and Rimington, J. (2000). Music technology in Illinois public schools. *Update: Applications of Research in Music Education*, 18 (2), 27-32.

Rudolph, Thomas E. (1984). *Music and The Apple II*. Unsinn Publications, Drexel Hill, PA.

Rudolph, Thomas E. (1994). Electronic Keyboards in the General Music Classroom. *Pennsylvania Music Educator News*. March.

Rudolph, T.; Richmond, F.; Mash. D.; and Williams D. (2002) *Technology Strategies for Music Education*. Hal Leonard Publishing Corp. Second Edition. Milwaukee, WI

Focusing, Advocating and Using Technology. Teaching Music, April , 1994.

Taylor, R., editor. (1980) *The Computer in the School: Tutor, Tool, Tutee.* Teachers College Press. New York.

Walls, K. (1997). Music performance and learning: The impact of digital technology. *Psychomusicology, 16*(1-2), 68-76.

Webster, P. (2002). Historical perspectives on technology and music. *Music Educators Journal, 89* (1), 38-43, 54.

Williams, D., & Webster, P. (1999). *Experiencing music technology* (2nd ed.). Schirmer Books. New York, N.Y.

Chapter 2

Internet Basics

Music Education National Standards: 8
NETS (National Education Technology Standards): 1, 2, 4, 5

The Internet is playing an important roll in virtually every aspect of the music industry and music education. Both students and teachers alike have become frequent users of the technology. This chapter is designed to present an overview of the Internet and the most common terms and functions. Specific Internet applications in the music curriculum will be dealt with in Chapter 11.

Each chapter that follows in this text includes some Internet-based activities. In order to accomplish these activities successfully, the terms and information presented here should be familiar to you. For additional study and reference, helpful books about the Internet are listed at the end of this chapter.

The biggest change in technology that has occurred since the first edition of this book was published in 1996 is the explosion of the Internet in all walks of life and education. Music and music education have seen a tremendous increase in use of the Internet, or "information superhighway," commonly referred to as the Net. The word Internet is an abbreviation for interconnected networks, and there are many internets. The Internet is an internet made up of millions of computers connected around the world. The internet can transfer data over telephone lines, cable connections, and wireless communications. The Internet started as a military project in the 1960s and 1970s.

Network

For our purposes, a network is a group of computers linked together in some manner. This is the "net" portion of the word Internet. Computers in a classroom are often networked, or connected, together so that each computer can share common software. Many school computer labs—and even entire schools—network their computers. In addition to being able to share software, there are several other advantages to networking computers in a computer lab, music classroom, or school building. Particularly advantageous is using the network to communicate between computer users and to facilitate teacher record keeping, grading, and other administrative tasks.

In a network, instead of supplying each computer with its own copy of a piece of software, such as a word processor or music program, one copy is located on a central computer that serves all of the connected computers. The computer that contains the information or software is referred to as the server. Note that a special license must be purchased in order to legally use software in a network. This is usually referred to as a site license and is discussed in Chapter 16.

Also, when computers are connected together messages can be sent back and forth electronically, which is called electronic mail, or, more commonly, email. Teachers can send and receive messages from students who have access to the network. This can make receiving assignments, posting grades, and record keeping much more efficient.

Intranet

An intranet is typically larger than a network and is usually limited to serving an organization or school system. In my school system, teachers can communicate via internal email that is part of the school system's intranet. Software and other applications on our intranet are available exclusively to the schools and classrooms in our district. The restricted access to a school district's computers and software creates an intranet. The main purpose of an intranet is to share company or school district information and computing resources among the members of the staff. An intranet resembles a private, mini-version of the Internet. Users on an intranet also have access to the public Internet.

Internet

A network is a group of connected computers that can be found in a library or a music classroom. An intranet is a series of web pages and other services that are only available to an organization or school system. The Internet is a global, incredibly large collection of networks where millions of users share and exchange information and resources.

A common Internet term is online communication. You are online when you connect your computer to another via any network. A computer, modem, and communication software are required to use the Internet. A modem, short for modulator/demodulator, enables computers to send (modulate) and receive (demodulate) signals. When you purchase a computer it typically comes with communications software and a built-in modem. In other words, today's computers are Internet ready.

Don't get bogged down with the technical side of all of this. Many schools provide help from technical staff to get connected to the Internet. There is also help available from the companies who are in the business of selling connections to the Internet, so don't worry about getting stuck. As a last resort, if you have trouble getting connected, check with one of your students. They'll be able to show you how.

Internet History

The Internet's roots can be traced back to "a Pentagon research project to develop military computers sufficiently robust to survive World War III."[1] This project created a way for computers in other cities and countries to communicate with each other. The Internet connects millions of computers all over the world. The Internet should not be thought of as a singular entity. Rather, it links many different types of computers "some military, some academic, some commercial. These interconnected networks are the very basis of the Internet name."[2]

Gaining Access to the Internet

There are several ways to establish Internet access. The easiest way to get on the Internet is through your school or university. Most schools already have

Internet access and teachers and students can gain access through the school. Getting access at home is another story.

Internet Service Providers

If you don't have access through a university or school, the next best way to get online is to gain access through a commercial Internet service provider, referred to as an ISP. Some of the most popular ISPs are America Online (www.aol.com), Microsoft (www.msn.com), Earthlink (www.earthlink.net), and Juno (www.juno.com). There are many others. Expect to pay a monthly charge for access to the Internet from ISPs. For a list of local Internet access providers, consult your telephone yellow pages under Internet Services.

Connection Speed

When you set-up an Internet connection from home, your connection speed will become an issue. Suffice it to say, faster is better. And, of course, you usually will pay more for a faster connection. The cheapest, and slowest, way to sign on is using a traditional telephone line. Other options are DSL, cable, and wireless connections. All of these options can be researched by looking in your telephone yellow pages under Internet Service.

Internet Offerings and Educational Applications

There are essentially six areas in which non-music teachers music specialists can benefit from Internet. These are:
- Communicating with students, parents and other teachers
- Sending and receiving files to students and other teachers
- Participating in electronic discussion groups
- Conducting research for class assignments and lesson plans
- Searching for music-related products
- Downloading sound, MIDI, and video files for class and rehearsal use

All of these can be used by teachers and students to enhance learning. Exploration of Internet applications in music education is included in Chapter 11.

Electronic mail, or email, refers to sending and receiving messages over a network. Nowadays, just about everyone has an email address. Music teachers can compose and send mail to teachers in other cities, states, and countries who are connected to the Internet. There are many advantages to using email. It is faster than the U.S. Postal Service because electronic messages are sent at the speed of light. As soon as you write your letter, it is delivered—you don't need to look for an envelope or remember to put it in the mailbox. Email saves postage as well as time: an electronic message doesn't require the expense of an envelope or stamp. Of course, if you must pay a connecting charge for email service, a small additional expense may be incurred.

> **Teaching Strategy 4**
> Communicate with your students and parents of your students using email.

Communication with students and parents can be greatly enhanced via email. At back-to-school night and the beginning of the year request the email addresses of parents and students. With your email address book, you can create a group mailing list. Then communication can easily be typed and sent to a large list of addresses at one time.

Electronic Address Format

When you sign up with an online service or ISP, you usually receive an email address. It is also possible to sign up for a free email account from a host of providers including www.hotmail.com, www.yahoo.com, www.msn.com, www.mac.com, and others. Schools and universities also often offer email accounts.

Email is literally sent around the world to computer users. It is directed by the email address. My email address is terudolph@aol.com. Every email address consists of three parts. The first part is the user's name, in my case, I use terudolph as my user name, but I could have selected anything, like baseballtrumpet if I had wished, as long as no one else had used that name first.

The next part of the address is an @ sign and the user's location, called a domain. The email server or domain, is the commercial or educational institution that handles you email. In my case, "aol" stands for America Online. The final part of the name indicates the type of organization that owns the location. Most commonly you will see .com, which stands for "commercial." Educational institutions use the suffix .edu. There are three other suffixes: .gov for "government," .org, for "organization," and .net for "network."

With an email address, you can send and receive mail to other locations throughout the Internet. I find that I use email mail more and more. It is a convenient and expedient way to send and receive messages.

Electronic Mailing Lists and Discussion Groups

There are thousands of special interest groups, referred to as listservs or email lists that people can join. Many were created specifically for educators. These groups communicate with each other via email.

> ### Teaching Strategy 5
> Participate in email discussion groups (also referred to as listservs or mailing lists).

There are specialized groups that deal with every conceivable topic including electronic music, early childhood education, and many others. Teachers can subscribe to these mailing lists and post questions and receive information, all via online communications. You can research mailing lists by doing a web search or by visiting links provided by other sites.

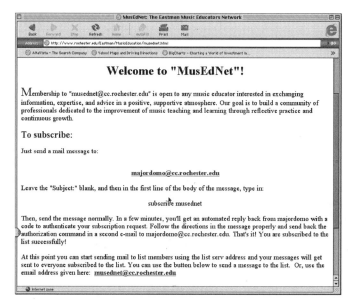

Figure 2.1 Sample music education mailing list
http://www.rochester.edu/Eastman/MusicEducation/musednet.html

Newsgroups

A newsgroup is similar to an email list. With email lists, everyone who subscribes to the list receives copies of emails that are sent to the list by any member. This can quickly fill up your email in-box. Newsgroup messages are housed on a central computer and users who subscribe log-on and read the messages.

> ### Teaching Strategy 6
> Use the Internet to access newsgroups to search for information for lessons and other applications.

The Internet is an excellent way to look for information especially for hard to find materials from various cultures throughout the world. Griswold[3] cites several examples of how the Internet helps his teaching. One unique way is by posting messages for Internet newsgroups. Griswold sent a message to an early music newsgroup (EARLYML@AEARN.BITNET) asking, "Does anybody out there know of works written for three sopranos and two alto recorders." The following morning, he reports, he received seven titles of possible pieces. These responses were from other music teachers who also subscribe to the same newsgroup. Once you gain access to the Internet and locate some newsgroups that interest you, you can read and post messages of your own. A good place to start to search for newsgroups is:

http://www.isd77.k12.mn.us/resources/staffpages/shirk/newsgroups.html.

The World Wide Web

The Interenet refers to the pathway for information. Initially, the primary mode of communication was text. In order to include graphics, sound, and video, the World Wide Web (www) was introduced in the 1990s. It was designed to make communication over the Internet easier and more friendly. The World Wide Web is in its infancy, having been introduced in 1992.

Here's how the World Wide Web functions: someone puts information in a specific location on a big computer, called a server; the information at that location is called a web site. This information can be a combination of text, pictures, graphics, animation, video clips, and sound. To access that information, you need to be connected to the Internet and have special software that allows you to see the information on your computer screen. The software that is used to display the information is called a web browser. There are many web browsers that can access the World Wide Web. The most popular browser is Internet Explorer for Macintosh and Windows. Internet Explorer is a piece of software that displays the contents of any certain location on the Web, referred to as a web page, on the WWW. The big difference between the Web and the Internet is the Web's ability to include graphics, video, and sound in addition to text.

Essential Terms for the World Wide Web

Basic Internet terminology is described in the section that follows. Briefly review these terms and feel free to return to the definitions as needed.

- **Bookmark:** A Netscape Navigator term for capturing the web address, or URL, of a web page so that it can be revisited in the future without typing in the specific URL, such as www.powertolearn.com. Think of it as a handy reference list of your favorite web site addresses. The term for Internet Explorer is "Favorite" (see below).

- **Browser:** Short for web browser. A browser is a software application used to locate and display web pages on a computer monitor. The two most popular web browsers are Netscape Navigator and Microsoft's Internet Explorer. Browsers can support text, graphics, audio, and video.

- **Download:** Refers to information that is copied from one computer to another. Conversely sending a file to someone else's computer is known as uploading a file.

- **Favorite:** An Internet Explorer term for capturing the web address, or URL, of a web page so that it can be revisited in the future without typing in the specific URL, such as www.powertolearn.com. Think of it as a handy reference list of your favorite web site addresses. The term for Netscape Navigator is "Bookmark" (see above).

- **Home page:** The main or front page of a web site. The home page usually serves as an introduction and a main index to the other documents or pages that are part of the entire web site. Note that the browser you use also uses the term home page. This is the page that is displayed when you open your web browser or click the home button.

- **Icon:** A graphic image that is used in place of text. For example, a graphic image of an arrow is used in the browser window to represent backward and forward movement.

- **Internet:** is a global network connecting millions of computers. The Internet has hundreds of millions of users worldwide. More than 100 countries are linked together via the Internet, enabling worldwide information exchange. To access the Internet, you need a way to connect. This can be done via your school's cable connection or via other means including local Internet service providers.

- **Link:** Short for hyperlink, is a line of text or a graphic on a web page that connects to another document or web site. A link is sometimes referred to as a "hot link" because when you click on it, you go to another document. The computer cursor also gives you information about links. When you pass the cursor over a link (without clicking the mouse), the cursor will turn into the picture of a hand with a pointing finger. This icon tells you that if you click the mouse, you will be sent to another location.

- **Protocol:** An agreed-upon format for transmitting information or data. There are a variety of standard protocols from which Internet programmers can choose. Each has advantages and disadvantages. For example, there are specific protocols for email transmission, transferring files between computers, and displaying text, graphics, sound, and video.

- **URL:** An abbreviation for "uniform resource locator." URL refers to the global address of documents and other resources that are located on the World Wide Web. The URL is the address of a web page. For example, the URL, or web address, of the Technology Institute For Music Educators (TI:ME) is http://www.ti-me.org. This URL has several parts. The "http" portion refers to the protocol, in this case, HyperText Transfer Protocol. A protocol is a an agreed-upon format for transmitting data between two devices. The www is an abbreviation for World Wide Web. The portion after the www is the domain name, in this case ti-me.org.

- **Web site:** Usually several different pages of information linked together via a main index page, usually referred to as the home page; look for a link that says home on a web site and it will return you to the home page.

- **Web page:** Refers to a single document. A web site is usually made up of multiple web pages .

- **World Wide Web:** One of several ways that information can be communicated over the Internet. Documents that are supported by the World Wide Web are specially formatted to incorporate text, graphics, audio, and video. Not all Internet computers are part of the World Wide Web. However, it is the most popular and fastest growing part of the Internet.

Music Education Web Sites

Many web pages will be of interest to music educators. Nearly every music organization has a web site. To find a web site, start by contacting the organization or looking up their web address. For example, the MENC, the National Association for Music Education has an informative web page at: www.menc.org. The National Association of Jazz Educators web site address is www.iaje.org. These web pages include a variety of information and links to other services on the Net.

If you are looking for a place to start, consider a site that offers links to a wide variety of music and music education web pages. The K-12 Resources for Music Education web site has a wealth of links to helpful sites for music educators. This site has been accessed more than 1 million times as of this writing. To get there, type the following address into your web browser: http://www.isd77.k12.mn.us/resources/staffpages/shirk/k12.music.html. Every character must be entered exactly for the web page to load. This is why saving web addresses is a good idea!

Figure 2.2: K-12 Resources for Music Educators
http://www.isd77.k12.mn.us/resources/staffpages/shirk/k12.music.html

Another excellent source of music education links is the J.W. Pepper and Son web site. It includes resources for music educators in various categories. This is an excellent place to locate other helpful web sites. Type in this address: www.jwpepper.com/resources.html.

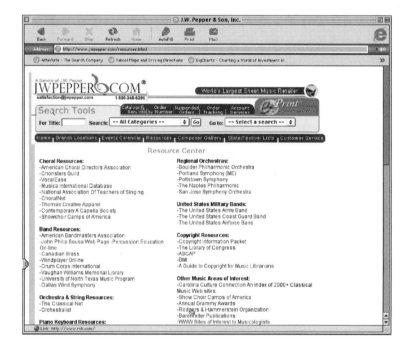

Figure 2.3: J.W. Pepper web page – Resource Center
http://www.jwpepper.com/resources.html

The TI:ME web site (www.ti-me.org) is also extremely helpful. TI:ME is dedicated to helping music educators integrate technology in music teaching. The site has a wealth of information for members and non-members including links, articles, newsletters, and more.

Figure 2.4: The Technology Institute for Music Educators web site

Message Boards

An excellent way to communicate with other music educators is to participate in message boards, sometimes referred to as electronic bulletin boards. A message board is typically hosted on a web site by specific organizations. For example, The MENC calls its message boards "channels" and can be accessed from its home page at www.menc.org. Members can post messages for others and read messages posted by others. You can usually find message boards on the home page of a web site.

Teaching Strategy 7

Use music education-related message boards to communicate with other educators with similar interests.

Some organizations that have message boards for music educators include MENC (The National Association for Music Education) www.menc.org, OAKE (the Association of American Kodaly Educators) www.oake.org, TI:ME (the Technology Institute for Music Educators) www.ti-me.org. Typically, you have to be a member of the organization to post messages, but anyone can read and view the messages. If you have a question that you would like an answer to, message boards can be helpful.

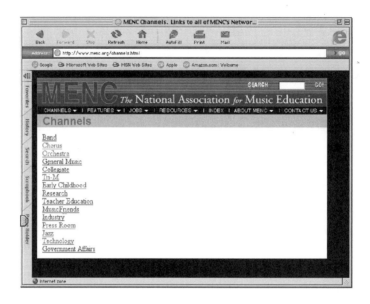

Figure 2.5: MENC Channels Listing (message boards)

Shopping for Products

Many companies and publishers are turning to online avenues to offer their products to consumers. Online music catalogs are becoming popular. It is now possible to search music catalogs online, view printed music, and listen to sound clips.

> **Teaching Strategy 8**
> Select music, shop for products, and find compact discs online.

Once you are connected to the Internet, the options are endless and the benefits significant.

Searching the Web

Due to the vast quantity of information on the Internet, specialized web sites have been developed to assist with searching the Web. When you look for a specific piece of information or a general topic, web-searching tools can be used to find links related to keywords that are entered. Each searching tool, also called a search engine, attempts to provide information that matches your request. There are basically two types of search engines:

- Spiders, or crawlers, that go out and memorize every word on web pages. Google (www.google.com) , alltheweb (www.alltheweb.com), and Alta Vista (www.altavista.com) are examples of this type of search engine.

- Search directories that are selected by real people. A team of reviewers looks at web pages and puts the quality sites into appropriate categories. Yahoo! (www.yahoo.com) and Excite (www.excite.com) are in this category.

Teaching Strategy 9

Use the Internet to research any topic. Use your search engine to find articles, specialized information, lesson plans, and so forth.

It is important to note that no search engine has indexed all of the pages on the World Wide Web. Search engines look for pages and then store their entire contents so they can be retrieved. Sometimes web pages move their location and/or are removed from the Web. Hence, from time to time, you will click on a link provided by a search engine and it will be a bad link, evidenced by an error message. There is nothing you can do when this happens except to try other links or use a different search engine.

Searching Tips

Here are some general guidelines that will help you efficiently search the Web.

- When you are looking for a general topic area, consider a topic-oriented search directory such as Yahoo! or Excite.

- When you are looking for a specific, obscure piece of information, try one of the spider search engines such as AltaVista or Go Network.

- Learn how the different search engine work. Read their help pages on how to conduct an advanced search.

- Save several search engines in your Favorites for quick access and reference. If you don't find the information you need with one search engine, try others. Most of what you are looking for is probably somewhere on the World Wide Web.

- Consider search engines that reference a vast amount of web pages such as www.google.com and www.alltheweb.com.

Suppose you were planning a lesson and needed information on Mozart and the Classical era. Articles, lesson plans, and other related information and files can be found online. If you have a need for a particular article or information on a topic you are teaching, finding it online can be a fast and easy way to locate information. So try it! Enter a keyword or two and see what sites the search engine locates.

Specialized Search Engines

If you don't find the information you are looking with a general search engine such as Yahoo, then consider using a specialized search engine, such as those designed just for educators. There are special search engines that try to completely meet the needs of certain populations. To find a topic-specific search engine, try the All Search Engines web site: www.allsearchengines.com. Go to this site and then click on the education link.

Music Education Search Engines

There are also search engines that are designed specifically for music and others designed for music education. An example of a search engine for music education is The Music Education Search Site. This site includes links to lesson plans, composers, and more.

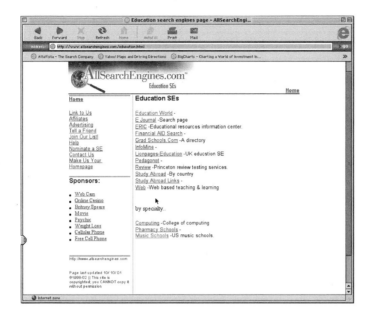

Figure 2.6: Education search engines
http://www.allsearchengines.com/education.html

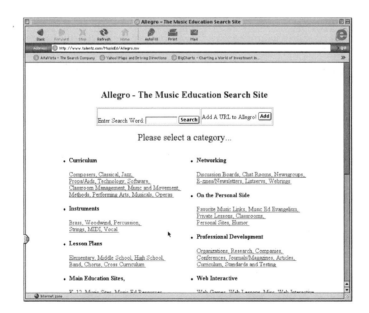

Figure 2.7: Allegro – The Music Education Search Site
http://www.talentz.com/MusicEd/Allegro.mv

It is possible to search for information on many topics such as song lyrics, composers, and vendors of music products to name a few.

Search Engines for Kids

There are also search engines designed for children. For example, Yahoo, the popular search engine, has a special version available for kids called Yahooligans. The address is www.yahooligans.com. Others include Cyber kids at www.cyberkids.com, and Ask Jeeves Kids (www.ajkids.com). These sites are designed for students with functions to eliminate inappropriate sites for kids and other helpful features.

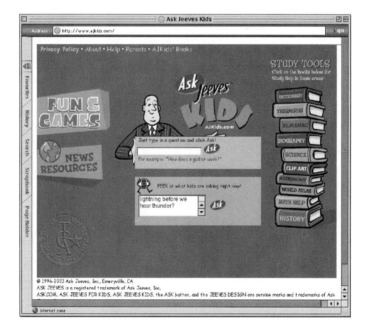

Figure 2.8: Yahooligans, a web search engine designed for students

Web Browser Plugins

When you visit a web page using a browser such as Internet Explorer, you may encounter many types of media. There are audio files, MIDI files, graphics files, and other types of files. Sometimes the media will load and function properly. Occasionally you will encounter a message telling you that you do not have the proper plugin to view the media. The reason for this is that web browsers use small add-on programs called plugins to interpret certain types of media files. A plugin extends the capabilities of a web browser, such as Netscape Navigator or Microsoft Internet Explorer, allowing the browser to run multimedia files such as audio files and movies.

If you don't have a certain plugin, it is usually easy to download into your computer. Often the message telling you that you need a particular helper or plugin also has a link to a web site where you can obtain it.

Teaching Strategy 10

When using the Internet with students be sure to check web sites ahead of time so that the proper plugins will be installed. Also, check to be sure your institution's web connection permits the downloading of plugins.

Capturing Text and Graphics from Web Sites

When visiting web pages, you will often want to print the information for reference. Printing the contents of a web page—text and graphics—is as simple as selecting Print from the File menu.

Teaching Strategy 11

Print the contents of web pages for reference and student handouts.

It is also possible to capture just the text from a web page. Perhaps you want to select some biographical information on a composer for a handout or performance program. Simply select the text and choose copy from the edit menu and paste the text into your word processor. Using this technique you can create customized handouts and reference materials for your classes. In addition, you can also capture pictures from web pages such as a portrait of a composer. In most cases copying a picture is simple.

Windows and Mac users with a two-button mouse should right click over the desired picture or graphic. Macintosh users with a one-button mouse (the standard Mac mouse) should click and hold down the mouse button for several seconds. A pop-up window will appear with several options. It is possible to copy the image and paste it into another location, just like text described above. Downloading the image to disk refers to making a copy of the file on your hard drive. When you copy a graphic it is placed on the computer's clipboard, which allows you to paste it in another application such as a word processor. When you download an image to disk, a copy of the file is placed on your computer's hard drive.

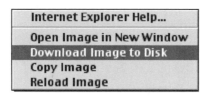

Figure 2.9: Downloading an image using the mouse-click method in Internet Explorer

Downloading MIDI, Sound, and Video Files from the Web

In addition to copying text and graphics, it is also possible to capture video and audio files. Let's suppose you need a particular musical example to play for a class and you don't find it in your library. There are many services that can transfer music and sound files to your computer so you can use them for class demonstration or any other related use. If you have access to the Internet, you could search for a specific file and transfer a copy to your computer. The same mouse capture technique described above to copy a graphic can also be used to copy an audio or video file. Simply right-click (Windows) or click and hold the mouse button (Mac) to capture a copy of the file that is displayed on the web page. After it is copied to your hard drive, it can be opened in music applications. Consult Chapters 8 and 11 for additional activities to practice downloading and opening audio, MIDI, and graphic files.

Copyright Caution

Be careful to download files correctly. Chapter 16 deals with the topic of copyright and digital media, look there for details on copyright law. Review that chapter for more in-depth information. It is sufficient to say here that you should read any notices on a web page and if the media is copy protected, you can't copy it without permission.

Summary

The online world offers a wide range of applications for music educators including signing on directly to computer networks such as the Pepper National Music Network, accessing commercial online services such as America Online and CompuServe, and accessing the Internet via a provider. This chapter is meant to be an introduction to some of the online possibilities. Consult the books and articles listed at the end of this chapter for additional information.

Review Questions

1. Define a network and give an example of how it can be used in education.
2. Define an intranet.
3. Define the Internet.
4. What is an ISP?
5. Identify the parts of an email address, for example myname@ispnet.com
6. What is an email mailing list and how can it be used by music educators? Provide the web address of one email mailing list appropriate to your area of specialization.
7. Define URL and identify the various components of a web address.
8. Give several examples of music education web sites. List benefits of using these sites.
9. Describe how to save a web address using a web browser.
10. Define a web search engine and give several examples of when a search engine could be helpful to the music educator.
11. Is all of the information on the Internet accurate and appropriate? Support your answer.

12. List one or more search engines designed to be used by children.
13. What is a web browser plug-in? Give an example of one and the web site where the application can be obtained/downloaded.
14. What is a message board and how could it be used by educators?
15. What does it mean to download files?
16. What are the steps to download a graphic or file?

CD-ROM Activities

- Project 2.1: Make a list of ways that you and others you know use the Internet for teaching and learning.
- Project 2.2: Save several web page locations as Favorites or Bookmarks. Organize these website locations into appropriate categories and folders.
- Project 2.3: List several email lists that can be helpful to music educators.
- Project 2.4: Use a search engine to find information relating to lesson plans you are teaching.
- Project 2.5 Complete the tutorial on how to download and install plug-ins for web browsers.

Reference

Campbell, D. & Campbell, M. (1995). *The Student's Guide to Doing Research on the Internet*. Addison-Wesley Publishing Co., New York.

Cunningham, C. and Billingsley, M. (2002) *Curriculum Webs: A Practical Guide to Weaving the Web into Teaching and Learning*. Pearson Allyn & Bacon, Upper Saddle River, NJ.

Ehn, Hope (1994). *Online Resources for Classical and Academic Musicians*. Von Huene Workshop. Brookline, MA.

Grescham-Lancaster, Scot (1994). Magical mystery tours. *Electronic Musician*, October, 1994. pp 47-62.

Griswold, Harold E. Multiculturalism, music and the information highways. *Music Educators Journal*, November, 1994. pp. 41-46.

Glossbrenner, A. and Glossbrenner E. (1998) *Search Engines for the World Wide Web*. Peachpit Press, Berkeley, CA.

Harris, Judi (1994). *The Way of the Ferret*. International Society for Technology in Education. Eugene.

Kehoe, Brendan P. (1992) *Zen and the Art of the Internet: A Beginner's Guide*. Prentice Hall. Englewood Cliffs, NJ.

Kongshem, Lars. The executive educator's complete guide to the Internet. *The Executive Educator*. April, 1994. pp. 55-70.

Pew Internet and American Life Project (2002, August 14) *The digital disconnect: The widening gap between Internet-savvy students and their schools*. Retrieved August 20, 2002 from http://www.pewinternet.org/reports/toc.asp?Report=67

Rudolph, Thomas. (1998). Jazz education resources for the World Wide Web. *Jazz Educators Journal*. November.

School Band and Orchestra Magazine. (April, 2001). SBO Report: Music Education Web Sites.

Sivin-Kachala, Jay; Bialo, Ellen; Rosso, James Lewis, (2000). *Online and Electronic Research by Middle School Students*. Interactive Educational Systems Design, Inc. http://www.mff.org/publications/publications.taf?page=293

Thibault, Matthew. (2001). Music through the Internet. *Teaching Music*. August.

Williams, Bad. (1999) *The Internet for Teachers, 2nd Edition*. IDG Books Worldwide. Chicago, IL.

Chapter 3

Computer Terms, Devices, and MIDI

Music Education National Standards: 8
NETS (National Education Technology Standards): 1

This chapter presents an overview of technology terms and concepts as well as an introduction to MIDI. Music educators need not be technological experts, but an understanding of the basic concepts and terms is necessary. For further study, consult the list of books and articles at the end of this chapter. If you are familiar with all the headings and concepts in this chapter, feel free to skip ahead!

An Introduction to Hardware and Software

It is very easy to be confused by the vast array of terms and concepts. The most essential terms are described below. If you are new to using computers and digital music equipment then read on! This chapter will familiarize you with terms that will be used throughout the text.

Digital and Analog

Today's computers and electronic instruments are all digital devices. Digital means that information, a sound wave for example, is represented as a series of numbers. Analog, an abbreviation for analogous, means that information is stored in a way that is similar to, or resembles, the original.

Digital information is generally more useful to musicians than analog. Numbers are more easily manipulated than are grooves on a record or magnetized particles on a tape. Why weren't numbers used before? Simple. For numbers to represent sound, the numbers have to be generated at an amazing rate of speed. Before computers were available, digital representation of sound wasn't feasible because the existing technologies were too slow.

The example I use most frequently to explain the difference between analog and digital is to refer to the two types of watches we wear on our wrist. A digital watch displays the time of day as a series of numbers. An analog watch gives us an analogous representation of the sun moving through the sky. Twelve noon is straight up, three o'clock is where the sun usually is at 3:00 p.m., and so forth.

Figure 3.1: Analog and digital watches

Phonograph records are analog while compact discs are digital. The phonograph record reproduces sound when vibrations are created as the needle moves along the grooves on the record. The grooves are analogous to the sound waves originally produced. On a compact disc (CD) the sound wave information is stored as numbers, hence it is digital.

Why didn't Thomas Edison, in 1877, use digital technology when he was experimenting with the phonograph? Well, there were no devices capable of generating numbers at the tremendous speed required for sound and reproducing a musical performance. Thomas Edison used the most advanced technology at his disposal: analog technology. Thomas Edison made the first sound recordings in 1877 using a telephone repeater system. The first recorded sound was Edison's voice saying "hello." The sound vibrations made indentations on a sheet of paper passing over a rotating cylinder. The indentations on the paper were analogous to the original vibrations. The process of recording music using discs with grooves continued for 100 years until the digital process was invented in the 1970s.

Today we have both analog and digital cassette tape recorders. The older, analog machines store information by arranging magnetic particles on a tape in forms analogous to the sound waves originally produced. Digital cassette recorders store sounds as a series of numbers.

Early electronic keyboards, in the 1950s, '60s, and early '70s, were analog instruments. They manipulated electrical current to produce an analogous representation of sound. Sound waves were produced by varying electrical current. Today, most electronic keyboards use digital means to create sound.

The analog process of storing sound waves and other musical information was invented first. In many ways it is less efficient and allows for far less control than digital technology. You can usually tell if a musical device, such as a tape recorder, is digital or analog when you fast forward, rewind, or change the playback speed. If you increase the speed and the pitch rises, then the medium is analog. If the pitch and speed can be controlled independently, then the device is most likely digital.

Hardware

I like to tell my students that if they drop something on their foot and it hurts, "it" is most likely hardware. Hardware can be touched or held. Hardware is a device usually in a hard case like a monitor, computer, printer, or an electric keyboard. In other words, it is the *physical* part of the system.

Chips and Microprocessors

Inside all digital devices today, including microwave ovens, digital television sets, and automobiles, are small silicon chips, each about the size of your fingernail. On this fingernail-sized material are thousands and thousands of electrical circuits. In fact, if you take the case off of an electronic keyboard or computer, you will find that it is 90% air. The microscopic circuitry on these chips contains information that at one time would have required an entire room for storage.

The key component of all digital electronic devices today is the microprocessor, or brain. The microprocessor is usually contained on one chip. Microprocessors in personal computers have numbers to indicate how fast they can process information; the higher the number, the faster the microprocessor, the "smarter" the computer. For example, the Macintosh microprocessors used today are called PowerPC G3, Power PC G4 and the newly minted (as of this writing) G5. Windows computers typically use processors that are also listed by number, for example, the Pentium 3 and the Pentium 4. The PowerPC G3 is slower than the G5 and the Pentium 3 is slower than the Pentium 4. As a rule of thumb, the more speed the better. Speed of processors is represented as GHz (gigahertz) or MHz (megahertz). Expect to pay more for a more powerful brain or microprocessor.

Computer System Types

Basically, there are three types of computers: desktop, consumer desktop, and portables usually referred to as laptops. Desktop computers typically have two distinct parts: a case that houses the computer's processor and a separate monitor. Consumer desktops are all-in-one devices that house both the computer's processor and monitor in one package. They are designed to be placed on a desktop. Laptops are all-in-one computers that are small and light enough to fit comfortably on a lap. Their advantage is portability.

The best choice for most music applications is to use a desktop computer system with expansion slots. Typically, this means a separate monitor and CPU (central processing unit). These computers have internal slots where expansion cards can be inserted. Some desktop models designed for the consumer markets, such as Apple Computer's iMac, do not have internal slots. Laptops do not typically have expansion slots, so they are not as usable as desktop models. The best all-around system for a music is a desktop model with expansion slots.

Computers

One of the most common questions asked is which computer should be used for music education. The choices are Macintosh or computers than run Microsoft Windows (Dell, Compac, IBM, Gateway, etc.). There are some differences between Macintosh and Windows computers. However, either can be used as the central component for all music and music education applications. Software is available from entry to professional level for both computer platforms, and many software titles are available for both Macintosh and Windows, referred to as cross-platform software.

My advice is to purchase the computer model for which you can get the most help, support, and advice. If your educational institution supports a particular brand or platform, then go with this equipment. If you are planning to use the computer in your home, ask around to see if there are people you know that use a particular brand of computer for music. The key is finding an individual or company to use as a model and a basis for comparison. It is also helpful to use equipment similar to your friends' and colleagues' so you can call on them for advice and help when needed.

Computer Memory: RAM

There are essentially two types of memory used in computers and other digital instruments: RAM and ROM. RAM stands for Random Access Memory. RAM is the space available in the computer's memory to hold information. RAM is reusable and can be erased. The more RAM a computer has, the better.

When you buy a piece of software it will say something like: "Requires 128 MB of RAM." This means that the computer must have at least 128 megabytes of available RAM or else the program cannot run.

To understand where the word megabyte (abbreviated MB) comes from, let's begin with how computers store information. Computers use a binary language, or the digits 0 and 1. The smallest piece of information is a bit: a zero (0) or a one (1). The word bit is an abbreviation of Binary Digit. A series of eight bits is called a byte. Computers store information in bytes. The size of each computer's memory depends on how many bytes the computer can store. The letter A is one byte. Obviously, many bytes are needed to store large documents and music files.

The next denomination is a kilobyte. One kilobyte equals approximately 1,000 bytes. For example, 48K means 48 kilobytes or 48,000 bytes. Next is megabyte or million bytes. A computer's memory is referred to as a certain number of MB, that is megabytes, of RAM. It is sometimes abbreviated as

MB. This means the device can store a particular number of megabytes or so many million bytes of information.

The bottom line is to remember that you *must* have enough memory in your computer to run the software you want to use. If a program requires 4 MB of RAM then you must have at least that much memory. So first determine what software you intend to use with your computer and find out how much memory is required. The memory requirements for software are listed on the back of the package or on the company web site. Then be sure to have at least the minimum required RAM.

ROM

RAM (random access memory) refers to the computer's memory for software that is erasable. ROM, or read only memory, is information that cannot be erased. Most digital devices come with some type of ROM. The computer has ROM installed so that it can interpret and translate human language into binary (numerical) language that the computer understands. Many electronic keyboards have a standard set of sounds in ROM that cannot be erased.

Software/Applications

Software is the instructions that controls the way the computer or digital device functions. The terms software, application, and program are interchangeable; each refers to instructions the computer or device follows. Without software, the computer could not operate. All digital devices require software to run.

A person who writes software is called a programmer. A program or software is usually purchased on a disk and used simply by starting the program or loading it into the computer's memory.

Computers and electronic devices require information to function. When we turn on a computer, it loads information so it can run properly. Loading refers to the process of copying information from a storage device such as a disk to the memory of the computer or RAM.

An application is a specific piece of software. The program that you use to type a letter is an application. When you peruse through the software catalog to select a music printing program, you are also looking for an application. The terms application and program are interchangeable.

The Display Screen (Monitor)

Just about every electronic device today, from a microwave to a computer, has some sort of display. A display may be as simple as a few numbers on the front of an electronic keyboard or as elaborate as a full-page computer screen. Most entry-level computer screens measure 15–17 inches diagonally. Computer screens are sometimes referred to as monitors. For music applications such as score writing, get the largest monitor possible. The larger the monitor, the more that can be viewed at one time.

In the computer and music industry, the term monitor can mean two entirely different things. A *computer* monitor is a television-like device that displays information. In a sound system, an *audio* monitor is a speaker that allows the performer to hear or monitor sound. Singers often use monitors for live performances. You are likely to have both in your music studio: a monitor display screen for the computer and an audio monitor or amplifier for sound.

Computer Operating Systems

When you purchase a computer, it comes with an installed operating system. The operating system performs basic tasks such as sending and receiving information to devices connected to the computer. You can usually tell what operating system is installed in your computer when it starts up, because the operating system is usually displayed during start-up.

Operating systems provide the necessary commands so software can run. Software is written to run on a particular operating system. So when you are selecting software, you must be sure that it is compatible with the operating system installed in your computer. For Windows PCs, operating systems include Windows 95, Windows 98, Windows NT, Windows XP, and others. So when someone asks what version of Windows you are running, they are referring the operating system installed in the computer.

Macintosh computers also have had a long history of Operating Systems and versions. As of this writing, the most current operating system is OS X (pronounced O.S. ten). Apple operating systems over the years followed a numbering system: OS 8, OS 8.6, OS 9, and OS X.

Upgrading the Operating System

It is possible to upgrade the operating system of your computer to the latest version. If you use a computer that is running Microsoft Windows, you can check for the most recent OS by going to http://www.microsoft.com/windows. There is an interesting history of Windows operating systems by clicking on the Windows History Link: http://www.microsoft.com/windows/WinHistoryIntro.mspx. Information on the most current operating system for Macs can be found at www.apple.com.

Upgrading typically costs money to purchase the new operating system on disc. Usually it is best to purchase and use the most recent operating system that is offered for your computer. However, there are considerations that impact the decision when is it best to make the switch. The first step is to find out if the hardware and software you are using are compatible with the new OS. You can check the manufacturer's web site for this information. Be sure that you will be able to run the programs you need on the new operating system before making the switch.

Peripheral Devices

The term peripheral refers to external devices that are connected to the computer. A CD or DVD drive and a hard disk drive can be thought of as peripherals to the computer itself. Other peripherals include scanners and printers.

Interface Options: SCSI, USB, and FireWire

Today's computers have a variety of ways to connect devices described in this chapter. These include SCSI, USB, and FireWire. Someone at a workshop asked me, "How do you know which connector is USB?" I answered, "Just keep trying the plugs and when the cable fits, you found it!" I say this tongue in cheek of course, but it always gets a laugh. The basic concept is your computer must be capable of connecting to the device. For example, if your computer does not have a USB connector, you cannot use USB devices.

The oldest most common way to connect devices is using SCSI, an acronym for "small computer system interface." Pronounced "scuzzy," SCSI is a interface standard used by computers for connecting peripheral devices such as hard disks, scanners and other devices to computers.

USB, which stands for "universal serial bus," can connect up to 127 devices, such as the computer mouse, modems, printers, and other devices.

The fastest data transfer rate, as of this writing, is FireWire. Products supporting this standard go under different names, depending on the company. Apple, which originally developed the technology, uses the trademarked name FireWire. Other companies use other names, such as ilink and Lynx, to describe these products.

Computers usually have several ways to connect devices including USB, FireWire, and so forth. More is better.

Printers

You may have heard the saying: garbage in, garbage out. This saying comes from the computer industry and relates to the terms input and output. When we are in the process of typing a letter using a computer, as we type we are inputting information. A printer is a type of output device. Printers produce paper copies of information created using the computer. The piece of paper that is produced is referred to as a hard copy. There are two basic types of printers: ink jet and laser. Ink jets are cheaper; lasers are better for high-end use. Printers usually connect via USB.

Storage Devices

Computers have a variety of ways to store information. These include floppy disks, hard disks, CD, and DVD. These devices all store data for future use. The difference is the manner in which they store information and the size and cost of the storage device. As you can imagine, the newest technology is the most expensive and the more storage capacity, the higher the cost. The computer's memory (RAM) and storage capacity are *both* expressed in megabytes (MB) or gigabytes (GB).

Inside of every computer is a hard disk drive also known as a hard drive. The terms "hard disk" and "hard drive" mean the same thing. The term hard drive refers to a type of hard magnetic surface that is used to store files and programs, hence the term hard disk. After you have typed a letter or composed a piece of music with the computer, you will want to keep a copy of it, so you save it to disk. Saving is the process a computer uses to make a copy of information on a storage device. When you type a letter on the computer and save it to disk, a file is created. A file is the basic unit used to store information. A hard disk can store thousands of files.

The term hard disk was used initially to differentiate between floppy and hard drives. No matter what medium or type of hard disk is used, it will degrade over time and will be, after a while, prone to crash. A crash is when a disk is no longer readable and cannot be used. Crashes occur without warning. Therefore, then working with digital files of any kind, be it on a computer or any other hard drive-based system, it is extremely important to have a means to copy, or back-up, the digital files. It is extremely important to have a basic understanding of how digital files are stored and precisely how to copy or to back-up the files in case they are lost or damaged.

So, on to technicalities: There are two basic types of drives: internal and external. The internal drive is located inside the computer or hard disk recorder while the external is connected to the device via a cable.

Figure 3.2: External hard disk

Floppy Disk

The floppy disk is a disk in a 3.5 inch case that is used to transfer and copy relatively small files from computer to computer. A floppy disk can hold approximately one megabyte (MB) of information. Because digital audio files are frequently much larger that one megabyte, a floppy disk is not a viable storage option. Floppy disks are still used in some computer systems. In recent years, due to the ever-increasing size of computer files, the floppy is being replaced by other drives that are capable of storing much more information.

Hard Disk Drives

A hard drive is the heart of any computer system. The hard drives used in today's computers are small units that use a hard magnetic surface. Hard drive storage is measured in megabytes (MB) or gigabytes (GB).

Computer drives are frequently identified by the amount of storage and how it connects to the computer. For example, 40 GB IDE hard drive. IDE stands for "integrated drive electronics," which is a type of hard drive that entered the market in 1988. This drive technology is one of the most popular types used. The 40 GB stands for 40 gigabytes of storage. More is better when it comes to storage. Some hard drives connect via USB. Both Macintosh and Windows computers now offer USB as a standard feature.

Hard Disk Space

When purchasing a computer, get the largest capacity drive you can afford. No matter what, the space on the drive will fill up quickly and more space is always needed. Drive space continues to increase with every new module that is introduced to the market. So get the most storage possible.

Removable Drives

There are several types of drives that use a removable disk to store files. These are similar to the 3.5 inch floppy drives, but the storage capacity is much larger. Removable disk formats include Zip, Jaz, and Superdisk. The advantage is that many drives can be purchased and stored for back-up and other purposes.

Magnetic Media Storage Considerations

No matter which type medium is used, it must be carefully handled and stored to ensure longevity. Every type of storage media has its problems. Back in the days when reel to reel tapes were used in the studio, the tapes had to be stored in a specific way or the information on the tapes would degrade. The same is true for disks. Follow these guideline to ensure that disks will not degrade over time:

- Use an indelible marker on the disk label. Do not use a pencil or eraser as particles can damage the drive.
- Store disks in a dry and cool place.
- Don't touch the exposed part of the disk.
- Keep disks away from magnets and magnetic fields.

Optical Drives

Optical drives use laser technology to store information. Optical storage is less volatile than magnetic storage media used in hard drives and removable tape drives. With the advance of inexpensive optical disc burners this technology is now an affordable option for backing-up and archiving files. Like the Zip drive, optical drives are not fast enough to record digital audio. One interesting note on the spelling of the word disk (disc): magnetic media are usually spelled with a "K" and optical media with a "C."

CD-ROM

CD-ROM stands for compact disc-read only memory. A CD-ROM drive connects to a computer or comes built-in and uses five-inch discs that look identical to audio compact discs. The distinction is that CD-ROM players can only be connected to computers. The ROM (read only memory) means that the information on a CD-ROM is permanent and cannot be erased. Therefore, a CD-ROM contains information that can be read by a computer but the information cannot be erased or changed.

The performance of a CD-ROM drive is rated in terms of X speed. The X speed of the drive refers to the number of times it spins in comparison to a standard audio CD. For example, a 1X drive spins at the same rate as an audio CD. Speeds currently range from 1X to 64X and more. The greater the spin rate, the faster you can access your information.

CD-R and CD-RW

The next evolution after CD-ROM was CD-R or CD-Recordable drives. These drives, called CD burners or writers, can read CDs and CD-ROMs and also write once to blank CD-Rs. Once a CD-R is burned it cannot be erased.

The CD-RW, or CD-Re-writable drive, can burn the same CD several times. A CD-RW drive can burn a standard CD or CD-ROM. It can also write to re-writable disks that can be erased and over written multiple times. CD-RW disks cost more, but can be rewritten up to 1,000 times. A CD-RW drive can be very helpful as a means for backing-up and archiving files.

One drawback of CD-RW disks is that they can only be read on a CD-RW drive. Another of the many advantages of using a CD burner is that the discs can be read by CD-ROM drives in both Macintosh and Windows PCs, so file exchange with other computer users is easy.

DVD and DVD-R

DVD, which originally stood for "digital versatile disc," is the latest generation of optical disc storage technology. It can be thought of as the big brother or sister of CD-ROM and CD audio. It is the same size disc as a CD, but can hold many times the amount of information including video, audio, and computer files. It also differs from the CD technology in that it records on both sides of the disc.

The goal of DVD is to be the standard digital format for all uses—CD, videotape, and CD-ROM. There are two types of DVD in use today: DVD-Video and DVD-ROM. DVD-Video is an enhanced video cassette format offering higher quality picture resolution and better quality sound. DVD-ROM discs hold computer information and can be read by DVD drives. Some computers are including DVD-ROM drives as standard equipment. One advantage to DVD-ROM is that it can also read CD-ROM discs.

Similar to the CD-ROM drive mentioned previously, DVD-ROM drives come in several formats. DVD-R index drives can write once to a DVD disc. DVD-RW drives can write several thousand times to a single disc. DVD-RW drive can be an excellent unit for back-up and archive of digital audio files.

Backing Up

A hard drive is a powerful, fragile device. The drive surface can become corrupted and will some day crash. Often times this happens without any warning. So, given the reality of hard drive technology, the question is not if you are going to back-up data, but how. Many computers today come with several different drives such as a floppy, hard disk, CD-ROM, or DVD-ROM. With multiple drives, it is possible to copy files from the hard drive to another, removable medium such as a floppy or CD-ROM. It is also possible to add an additional external drive for back-ups.

I recommend purchasing automatic back-up software that will make copies of your computer on a regular basis. Retrospect (www.dantz.com) is an excellent solution for Macintosh and Windows. I have this software on my home system and it backs-up my computer's hard drive every night.

MIDI

MIDI, an acronym for "musical instrument digital interface," is a digital computer language that is used to transmit information between electronic instruments and computers. MIDI is a universal language and when it is built into electronic instruments it allows them to communicate with each other and with MIDI-equipped computers. MIDI was developed in 1983 (as of this writing, it is 20 years old!). It increases the compatibility of all electronic equipment in order to extend the capabilities available to musicians while slowing the rapid rate of hardware obsolescence. MIDI, in its simplest terms, allows someone to buy keyboards and other devices from different manufacturers and use them together. MIDI equipment from Yamaha, Korg, Roland, or any other manufacturer can be interconnected and used together in a studio or live set-up.

In addition, MIDI can be used to communicate between electronic instruments and computers opening up an entire world of applications. The various software and educational applications of MIDI will be reviewed in detail in the chapters that follow.

What MIDI Transmits

An analogy can be made between MIDI and the eventual sound it produces and a piano roll and a player piano. A piano roll by itself can make no sound. It is basically a primitive program that records the performance data or notes to be played—rhythm, volume, pedals, and so on. In order to hear the sound, the roll must be connected to a player piano. Then, the piano roll tells the piano what notes to play. In a similar manner, MIDI is analogous to the piano roll in that it tells the MIDI instrument or device what notes to play as well as other information such as volume and so forth.

The language component of MIDI breaks down the musical performance into separate parts and represents these parts digitally. Think of MIDI as a lightning-fast analyzer. When a MIDI keyboard is played, the computer chip inside the instrument reads the performance and sends a host of information. This information includes:

- What keys are being pressed down. Each key has been assigned a specific MIDI number called a MIDI note number. For example, middle C on the piano is 60.
- The start or attack of each note. This is called note on.
- When the keys are let up or released, referred to as note off.
- How fast or hard the key is pressed, which controls the volume, referred to as velocity.
- Any use of the pitch bender to create tremolo or vibrato. This is called pitch bend.
- What timbre or program is used.

This information is analyzed at a very fast speed. The main concept to understand is simply that MIDI sends and receives information about the performance. There is no sound recorded—digital or audio. The sound that is heard is solely dependent upon the type of MIDI playback device used.

MIDI Channels

MIDI was originally designed to transmit on 16 different channels. Channels are used to keep information separate from one another. Think of each MIDI channel as being capable of transmitting a different instrument sound or timbre. Just like a television set receives different programs on different channels, MIDI can transmit to the MIDI instrument the information it requires to play back separate timbres on different channels. If you want try to recreate the sound of a string trio (violin, viola, and cello) for example, then you will need to send the information for each instrument on a separate MIDI channel.

So, in effect, it is possible to play back 16 different instrument sounds simultaneously through MIDI. In order to send 16 different timbres through MIDI, one could connect 16 different MIDI instruments or MIDI sound modules and set each one to receive only one specific channel. However, is it more convenient to use a multitimbral MIDI instrument or sound module (see Chapter 4). Multitimbral means more than one instrument timbre can be produced at the same time. In order to achieve multitimbral sound via MIDI, each individual timbre must be placed on its own channel.

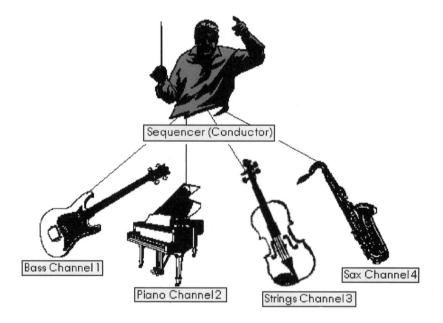

Figure 3.3: MIDI channel assignments

General MIDI (GM)

MIDI was created to standardize the transmission of information among electronic instruments made by different manufacturers. Originally, when a MIDI file was created with one brand of instrument, it would likely sound totally different on another. The problem was that each manufacturer used a different numbering system to access the various sounds. The piano might be 41 on a Korg, 120 on a Yamaha, 45 on a Roland, and so forth. Because MIDI does not transmit the actual sound, only the number of the sound, it was difficult to share MIDI files and have them play the intended instrument sound.

The electronic keyboard manufacturers got together to address this need and developed a standard sound set that all instruments would adhere to and named it General MIDI. For example, on all General MIDI instruments and computers, number 1 is *always* a piano, number 57 is always a trumpet, and so forth. General MIDI automatically sets MIDI channel 10 to drums. This also was advantageous for music being sent over the Internet in MIDI file format. Today's Macintosh and Windows computers have built-in General MIDI capability, so they can playback MIDI files in General MIDI or GM format. The basic 128 General MIDI sounds are listed in the following graphic.

Acou Piano	1	Nylon Guit	25	Strings	49	Piccolo	73	Ice Rain	97	FX-Fret	121
Brght Piano	2	Acou Guit	26	Slow Strg	50	Flute	74	Sound Trk	98	Fx-Breath	122
Elec Grand	3	Jazz Guit	27	Syn Strg 1	51	Recorder	75	Crystal	99	Sea Shore	123
Honk Tonk	4	E Guit Cln	28	Syn Strg 1	52	P Flute	76	Atmosphere	100	Bird Tweet	124
Rhodes	5	E Guit Mut	29	Choir Aahs	53	B Bottle	77	Briteness	101	Telephone	125
Elec Piano2	6	O-D Guit	30	Vocal Oohs	54	Shaku	78	Goblin	102	Helicopter	126
Harpsichord	7	Dist Guit	31	Syn Voice	55	Whistle	79	Echoes	103	Applause	127
Clav	8	Guit Harm	32	Orch Hit	56	Ocarina	80	Sci Fi	104	Gunshot	128
Celeste	9	Acou Bass	33	Trumpet	57	Sqr Wave	81	Sitar	105	DRUMS	
Glockenspl	10	Fing Bass	34	Trombone	58	Saw Wave	82	Banjo	106		
Music Box	11	Pick Bass	35	Tuba	59	Calliope	83	Shamiron	107	Standard	
Vibraphone	12	Ftless Bass	36	M Trumpet	60	Chiff Lead	84	Koto	108	Room	
Marimba	13	Slp Bass 1	37	Fr Horn	61	Charang	85	Kalimba	109	Power	
Xylophone	14	Slp Bass 2	38	Br Section	62	Vox Lead	86	Bag Pipe	110	Electronic	
Tube Bell	15	Syn Bass 1	39	Syn Br 1	63	Fifth Lead	87	Fiddle	111	Rap (808)	
Santur	16	Syn Bass 2	40	Syn Br 2	64	Bas & Lead	88	Shanai	112	Jazz	
										Brush	
DB organ	17	Violin	41	Sop Sax	65	New Age	89	Tinkle	113		
Per organ	18	Viola	42	Alto Sax	66	Warm Pd	90	Agogo	114		
Rock organ	19	Cello	43	Ten Sax	67	Poly Synth	91	Stl drm	115		
Ch organ	20	Ctra Bass	44	Bari Sax	68	Pd Voice	92	Wd block	116		
Reed organ	21	Tremelo	45	Oboe	69	Pd Bowed	93	Taiko drm	117		
Accordian	22	Pizzicato	46	Eng Horn	70	Pd Metal	94	Mel toms	118		
Harmonica	23	Harp	47	Bassoon	71	Pd Halo	95	Syn drums	119		
Band Neon	24	Timpani	48	Clarinet	72	Pd Sweep	96	Rev cymbl	120		

Figure 3.4: General MIDI sound list

General MIDI established a standard location or number for sounds. The GM standard also includes a minimum of 24 polyphonic, or multitimbral voices. This guarantees that a General MIDI (GM) instrument or computer can play back a minimum of 24 different sounds at the same time, referred to as 24-part multitimbral.

The downside of General MIDI is that even though number 57 is a trumpet, it may sound quite different when played on different brands of instruments and computers. For this reason, most MIDI keyboards include other banks of sounds that can be used in conjunction with GM. These other banks have additional sounds that compliment General MIDI and utilize the specific strengths of the instrument.

GS and XG Specifications

Both Yamaha and Roland have developed extended General MIDI specifications to include sound effects and other enhancements. Roland developed the GS format and Yamaha the XG format. These formats are downwardly compatible, which means they will play on any GM instrument. However, when played on their own or compatible equipment that includes the GS or XG enhancements, additional voices and sound characteristics that are not available under GM are possible. Some computer game companies have also utilized these enhanced GM formats.

General MIDI 2 (GM2)

General MIDI 2 is a group of extensions made to the original General MIDI specification. It increases the number of available sounds and the amount of control available for sound editing and musical performance. All GM2 devices are fully compatible with General MIDI.

MIDI Interface

In order for computers and electronic instruments to communicate via MIDI, a way to connect or interface them is needed. The device that accomplishes this task is called a MIDI interface. There are many different types of MIDI interfaces for a wide variety of applications. Many Windows computers include a MIDI interface built right into the internal sound card. Also, some electronic keyboards and MIDI devices come with built-in MIDI capability. Macintosh computers require an external MIDI interface to be connected to the computer. Diagrams and descriptions of how to connect these devices are discussed in Chapter 13.

Figure 3.5: External MIDI Interface: Fastlane by Mark of the Unicorn

To connect two MIDI instruments together or to connect a MIDI keyboard or sound module to a computer, MIDI cables must be used. Usually at least two MIDI cables are needed, one for input and one for output. Remember, MIDI only transmits MIDI data. You cannot connect your MIDI cable to a speaker. It is the actual MIDI instrument that produces the sound.

Standard MIDI Files

MIDI performance information is stored in computer file format. A few years after the advent of MIDI, every instrument manufacturer and software publisher had its own proprietary MIDI file format. This meant that it was not possible to share MIDI files between different software programs, MIDI instruments, and different brands of computers. The industry addressed this problem by developing a standard MIDI file format, referred to as SMF. A MIDI file that is in SMF format can be shared between different computers and MIDI-compatible instruments. For example, a MIDI file saved in SMF format on one instrument or program can be read by other programs produced by different publishers and manufacturers. This makes it possible to create files that can be read by any software. Most SMF files produced today are also General MIDI compatible, making them instantly playable on any General MIDI compatible instrument or on a computer.

Summary

This chapter offers a very basic introduction to the many terms and concepts used in the computer industry and an understanding of MIDI. If you want more in-depth information, I recommend that you purchase one or more books for further reading. See the list in the reference section at the end of this chapter. Many titles are available at local bookstores and via online services such as www.amazon.com. There are also many excellent hands-on courses offered at colleges and through continuing education programs at high schools. These courses can be extremely helpful, especially for the novice computer user.

Review Questions

1. What is the advantage of digital technology? Give one example of a device that is analog and one that is digital.
2. Define the terms hardware and software. How can you tell one from the other?
3. What do the abbreviations MB and GB stand for?
4. What is the function of a computer's operating system?
5. How can you find out the latest version of a particular computer operating system?
6. There are several types of data transfer standards that are used with computers. List them and describe the differences among the standards. For example, SCSI, USB, and so forth.
7. What is the difference between a CD-R and a CD-RW drive?
8. What is the definition of DVD? What is the difference between DVD and DVD-R?
9. There are several types of removable drives. List the types of drives and comment on ways they can be used.
10. Define ROM and RAM.
11. What is the difference between the computer's RAM and the storage capacity of a hard drive?
12. What are the three types of computers?
13. What advice is given for when to buy a Macintosh or Windows computer?
14. What is backing-up and why is it important?
15. What is the definition of MIDI?
16. What information does MIDI transmit?

17. Explain the similarities and differences between a piano roll and MIDI.
18. What is General MIDI?
19. What is General MIDI 2?
20. What is the function of GS and XG configurations?
21. What is the function of a MIDI interface?
22. Define SMF.

CD-ROM Activities

- Project 3.1 Review the Chapter 3 Web links. Review the sites you visit.
- Project 3.2 Go to http://www.webopedia.com or www.hyperdictionary. com/ and search for definitions of the terms mentioned in this chapter.
- Project 3.3 Create a list of computer hardware that you would like to purchase for your music office or room. Include computer, monitor, and peripherals such as printers, scanners and the like.

Reference

Cortinas, Marty (2001). *The Macintosh Bible (8th Edition)*. Peachpit Press

Mash, David. (2002) *Mac OS X for Musicians*.
    http://www.mashine.com/members/articles/OSX.html

Simpson, Alan. (2001). *Windows XP Bible*. John Wiley & Sons.

White, Ron and Downs, Timothy. (2001). *How Computers Work (6th Edition)*. Que Publishers.

Williams, D. B. & Webster, P. (1999) *Experiencing Music Technology: Software, Data, and Hardware, Second Edition*. Schirmer Books, New York.

Chapter 4

Electronic Keyboards

Music Education National Standards: 2, 3, 4, 5
NETS (National Education Technology Standards): 3, 5

This chapter has a two-fold purpose. The first part describes the various types of electronic keyboards. The second part of the chapter deals with specific teaching applications using electronic keyboards as a performance and demonstration instrument. Electronic keyboards labs are dealt with in Chapter 12.

Electronic keyboards have been around for decades in one form or another, and today they can be found in millions of homes and classrooms. Several years ago, an eighth grade student of mine, the first trumpet player in my band, came up to me and asked, "Dr. Rudolph, I'm going over to the music store to buy an electronic keyboard, which model do you recommend?" I remember realizing that I had a unique opportunity. Many of my students had electronic keyboards at home. My thoughts focused on how I could incorporate these instruments into the curriculum.

Today, electronic keyboards of all shapes and sizes are finding their way into homes, schools, churches, and just about anywhere a keyboard instrument can be used. They are used in every facet of the music industry and school music programs. Classroom teachers find electronic keyboards to be more portable than traditional acoustic pianos. Performance groups, such as jazz bands and choruses, use electronic keyboards as accompaniment instruments, and electronic piano labs are continuing to gain popularity in schools. Computers are connected to electronic keyboards to create music composition studios and for many other applications. With the wide variety of electronic keyboards available, there is a model to fit virtually every music budget and application.

Teachers have reported that students respond positively to the use of technology.[1] Music teachers who have incorporated computers, electronic keyboards, and technology into their music curriculum have found it to be a productive tool. In addition, students working with technology have been found to have a higher level of achievement than those using traditional methods.[2] Claudia Appel in her article "Keyboard Instruction in the Music Curriculum," states:

> Keyboards present an optimum opportunity to use a popular and affordable medium for music class. It is an opportunity that we should choose to provide.[3]

Electronic keyboards can create the following benefits in the music classroom:[4]

- Keyboards can be used to support music literacy.
- Keyboards can foster creativity.
- Keyboards support technology education.

Obviously, today's electronic keyboards offer educators a unique opportunity. We must first address two issues: deciding what type of keyboard to purchase and formulating strategies to use electronic keyboards in a unique and appropriate manner.

Selecting an Electronic Keyboard

One of the problems associated with electronic keyboards is the difficulty in selecting the best model for a particular purpose. Selecting an electronic keyboard can be a confusing. The plethora of models are constantly updated and changed. To determine which electronic keyboard is best for your particular application some basic knowledge of keyboards is needed.

I will highlight the essential concepts that a music educator needs to understand in order to purchase the best keyboard for a particular teaching situation. It is not necessary to understand the technical jargon frequently used to describe electronic instruments. The critical point is to understand the various types of electronic keyboards available and some key characteristics in order to make an informed purchase.

MIDI Compatibility

It is easy to tell if an electronic keyboard or instrument is MIDI capable (see Chapter 3 for a definition of MIDI). Just look on the back panel of the instrument. If the keyboard has connectors labeled MIDI IN and OUT (referred to as MIDI ports), then the instrument is MIDI capable. Some keyboards also have a MIDI THRU port. MIDI THRU simply passes the incoming information on to the next instrument. The THRU port is handy when you are connecting several instruments together. MIDI is included with most electronic instruments today that cost more than $100.

Types of Electronic Keyboards

Some people use the word synthesizer to describe any keyboard that is electronic. Purists only call synthesizers those keyboards that create sounds by manipulating electrical currents. The term "synth" is often used in the industry as a generic term for an electronic keyboard. I limit the use of the term "synthesizer" to one specific type of electronic keyboard, the analog synthesizer. The more appropriate general term to use is electronic keyboard, as this is the one aspect all of these instruments do have in common.

Almost every electronic keyboard on the market today can be placed into one of the following categories: sample player, sampler, digital piano, workstation, or analog synthesizer. Early electronic instruments in the 1950s, '60s and early '70s were analog synthesizers. They manipulated electrical current using oscillators and filters, to produce an analogous representation of sound. Today, most electronic keyboards use digital means to create sound.

Teaching Strategy 12

Go to the International Association of Electronic Keyboard Manufacturers web page (www.iaekm.org) and read about the various types of keyboards. Click on links to various manufacturers' web sites for addition information on keyboards.

Sample Players: Portable Electronic Keyboards

There are portable electronic keyboards designed for the home or non-technically oriented user. These are the least expensive type of electronic instrument. Typically, these keyboards have buttons with labels such as "trumpet" or "violin." They are considered sample players because they reproduce samples of instruments that were recorded digitally. There are no potentially confusing, complex looking windows with numbers. The player selects a sound merely by pressing a button. These instruments can be placed on a tabletop or stand and are easily transported from place to place. Most models of portable electronic keyboards are equipped with features that create automatic harmonies and rhythms. These instruments also contain built-in speakers so external amplification is not needed. Portable electronic instruments are sold in department stores, mail order catalogs, and music stores.

Figure 4.1: Yamaha PSR-350 portable electronic keyboard

Generally, portable electronic keyboards are the least expensive electronic instrument. Some models cost less than $200. However, to obtain quality sound production and other important options discussed below, be prepared to spend $400 or more. Be sure to listen to several models in the same price range before making a decision. Some models of portable electronic keyboards include:

- Yamaha PSR-350, and PSR-550
- Panasonic SX-KC611
- Casio CTK-573
- Roland EM-15

These instruments have recording capability in the form of a built-in sequencer. This recording device is designed for practice and enjoyment, not professional-level recording.

Intelligent Keyboards

There are portable electronic keyboards that have many advanced features and are designed to produce professional-sounding accompaniments, rhythms, and rhythm patterns. Most of these instruments are designed for professional use. The enhanced applications come with a price of course. Expect to pay in the $1,000 range for these instruments. These models have significant amounts of built-in features and therefore are usually referred to as intelligent keyboards. These keyboards are often used in stadiums to play the sound effects for athletic events.

Examples of intelligent keyboards are:

- Korg PA-80
- Roland EM-55
- PSR-1000

Figure 4.2: Roland EM-55 Intelligent Keyboard

Intelligent keyboards have built-in automatic accompaniment capabilities. The Yamaha PSR line, Roland E-series, and the Korg I-models are examples of keyboards with these built-in capabilities.

> **Teaching Strategy 13**
>
> Use an intelligent keyboard to create accompaniment parts for rehearsal and live performance.

The high end models such as the Roland E-86 and Korg I-5 come equipped with a disk drive. These intelligent instruments can create accompaniment parts including bass, drums, and piano similar to those created by intelligent software such as Band-in-a-Box without the need for an external computer. The advantages of using an intelligent keyboard are that they are very portable, they have built-in speakers and they are easy to use and operate. If a computer is not available, they can be used to create instant accompaniments for practice, rehearsal, and improvisation.

Programmable Keyboards: Synthesizers

Programmable electronic keyboards have the capability to alter and create new sounds as well as play back digital sound. The sound quality is very good and these instruments are frequently used for performance and in the recording studio.

Figure 4.3: Roland XP-30 programmable keyboard

You can usually tell if a keyboard is programmable by the type of display. If you find a window with numbers and parameters displayed, it is most likely a programmable keyboard. If, instead, it has buttons that say "trumpet," "violin," etc., then it is most likely a portable electronic keyboard.

Programmable keyboard models include:

- Kurzweil PC2
- Roland XP series
- Alesis QS series

Digital Pianos

A digital piano combines the realistic sound quality of sample players with the feel of an acoustic piano. In an effort to make the digital piano mimic the action of an acoustic piano, weights are inserted inside the keys, hence they are called weighted keys. Weighted keys are especially important if the instrument will be played by performers who prefer the feel of an acoustic piano keyboard. Most digital pianos are smaller and less expensive than traditional acoustic pianos.

- Yamaha YDP-101
- Kurzweil SP88
- Korg C3200
- Roland EP77

Figure 4.4: Kurzweil SP88

If you visit a piano outlet or manufacturer you will most likely see both acoustic and digital pianos on display. Digital pianos offer many more options than their acoustic counterparts, such as a built-in music recorder, the ability to play more than one timbre at a time, and the advantage of silent practice with the use of headphones.

Digital pianos are usually somewhat more expensive because of the weighted keys. They are also less portable. The cost usually starts around $1,200. Some examples of digital pianos include:

- Korg C series
- Roland FP series
- Yamaha YDP and Clavinova Series

The Workstation

The term workstation refers to an instrument that combines several functions in one package. Workstations look like programmable keyboards from the outside. But workstations also have a built-in MIDI sequencer and several effects processing devices so that digital echo and reverb can be added to sounds and sequences. In addition, there is typically a storage device, such as a disk drive, for storing sequences. Some keyboards even offer the option of digital recording.

Figure 4.5: Korg Triton LE workstation

The concept behind a workstation is to provide an all-in-one instrument: a performance keyboard and built-in sequencer and effects devices for creating and playing back sequences. A workstation can serve as the main component of the low-budget studio. Examples of workstations include:

- Korg Triton Le, Triton
- Kurzweil K2600

Samplers

Keyboards with sampling capability can record from external sources using a microphone and record from other sources such as compact disc and Macintosh (aiff) and Windows (wav) file formats. Some keyboards, such as the Korg Triton and Kurzweil K-2000, can function as a sample player, MIDI sequencer, and sampler. With these instruments, samples can be recorded and played back, and MIDI sequences can be recorded with mono and stereo samples. This means you can record a mono or stereo sample of up to 11 minutes long. The trade-off for all these features is cost. Keyboards with multiple options such as sampling and MIDI sequencing cost more, in the $2,000–$3,000 and up range.

Figure 4.6: Korg Triton sampling keyboard

Samplers also come in rack mountable versions such as the Akai S5000. In other words, you get all of the internal sampling capability without the keyboard. This type of sampler is designed for studio use.

Figure 4.7: AKAI S5000 Rack Mount Sampler

Analog Synthesizers

In the past few years, performers have shown a renewed interest in using electronic keyboards that emulate the original analog sounds from the 1960s and '70s. The price of these instruments is usually in the $1,000 range and up. These analog synthesizers are not designed to be an all-purpose instrument. Examples of analog synthesizers include:

- Roland V-Synth
- Korg MS2000
- Minimoog Voyager synthesizer

Figure 4.8: V-Synth from Roland

MIDI Sound Module

MIDI sound modules are electronic keyboards without keys. These are also referred to as rack modules as they are made to be placed in studio racks. Modules are less expensive than their keyboard counterparts. The advantage is being able to add additional sound sources to the studio at less expense. Most samplers and synthesizers can be purchased in module format. There are MIDI modules designed for specific purposes that can be added to a digital studio. Some modules have only piano sounds, others specialize in orchestral sounds, bass and percussion sounds, and so forth. This is often the best way to expand the sound capabilities of your studio. Some available sound modules include:

- Alesis QS7
- Korg NS5R
- Roland JV-1010

Software Synthesizers

If you buy a Macintosh or Windows computer today, it will be equipped with at least rudimentary sound synthesis capability. A Windows PC running Windows 95 or later comes equipped with a sound card that can generate mulitimbral sound output and MIDI data. Apple Computer includes QuickTime with all Macs. This free program adds to the computer multimedia sound capability that is General MIDI compatible. It is therefore possible to playback General MIDI files through the computer's internal sound synthesis capabilities.

It is also possible to purchase software synthesizers, often called software synths that provide a higher quality sound output than the built-in counterpart. A software synthesizer is a program that does the same thing as the external hardware of these synthesizers except that it uses the memory and storage capability of the computer. They give your computer the ability to generate high quality sound thereby eliminating the need for additional pieces of hardware. The computer's resultant sound producing capability can be added to the existing pieces in the studio.

Several companies produce software synthesizers including Roland, Bitheadz, and NemeSys. These companies offer a range of products including software that emulates analog and digital synths and samplers. Many of these professional sound synthesis programs can be purchased for under $500 and can be used as a MIDI sound source. Software synths can be used in conjunction with MIDI sound modules and keyboards.

Retro Lite is the perfect beginner's software for anyone wanting to get involved with music software synthesis at the low-end level. It comes with a combination of factory preset sounds ready to play back the classic analog synthesizer sounds of the past. Extensive MIDI implementation lets you control all parameters and make integration into existing MIDI setups. You can use the program "live" just like any other musical instrument, or use it as a multitimbral sound module running behind your favorite MIDI application. It can run on the computer alone or be used in conjunction with other MIDI gear.

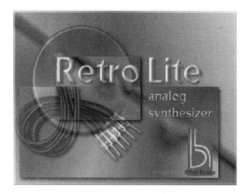

Figure 4.9: Retro Lite (Mac/Win) Software Synthesizer

MIDI Keyboard Controllers

MIDI keyboard controllers are keyboards that can transmit MIDI data but have a limited amount of built-in, or on-board, sounds. The primary function of a MIDI keyboard controller is to act as an output device and to control other MIDI modules in the studio and/or performance.

There are two categories of keyboard controllers: computer desk-top models and performance controllers. The desktop MIDI keyboard controller is designed to be used with a computer and a MIDI sound module or sound card. It is light and compact and can fit in a small space. These units can be purchases in a variety of models, from 1 and 1/2 octaves to 5 octaves or more. Examples of this type of keyboard include:

- M-Audio MIDI controllers such as the Oxygen 8 and Ozone
- Fatar CMK series
- Edirol PRC series controllers

Desktop MIDI keyboard controllers are less expensive than other MIDI keyboards because they have *no* sound producing capabilities of their own. This type of MIDI keyboard controller is a good choice when there is limited space or for a desktop MIDI set-up in an office or practice room. If you already own a MIDI sound module or your PC has a built-in MIDI compatible sound card, then a desktop MIDI keyboard controller could be your least expensive option. The cost of desktop MIDI keyboard controllers is in the $150–$250 range.

The second type of MIDI keyboard controller is designed to be used primarily in live performance to control many different keyboards and MIDI devices. These can also can be used in a MIDI recording studio. Examples of this type of keyboard include:

- Kurzweil PC88
- Fatar SL series
- General Music SK88
- Roland A-90

Kurzweil refers to its PC88 model as a "performance controller." The Fatar Studio 49 and Roland A-80 are also examples of advanced MIDI keyboard controllers designed to be used with a complex MIDI equipment set-up. A performance MIDI keyboard controller would be a good choice for live performance when many different MIDI keyboards and sound modules must be controlled at the same time, or in the recording studio with multiple MIDI devices. These MIDI keyboard controllers are designed for the serious MIDI user. Music educators would only consider a performance controller for use in live performance or with a very complex set-up of MIDI hardware. These devices are significantly more expensive than desktop MIDI keyboard controllers, in the $1,000–$3,000 range.

Part II:
Electronic Ke
Curriculum Ap,

Electronic keyboards can serve many areas of music e   ding classroom music as a performance instrument and for teac   monstration, instrumental and choral performing groups, and for keyboard instruction classes. This chapter deals with the use of electronic keyboards in the classroom.

Electronic Keyboards in the Classroom

Electronic keyboards are appropriate for use at all levels from elementary to college. There are three main approaches for using keyboards in a classroom music setting:

- One electronic keyboard in a classroom: using the keyboard as a teaching tool for classroom demonstration and accompaniments. With this option, the keyboard is controlled mainly by the teacher.
- Several electronic keyboards (2-6) in a classroom: using the electronic keyboard as a classroom instrument by integrating keyboards with other classroom instruments including Orff instruments, percussion instruments, and other non-electronic instruments.
- Electronic keyboard lab: purchasing enough keyboards so that the entire class can use the keyboards simultaneously. This will be discussed in depth in Chapter 12.

Teaching Strategy 14

Use an electronic keyboard to create accompaniments and rhythm ostinatos for the general music class.

If you were to you walk into Ken Peters' classroom in Chatham Park Elementary School in Havertown, Pennsylvania, you would be struck by the sight of several electronic keyboards and a computer in front of the room. As a third grade class enters the music room, Ken presses the spacebar on the computer and a complete orchestration/accompaniment, that he has recorded, is played for the class. Ken walks around the room as the students sing and move while the workstation generates the accompaniment. The class is having difficulty keeping up with the tempo. No problem. Because he is using a sequencer, Ken can adjust the tempo with the touch of a button, without changing the key. Later, students are having trouble singing a song in the key selected as it is a bit too high. Again, the electronic keyboard is an asset since Ken can change the key up or down to any interval. Within seconds the keyboard is now playing the accompaniment in a new key.

Many of the basic rhythm and chordal accompaniments can be generated using a portable electronic keyboard with built-in rhythms and accompaniments. The Yamaha PSR series is designed for classroom use.

Electronic Keyboards as a Classroom Instrument

In addition to using the keyboard as a teaching, demonstration, and accompaniment tool, the electronic keyboard can also be used by students in the general music classroom. A good first step for classroom music specialists is to integrate electronic keyboards into the existing music curriculum. In other words, treat the electronic keyboards as another classroom instrument but utilize its unique characteristics.

Teaching Strategy 15

Integrate electronic keyboards as part of the classroom music experience. Begin by using the electronic keyboard as an additional classroom performance instrument.

Jackie Wiggins, an elementary classroom specialist and author, advocates integrating electronic keyboards into the classroom curriculum. She recommends using the keyboard with elementary students both as a medium for creating music and in live performance.[5] Wiggins recommends electronic keyboards as another option for the students to use along with traditional classroom instruments such as Orff and percussion instruments. The advantage of this approach is that as few as 1–3 electronic keyboards can be integrated into the classroom music curriculum.

An excellent resource for classroom integration activities is Jackie Wiggins' publication, *Synthesizers in the Elementary Classroom*.[6] Wiggins offers suggested lesson plans and ideas for incorporating electronic keyboards into the classroom. Some of the objectives of her lessons include:

- to learn to play chords and bass lines
- to learn to play and record a drum pattern
- to discover the differences between acoustic, electronic, and electrically amplified acoustic instruments
- to create an effective montage of electronic and acoustic sounds

Wiggins suggests using three or more keyboards and rotating the use of them throughout the class. Rotation gives all the students a chance to play the keyboard over a period of time.

> **Teaching Strategy 16**
> Use keyboard method books written specifically for integrating the electronic keyboards into the classroom music curriculum.

Sandy Feldstein and Debbie Cavalier have written a method book dedicated to integrating electronic keyboards into the general music curriculum titled *Keyboards in General Music*.[7] Book One presents many practical ways to integrate one or more keyboards as part of the general music curriculum. There are theory lessons for finding the keys and reading basic notation, and playing tonic, dominant, and subdominant chords. Singing and playing activities are provided as well as ensemble activities. A teacher's manual with detailed lesson plans is available. *Keyboards in General Music* is an excellent resource for the elementary classroom teacher who wants to integrate synthesizers into the curriculum.

Silver Burdett publishes *Making Music with MIDI*, a complete curriculum for integrating MIDI and electronic instruments into the elementary curriculum. These lessons are designed to be used with the MIDI Partner System. The instruments are produced by Fm7, Inc. and are designed especially for elementary students. A group of lessons is published by Silver Burdett that can be used with the MIDI Partner hardware or with existing electronic instruments in the classroom.

Classroom Demonstration

In elementary and high school classrooms, one electronic keyboard can be used to demonstrate sounds and acoustic concepts. This is easily and affordably accomplished with one electronic keyboard with either built-in speakers or connected to an external speaker/amplifier.

> **Teaching Strategy 17**
> Have students identify and classify sounds into instrument families (brass, strings, percussion, woodwind); specific instruments (trumpet, violin, marimba) and electronic sounds or sound effects (bird tweet, gun shot, etc.).

The sound quality of most moderately-priced keyboards is usually good enough to distinguish among various instrument sounds. However, there are some sounds that do not reproduce well on electronic instruments, for example, the saxophone and trumpet.

Electronic keyboards provide students with a way to experience different timbres and classify them by instrument type. For example, a list of the sounds of any General MIDI compatible keyboard can be displayed for the class. Students can be asked to select sounds and label them by category. With General MIDI the sounds are logically organized, keyboard sounds are 1-8, melodic percussion 9-16, organ 17-21, guitar 25-32, and so forth. General MIDI sounds include more than the four instrument families: strings, brass, percussion and woodwinds. General MIDI also includes:

- keyboard samples (organ, harpsichord, piano, electric piano)
- electric guitar/electric bass samples (slap bass, distorted guitar)
- synthesizer sounds (synth brass and synth strings)
- Instruments from various cultures (ocarina, koto, bagpipe, sitar, kalimba)
- vocal sounds (choir ahs, synth voice)
- sound effects (telephone, helicopter, gunshot)

An excellent demonstration of the different acoustic and electronic sounds, as well as demonstrations of electronic instruments, can be seen in Don Muro's video, *An Overview of Electronic Music Instruments*.[8] Muro's presentation clearly explains the basic concepts of electronic instruments in a lively, entertaining and educational setting.

Teaching Strategy 18

Use automatic accompaniment functions found on portable electronic keyboards as a performance and demonstration tool.

Most electronic keyboards contain some type of accompaniment feature whereby chords and rhythms are automatically performed. Rhythms can be played independently, as can bass lines and chords. Electronic keyboards usually include a variety of rhythmic styles such as tango, reggae, rock, etc.

These styles can be used to accompany songs and they can be used to discuss the various sounds and rhythms that distinguish one style from another.

> **Teaching Strategy 19**
> Use the automatic chord function on electronic keyboards to teach basic harmony functions and terms.

The rhythm and chordal accompaniments that are offered on even the most inexpensive electronic keyboards can be used to teach basic chord functions. Most portable electronic keyboards include a "single-finger" approach to playing harmonies. Each manufacturer has a slightly different manner in which to access the various chords. The Yamaha method is as follows:

- For a major chord, depress the key of the chord. If you want an F major chord, hold down the F key.
- For minor chords, hold down the note of the chord and the closest black key below it.
- For dominant chords, hold down the note of the chord and the closest white key below it.

Check the manual of your instrument to see how to access the various chords. This simple technique can be learned by students of all ages and is an excellent way to introduce the concepts of tonic, dominant, and subdominant harmony. Have the class sing a song and use the keyboard to play the rhythm and different choral accompaniments.

> **Teaching Strategy 20**
> Use the keyboard's record function to record accompaniments and to provide a tool to enhance music creativity.

Even keyboards that cost less than $100 usually have some type of recording capability. Most inexpensive keyboards are limited to one song or 1–2 minutes of recording. This function is an outstanding way for students of all ages to experience the thrill of hearing their own music played back for them.

> **Teaching Strategy 21**
>
> Use percussion sounds to accompany songs and for composition exercises.

Just about every electronic keyboard can also produce percussion sounds. For example, with a General MIDI keyboard, number 129 is the drum kit. Select 129 and your keyboard is turned into a palate of percussion samples. Each key has its own sound including snare, bass, tom-toms, cymbals and a wide variety of other percussion sounds. These sounds can be used to accompany pieces or for students to play rhythm patterns live on the electronic keyboard. Students can learn to play basic rhythm patterns and drum beats using the keyboard. My middle school general music students always enjoy making percussion sounds on their keyboards. In their own words, it is a "cool" activity.

The Keyboard Lab

Another approach to using keyboards is to install a complete lab of keyboards so that an entire class can use them for creativity, performance and other activities. Obviously, the cost is significant as keyboards need to be purchased for all students. It is possible to put two students at each keyboard reducing the minimum to 10-15 keyboards. The specifics of developing a keyboard lab will be addressed in Chapter 12. Labs can be used from intermediate grades on up. Each level has different needs and the equipment should be selected to suit these needs. Please refer to Chapter 12 for an in-depth discussion of the keyboard lab approach.

Getting Started

Many music departments have difficulty funding technology. There are ways to get started with a shoestring budget.

> **Teaching Strategy 22**
>
> Begin using electronic keyboards by inviting students to bring their personal instruments to school.

Many students have keyboards at home. Invite your students to bring their personal instruments in to school for instruction. An electronic keyboard class could be held before or after school. This builds enthusiasm for the program and for the eventual goal of purchasing a lab of instruments for the school.

Instrumental Applications

Keyboards are a valuable asset to instrumental ensembles as well. A keyboard can be used by the teacher as a demonstration instrument or as a member of an instrumental ensemble. Bands and orchestras can use an electronic keyboard as a bass instrument or to fill in for instruments such as a harp or celeste.

> **Teaching Strategy 23**
>
> Use electronic keyboards to play accompaniments for small and large group lessons.

Beginning instrumental lessons can be enhanced by using an electronic keyboard. Simply select a rhythm pattern such as rock, jazz, or reggae, choose the appropriate tempo, and have the students play along. Not only will they be motivated to play with a pop sounding beat, they will gain valuable experience by attempting to play in time.

> **Teaching Strategy 24**
>
> Use keyboards to replace instruments not in an ensemble.

What school ensemble has perfect instrumentation? There are always places where an electronic keyboard can fill in. One of the most common ways school instrumental ensembles use electronic keyboards is as a substitute for the bass part. Another approach is to use electronic keyboards to imitate missing instruments in the group. Instruments such as the bassoon, French horn, and cello can be imitated by the electronic keyboard. Keyboards can be used as "musical chameleons," changing roles and functions as the need arises. The electronic keyboard works best as a musical "pinch-hitter" for instruments missing from the ensemble, not as a permanent substitute.

Teaching Strategy 25

Use the transpose function on the keyboard to read transposed parts and play the actual pitch.

Electronic keyboards can be transposed by any interval. A keyboard can play any part in the band or orchestra without transposing the part. For example, if a bass clarinet is called for and you have no one to play the part, a keyboard player can dial up a clarinet sound and transpose the keyboard to play the appropriate transposition. This is easy to do. If you need a Bb instrument, such as a trumpet or clarinet, transpose down two half-steps. For an Eb instrument, such as saxophone, transpose down nine half-steps. For an F part like a French horn, transpose down seven 1/2 steps. Once the transposition is set, the actual part can be played without sight transposition or rewriting.

Teaching Strategy 26

Use the keyboard to provide percussion sounds and sound effects called for in compositions, i.e. the cannon shots in the 1812 Overture.

Electronic keyboards are quite handy for producing sound effects such as the cannon shots in Tchaikovsky's 1812 Overture and the bird sounds in Respigi's Pines of Rome. They also make excellent substitutes for large, expensive percussion instruments like the gong, chimes, and timpani. Even some professional symphony orchestras are using programmable keyboards and sample players in live performance for sound effects and electronic sounds.

Keyboards and Choral Rehearsal

Electronic keyboards can also be an asset to the choral director. Some of the classroom and instrumental teaching strategies mentioned above can be applied to choral groups.

> ### Teaching Strategy 27
> Use an electronic keyboard as a portable live performance instrument to imitate piano, harpsichord, and church organ.

For live performance, a good electronic instrument with velocity sensitive keys can produce amazing sounds for choir accompaniment. Especially in the $500 plus range, keyboards connected to a good amplification source can produce excellent piano, harpsichord, and organ sounds as well as sound effects and percussion instruments.

> ### Teaching Strategy 28
> Use the transpose function of electronic keyboards to adjust the key of a selection when needed.

How often does the situation arise when a piece is just a step too high or too low? With an electronic keyboard, the key can be adjusted by half-steps in either direction.

Electronic Keyboards and the Internet

There are many web sites on the Internet that support the use of electronic instruments in the classroom. An excellent site that includes information on the types of keyboards and manufacturers web site links is the International Association of Electronic Keyboard Manufacturers (www.iaekm.org).

> ### Teaching Strategy 29
> Visit web sites to research information on electronic instruments and manufacturers, and learn about the world of music technology.

The main section of the web site includes articles, product information, and educational resources. The site also includes a glossary of music technology terms simply and well defined.

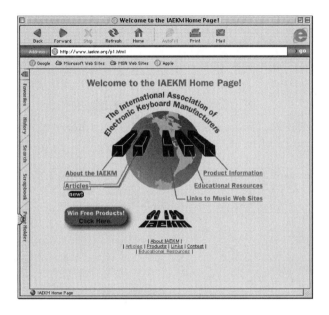

Figure 4.10: International Association of Electronic Keyboard Manufacturers (www.iaekm.org)

Figure 4.11: Glossary of Terms (www.iaekm.org)

History of Electronic Instruments

There are several exceptional web sites that give an overview of the history of electronic instruments. Two sites to consider are the Synthmuseum (www.synthmuseum.com) and a site that includes sounds, photos, and information on every facet of electronic music from www.obsolete.com. Both sites offer a wealth of information on the roots of electronic music production.

Teaching Strategy 30

Visit web sites to do research on the history of electronic instruments and to listen to recorded samples of various instruments.

Figure 4.12: Synthmuseum.com

Summary

Electronic keyboards can have a positive impact on classroom, instrumental, and choral music education. A keyboard can be used as a teaching tool, performance instrument, and recording device. Once the best keyboard is selected, you can find many new and exciting ways to make electronic keyboards an important and essential part of the music learning process.

Review Questions

1. What benefits do electronic keyboards offer the music curriculum?
2. How can you tell if a keyboard is MIDI compatible?
3. What are the advantages of portable electronic keyboards?
4. What are the characteristics of a programmable synthesizer?
5. Digital pianos are primarily designed to serve what function?
6. What are the basic functions of a workstation?
7. Define software synthesizer.
8. What is the advantage to using a MIDI sound module?
9. What is a MIDI keyboard controller?
10. Give two examples of applications for electronic keyboards in the music classroom.
11. Give an example of how electronic keyboards can enhance the instrumental or choral rehearsal.
12. Give an example how a teacher can use an electronic keyboard in the classroom.
13. List two method books designed to be used with electronic keyboards in the music classroom.
14. List one or more web sites that can be used to research information on electronic keyboards.

CD-ROM Activities

- Project 4.1: Review the Chapter 4 Web links. Write a short review of the sites you visit. Go to the IAEKM site (www.iaekm.org) and review the information presented on the various keyboard models.

- Project 4.2: Review the keyboard models presented in this chapter and select the model that best suites a particular need: performance, classroom, and provide a rationale for why the model best suits a particular need.
- Project 4.3: Review the list of electronic instrument strategies listed in this chapter. Select one or more of the strategies and describe how it could be applied in a classroom/rehearsal setting.
- Project 4.4: Prepare a report on the history of electronic instruments. Start with the web sites listed in this chapter or others that you find on the internet. Find photos, sounds, and text describing the evolution of electronic instruments.
- Project 4.5: Review the steps how to reset a MIDI keyboard to the factory presets and/or how to set the keyboard to General MIDI mode.

CD-ROM Lesson Plans

Lesson 4.1 Exploring General Music: poem orchestration, page 8.

Lesson 4.2 Excerpt from Roland's Music Mentor series: Performance Controllers and Expression Features.

Lesson 4.3 Teaching Strategies: Technology (MENC) Create a free-form sound story using a variety of tone colors, page 22.

Reference

Appell, Claudia, J. (1993). *Keyboard Instruction in the Music Classroom*. *Music Educators Journal*, May pp 21-24.

Cavalier, Debbie. (2001). *Exploring General Music in the Keyboard Lab*. Carl Fisher, New York, NY.

Chamberlain, Linda, L. (1993). *Success with Keyboards in the Middle School*. *Music Educators Journal*, Reston, VA. pp. 31-35.

Eiche, Jon F. (1987) *What's a Synthesizer?* Hal Leonard Books. Milwaukee, WI.

Emmons, Scott, et al. (2002). *Silver Burdett Making Music with MIDI*. Scott Forsman, NJ.

Feldstein, Sandy & Cavalier, Debbie. *Keyboards in General Music*. CPP/Belwin, Inc. Miami, FL.

Freff. (1989) *What's a Sampler?* Hal Leonard Books. Milwaukee, WI.

Hilley, Martha F. and Pardue, Tommie (1996). *Strategies for Teaching Middle-Level and High School Keyboard.* MENC, Reston, VA.

Idea Bank (1986). Idea Bank: Does CAI really work?. *Music Educators Journal*, December.

Moore, Brian. (1991) *Technology - A Resource Providing New Ways for Music Educators. New Ways in Music Education*, Fall, 1991. Yamaha Corporation of America, Grand Rapids, MI.

Muro, Don (1991). *Video: An Overview of Electronic Musical Instruments.* J.D. Wall Publishing, Merrick, NY.

Rudolph, Thomas E. (1989). Using Synthesizers in the Instrumental Music Program. *New Ways in Music Education*, Winter. Yamaha Corporation of America, Grand Rapids, MI.

Rudolph, Thomas E. (1993). *Technology for Teaching: Selecting A Synthesizer.* Parts I and II. *Music Educators Journal*, January pp 56-58, and February, 58-60.

Rudolph, Thomas E. (1994). Electronic Keyboards in General Music. *Pennsylvania Music Educators Journal.* March.

Rudolph, Thomas E. (1994). Keyboard Labs in General Music. *Korg Educational News*, June 1994, Vol. 1.

Wiggins (1991). *Synthesizers in the Elementary Classroom.* Music Educators National Conference. Reston, VA.

Wiggins (1993). *Elementary Music with Synthesizers. Music Educators Journal.* Reston, VA. pp 25-30.

Chapter 5

MIDI Controllers and Electronic Instruments

Music Education National Standards: 1, 2
NETS (National Education Technology Standards): 2, 3

This chapter presents an overview of various types of non-keyboard MIDI instruments and electronic devices that can be used to enhance the learning experience in the classroom or in performance.

A controller is any device that "controls" one or more MIDI instruments and/or sound modules. In addition to MIDI keyboard controllers (see Chapter 4) there are MIDI devices designed for percussionists, violinists, guitarists, wind players, and vocalists. All of these devices provide a wide range of opportunities in performance and classroom.

Non-keyboard MIDI instruments are referred to as alternate MIDI controllers. They are an alternative to using the most common MIDI controller, the MIDI keyboard. Alternate MIDI controllers can be placed into five distinct areas:[1]

percussion controllers
string controllers
wind controllers
guitar controllers
unconventional controllers

In addition to the above five categories of alternate MIDI controllers, one additional area will be covered in this chapter: electronic instruments that do not have MIDI output but can be of use in the music curriculum and performance.

Electronic Percussion

One of the most popular applications of MIDI is in the area of electronic percussion. Electronic percussion is a term used to describe any device that produces sound electronically. Many of these instruments are also capable of being connected to other devices via MIDI. There is a wide variety of electronic percussion devices from which to choose. These include drum machines, electronic percussion MIDI controllers, and MIDI drums sets. All of these share several advantages: they are compact, can produce a wide range of sounds, and can be used in conjunction with other instruments.

Drum Machine

The drum machine is one of the oldest electronic percussion instruments. Its predecessors were the rhythm generators that began to appear in home organs in the 1960s. The first programmable drum machines were introduced in the 1970s by the Oberheim and Lynn drum companies. Essentially, drum machines, or drum computers, are devices that can store, record, and play back percussion sounds. They can also be interfaced via MIDI with other instruments. Think of a drum machine as a specialized percussion playback unit with a built-in recorder. Drum machines have a series of pads that are played with the fingertips. Rhythm patterns can be created and recorded. Even the most inexpensive drum machines can store hundreds of patterns.

Just about every major electronic keyboard manufacturer produces drum machines. Today's drum machines are designed to create and record drum patterns for use in live performance or a MIDI studio. Some examples of drum computers include:

- Boss DR-770 DR Rhythm
- Alesis SR-16
- Roland R8

Figure 5.1: Boss DR-770 Drum Machine

The drum machine reproduces digitally recorded samples or sounds of percussion instruments. In other words, actual sounds from acoustic percussion instruments were digitally recorded and stored inside the drum computer's memory. Using a drum machine, claves, bongos, maracas, and other instrument sounds can be instantly accessed both for live performance and for recorded playback.

Since many patterns can be stored, drum parts can be created for entire songs including introduction patterns, fills, and ending patterns. With a drum machine, rhythm patterns can be recorded in real time (playing in time with the drum machine's metronome) or step entered one note and its duration at a time.

Teaching Strategy 31

Use a drum machine to record and store drum patterns for use in the general music classroom or ensemble rehearsal to accompany songs and movement activities.

The drum machine is not necessarily essential equipment in today's MIDI studio because most MIDI keyboard workstations and most electronic MIDI keyboards can generate and record drum sounds and rhythms. However, they are very portable and make a wonderful addition to the music classroom, jazz ensemble, or other performing group.

MIDI Percussion Controllers

The drum machine can be played with the fingertips. If you want to play with drum sticks, mallets, or the hand, you will need a MIDI percussion controller. These are specialized electronic instruments designed to be played with a drumstick, xylophone mallet, or bare hand. Percussion controllers are devices that when struck by a stick, hand, or pedal can generate sound or control an external MIDI device.

Teaching Strategy 32

Use a MIDI percussion controller to produce the sounds of large, expensive percussion instruments such as the gong, conga drum, and timpani.

Most percussion controllers are capable of generating their own sound, both pitched and unpitched, and they can control external MIDI keyboards and MIDI sound modules. MIDI percussion controllers can be used to produce sounds of instruments that are too expensive or not available in a performance ensemble. For example, a percussion controller could be used to produce the sound of timpani, chimes, or gong. They are also quite compact, and where space is a major concern, they can be a distinct advantage.

There are various models of percussion controllers from which to choose. Some are designed for the professional and others for the music hobbyist. The basic difference is price. Professional MIDI percussion controllers usually cost more than $1,000 while those made for the consumer market are usually priced in the $200-$300 range.

The oldest and most common type of percussion controller is a series of pads that are played with drumsticks. The Roland SPD-20 is an example of a MIDI percussion controller. The user can assign each of the eight pads on the instrument to a separate sound or timbre. The SPD-20, formerly the Octapad, is designed to take up a small amount of space. It is an excellent way to reproduce the sounds of timpani for a musical pit orchestra or on the field for a marching band show. In Chapter 8, MIDI sequencers will be introduced. The drum controllers can be used with these applications to input drum parts.

The SPD-20 has a wealth of built-in sounds featuring realistic acoustic drum sounds, ethnic and world instruments, classic electronic drum sounds, and unique sound effects. It is MIDI capable so it can also control external MIDI devices. The Roland SPD-20 can be used in performing ensembles and in the music classroom. It is designed for professional use. It does need to be connected to an external amplifier as there are no built-in speakers.

Figure 5.2: Roland SPD-20 percussion controller

MIDI Percussion Controllers for the Classroom

Yamaha has a less expensive line of drum controllers (the DD series) with on-board sounds, so an external MIDI module is not required. The lower cost ($100-$300 range) make these affordable by most school budgets. The other attractive feature of the Yamaha DD series is they have built-in speakers. This makes it a most desirable addition to the classroom and for small ensembles.

An additional interesting feature of the Yamaha DD35 is the use of guide lamps to help novices play the right notes at the right time. The DD35 takes full advantage of this feature with built-in activities using the lighted rings around the drum pads to make the DD35 fun and educational. The pads can be played with drum sticks or hands.

Figure 5.3: Yamaha DD35 Digital Drums

95

MIDI Drum Set

For the percussionist who wants a digital drum set that resembles and can be played like a traditional drum set, there are several options. Roland makes V-Drums and Yamaha offers the DTX Digital Percussion System. Other companies also offer MIDI drums sets.

> **Teaching Strategy 33**
>
> MIDI drum sets can be used in the jazz ensemble to generate many different types of percussion and sound effects.

MIDI drum sets include a complete array of drum triggers and a sophisticated drum sound module designed for the serious percussionist. The cost of this professional option is in the $1,000-$2,000 range and up. The main advantage of this option is that the instruments can be set up in a similar fashion to a traditional drum set complete with pads for snare, tom-tom, bass drum, and cymbals.

Figure 5.4: Roland V-Drums

Because a percussion controller sends MIDI data, it can be connected to the input of a MIDI interface and used to input data into a sequencer or notation program. This is a natural way for percussionists to enter parts into a sequence.

Hand Percussion Controllers

Roland also makes the Handsonic (HPD-15), a compact and lightweight hand percussion unit that you can play with your hands. The unit can be an enhancement to jazz ensembles and other performing groups. It does not have built-in speakers, and therefore must be connected to an amplification source. The Handsonic includes more than 500 drum, percussion, and melodic sounds; built-in effects, a sequencer, inputs for kick and hi-hat pedals, and MIDI. The touch-sensitive playing surface is based on that of Roland's V-Drums and offers features such as positional sensing that alters the timbre according to where the pad surface is struck. Positional sensing also means sounds can be dampened by touching the pads or bent by pressing down harder. The Handsonic can be used to create the sounds of bongos, congas, and other hand percussion.

Figure 5.5: Roland HPD15

Groove Sampler

Groove samplers are primarily designed for use in rap and dance styles. The purpose of a groove sampler is to assemble audio loops into a composition or for live performance.

> ## Teaching Strategy 34
> Use a groove sampler to create "hip" sounding tracks for movement and improvisation.

Most groove samplers can also record audio that can then be triggered from pads on the unit. It is possible to record students speaking, singing, or performing on instruments into the groove sampler for playback. Different models have multiple editing and processing capabilities to alter or edit the samples once they are recorded. Audio output is controlled from a mixer section where volume is controlled in actual (real) time. It is possible to patch or send the audio signal to an audio mixer (see Chapter 9) to combine it with other devices. Some units also have a built-in tone generator to add bass or keyboard parts. In addition to the Roland SP-808 and MC-505, Akai, Ensoniq, and Yamaha also offer their own designs of groove samplers.

Figure 5.6: Roland SP 808 Groovebox

MIDI String Instruments

The Zeta Company produces a complete line of electronic string instruments including several models of electronic violins, violas, and cellos. These instruments are specialized electric string instruments that provide string players with an instrument that can be easily amplified for live performance.

> ### Teaching Strategy 35
> Use an electric violin equipped with a MIDI violin controller for live performance.

Zeta also produces a MIDI violin controller that connects up to four or five string Zeta violins and allows these instruments to send MIDI information to MIDI sound modules and synthesizers. To use these MIDI controllers, essentially two devices are needed—a Zeta MIDI violin and a MIDI violin controller. MIDI string instruments are excellent additions to an electro-acoustic ensemble and for live performance and for entering data into music software programs. Zeta makes professional-quality instruments. They do offer a special Educator series designed for teacher and student use. Expect to pay more than $1,000 per instrument.

Figure 5.7: Zeta Educator Modern Violin
(www.zetamusic.com)

> ### Teaching Strategy 36
> Use a MIDI string controller to replace instruments not available in the ensemble. For example, a violinist could play a MIDI violin, dial up a string bass patch and play the bass part.

Suppose the cello player in a string quartet can't make the concert. With an electric violin connected to a MIDI module, a violinist could play the cello part, using a cello sound in the correct octave. MIDI instruments also make it possible for string players to be added to jazz, rock, and other contemporary ensembles. These instruments are not designed to replace their acoustic counterparts, rather they are designed for string players to use in live performance and to control MIDI modules.

Guitar Controllers

Electric guitars can also send MIDI information when equipped with appropriate gear. Several available products make this possible, for example, Roland's line of guitar synthesizers. The Roland GR series comes in various configurations allowing guitarists to access a wide range of sounds including acoustic instruments, effects, and even percussion sounds. Connect any guitar to a guitar synthesizer and many additional sounds are made possible.

Roland also makes a special device, the GI-10 Guitar MIDI interface that converts a guitar's output to MIDI data. When the GI-10 is connected, a guitarist can plug into any MIDI module and access all of the available sounds. Also, with the GI-10, a guitarist can plug into the MIDI IN of a computer interface and input directly into a sequencer or notation program. This is an excellent device for guitarists who don't play the keyboard but want to record, play back, and store MIDI data.

MIDI Wind Controllers

There are electronic instruments called wind controllers that are designed for horn players. In a manner similar to the percussion, string, and guitar controllers mentioned above, MIDI data is sent to a sound module via an instrument that is fingered and blown like a wind instrument.

> ### Teaching Strategy 37
> Use a wind controller so students, especially woodwind players, can control a MIDI sound module or keyboard. This can be useful in the jazz ensemble and to produce sounds of instruments not included in the ensemble.

MIDI wind controllers have been around since the advent of MIDI, but none have caught on in a major way. Akai's Electronic Wind Instrument or EWI (pronounced EE-WEE) has fingerings similar to a recorder and a breath sensor so the instrument will respond to breath attacks. Yamaha makes a wind controller similar to the Akai unit, the Yamaha WX-5.

Figure 5.8: Yamaha WX-5 Wind Controller

Overall, wind controllers have not been as successful as originally thought, especially when compared with electronic keyboards and electronic percussion. Some jazz and commercial performers have embraced wind controllers. Jazz artists, including Michael Brecker and others, have featured electronic instruments on recordings and in live performance. Wind controllers do have many advantages as they can access a variety of timbres in an unlimited range. Because wind controllers are MIDI compatible, they can produce non-pitched sounds, chords, sound effects, and any other sound a MIDI device can produce.

There are two primary limitations of wind controllers. First, in most cases, they must be connected to an electronic keyboard or MIDI sound module to produce sound. Second, it takes practice to learn to play a wind controller and become familiar with each instrument's various performance parameters.

> **Teaching Strategy 38**
> Use a wind controller to imitate the sound of instruments not in the ensemble or to enter data into a music software program.

MIDI Saxophone

Some companies have taken traditional instruments and added sensors that can be used to transmit MIDI data to a synthesizer or MIDI sound module. The Synthophone (http://synthophone.home.att.net/) is an actual alto sax that has been modified to send MIDI data to synthesizers and computers. The instrument feels and plays like a sax, but in addition is also capable of producing some quite amazing new effects such as chords. The MIDI format of the Synthophone allows you to choose from a large selection of synthesizers, enables you to play into sequencers and even use notation programs that will turn your performance into notated scores.

MIDI Bass Pedals

Another type of MIDI keyboard controller is designed for keyboard players who play foot pedal bass. This instrument is used to drive a MIDI module and is primarily used to generate bass notes. The Roland PK-5 and the Fatar MIDI bass pedals are examples of MIDI bass pedals and they resemble a miniature church organ bass pedal unit. MIDI bass pedals are designed for live performance.

Electronic Instruments Designed for the Music Classroom

One fascinating electronic instrument that can be used in the classroom is the Q Chord by Suzuki. This is the redesign of the popular Omnichord that has been used in schools for many years.

The Q Chord incorporates the technology of a basic keyboard and electric guitar and combines both in a portable, easy to use way. The instrument is divided up into three sections; a touch sensitive strum plate, a rhythm section, and a chord button section. Each of these areas can be used independently or combined together. Many sounds are obtainable from the strum plate.

> ### Teaching Strategy 39
>
> Use the Q Chord in the classroom to create chords, melodies, and a variety of sounds and effects. It is an easy instrument to learn for students at all grades. Because there is a MIDI output, it can be connected to other MIDI devices and computers.

Figure 5.9: The Q Chord by Suzuki
(www.suzukimusic.co.uk/qchord.htm)

There are a number of accessories available for the Q Chord, the most notable of which are song cartridges. These plug into the instrument and, like karaoke, make it possible to play, as well as sing along to pop, country and western, religious, children's songs, party hits, and so forth. The Q Chord can be used as a stand-alone instrument, as it has built-in speakers. It is possible to connect it to an external amplifier using its built-in audio outputs. MIDI output is also possible so the Q Chord can connect to other MIDI instruments or to a computer if needed.

The MIDI Partner System

Silver Burdett introduced a specialized set of MIDI instruments called the MIDI Partner System. These electronic instruments are designed for the music classroom. The instruments include a MIDI recorder, MIDI xylophone, and MIDI keyboard. They are connected to a central player station and have the capability of playing live and for recording. Silver Burdett has created a complete curriculum that integrates these instruments into the general music class and works in conjunction with their music curriculum, *Making Music*.

The MIDI Partner System can be used to enhance and expand instrumental performance possibilities for elementary students. The design is modular so instruments can be added. One, two, three, or more MIDI instruments can be used for performance.

> **Teaching Strategy 40**
>
> Use the MIDI Partner System in the elementary music classroom to add electronic instruments as a performance option for students.

Pitch-to-MIDI Converters

If you want to use an acoustic instrument to produce MIDI sounds and effects, you will need a pitch-to-MIDI converter.

> **Teaching Strategy 41**
>
> Use a pitch-to-MIDI converter with an acoustic instrument to trigger MIDI modules and other sound sources.

There are pitch-to-MIDI converters that take acoustic sound played into a microphone and convert the sound vibrations into MIDI data. Any acoustic instrument or the human voice can be used. Play or sing into a microphone and the sound is converted to MIDI data. Because the conversion process from acoustic sound to MIDI is quite complex, most pitch-to-MIDI converters are only 90-95% accurate. However, pitch-to-MIDI converters do offer a viable alternative to entering MIDI data and controlling MIDI modules with acoustic instruments and the voice.

An excellent, all-purpose MIDI converter is Amadeus II. Connect a standard microphone to Amadeus II and any acoustic sound can be changed into MIDI data. The voice can also be used to generate MIDI data. Simply sing into Amadeus II using a standard microphone and the pitches are converted to MIDI information.

The advantage of using an acoustic instrument or voice to input MIDI data is that the performer does not need to learn a new instrument. The disadvantage is the significant amount of equipment needed. Also, the technology of converting acoustic sound to MIDI data is inexact. Sometimes, especially if many fast notes or a combination of single notes and double stops are played, the converter can become overloaded and even sound some notes that were not played. Try out a MIDI converter before purchasing to be sure that the device can deliver your required performance level.

Acoustic Pianos and MIDI

One of the most fascinating areas of acoustic/MIDI application is retro-fitting or adapting an acoustic piano to send and receive MIDI data. Several companies, including Yamaha and Piano Disc, produce the necessary hardware to convert the vibrations of acoustic piano strings to MIDI information. As you can imagine, retrofitting an acoustic piano to convert its vibrations to MIDI is expensive—in the $4,000-$8,000 range. However, if you prefer using an acoustic piano and have sufficient budget money available, there are some applications that can be realized in education.

> ### Teaching Strategy 42
> Use an acoustic piano retro-fitted to send and receive MIDI information to play and record sequences for student demonstration and performance.

The first step is to have the acoustic piano retro-fitted to send and receive MIDI information. Then MIDI files must be purchased or created to be used for listening or practice. Another option is to purchase an acoustic piano that is designed to function in the dual role of acoustic piano and MIDI device. If the school budget can afford it, this is an outstanding way to play back sequences in live performance enabling the teacher to have the best of both worlds: the sound and feel of an acoustic piano with the power and flexibility of the sequencer. This is the modern day version of a player-piano.

There are two major players in the acoustic piano-MIDI world, Piano Disc and Disklavier by Yamaha. Both companies make the necessary hardware and MIDI data files to play on the specially equipped pianos. The Piano Disc Company will convert an existing acoustic piano or provide new instruments that are MIDI compatible. Yamaha produces the Disklavier, a special acoustic piano model capable of sending and receiving MIDI data.

Unconventional Controllers

Unconventional controllers abandon any duplication of acoustic instrument design and may vary widely in their use of MIDI to control sound as well as in the manner in which they are played, referred to as the interface.[2] Examples of unconventional controllers designed for professional performance use include the Chapman stick and the Theremin with MIDI capabilities.

Teaching Strategy 43

Use unconventional MIDI controllers in the classroom or in live performance. They will take some time to learn, but will open up a new world of possibilities.

Chapman Stick

The Chapman Stick comes in a variety of formats and is designed for the performer. The instruments use strings like a guitar and are designed by Emmett Chapman. They are designed to take advantage of his unique two-handed tapping method. With both hands as equal partners on the fretboard, each hand can play independent lines, or the two hands can work in concert to form interlaced arrangements. The Stick method enables live execution of complete musical concepts, including bass, chords, melody, and effects.

Guitarists can play lead lines backed by their own rhythm and counterpoint from all registers. Bassists can support a group with driving low frequencies while filling in the spaces with chordal upbeats and melodic patterns. Keyboardists can discover subtle elements of expression with their fingers directly engaging the vibrating strings. Percussionists can apply familiar rhythmic techniques to the world of harmony, simply by measuring distances between the hands and between the fingers on each hand.

Even novice musicians can discover the ease of making fully realized song arrangements and harmonically meaningful improvisations with this instrument. The success of Chapman's tap-and-hold method can be attributed to a basic advance—that of equal access by all fingers of both hands to the strings.

Figure 5.10: 10-String Chapman Stick
(www.stick.com)

The Chapman stick is something that will take time to learn and is on the expensive side, costing in the $1,000 and up range. The Chapman stick could be used as a classroom instrument or by bass, guitar, and percussion players in any ensemble.

Theremin MIDI Controllers

Since the 1920s the theremin has intrigued people with its space-controlled, highly expressive sound. The instrument is played by waving your hands near the instrument's antenna.

There is a theremin that combines classic tone and playability with the latest music technology, the Etherwave theremin by MoogMusic, Inc. These devices cost in the $500 range and can be used in the classroom or performing ensemble to perform sound effects and related sounds. To hear samples of these fascinating instruments, go to www.moogmusic.com.

MoogMusic also produces an Ethervox theremin that has MIDI technology built in. It can be integrated easily into a MIDI studio, music classroom, or stage setup. Several menu options let you match your Ethervox's MIDI data to the other resources in your MIDI setup. The Ethervox's MIDI data can be played back through the Ethervox itself, or through any MIDI sound generator that is capable of wide-range pitch-bend.

Figure 5.11: Ethervox MIDI Theremin
(www.moogmusic.com)

Thus you can create a virtually limitless array of dramatic and expressive continuously varying musical gestures simply by moving your hands around the Ethervox's antennas. Because the Ethervox produces MIDI data, it can be recorded into a MIDI sequencer. MIDI theremins are priced in the $1,000-$4,000 range.

The airSynth

The concept of using hand motions to create sounds and effects has also been incorporated in a device called the airSynth by Alesis. The airSynth is played by moving your hands in the air, in a similar fashion to the theremin. Connect an audio output to the airSynth or airFX—such as a CD or a turntable, or any electronic instrument—wave your hand over the red sphere, and you can create sounds, literally out of thin air.[3] The device comes in a low-end version called the airSynth and a high-end model call the airFX.

Figure 5.12: The airFX by Alesis

The airSynth has its own on-board sounds that include staccato and percussive sounds, drum sounds, and more, that beg to be twisted, slapped, gyrated, and stretched by the musically adventurous. You can't program your own sounds, but there are ample sounds included to create a wide range of effects.

At the heart of the airSynth is Alesis'Axyz ("ax-is") technology, which powers the infrared, 3D sphere that allows a user to control up to five sound variables simultaneously by moving the hand left and right, forward and backward, and up and down over the product—complete with velocity sensitivity. The solitary front-panel knob can select, freeze, and release a given sound. Audio is handled with 24-bit RCA stereo outs, and it has RCA inputs that allow pass-through of external signals. This allows the user to control external signals from turntables, CD players, electronic instruments, and the like.

The current version is not MIDI compatible. It can be used for overdubbing, in live performance, or in the classroom to create sound effects. A threaded socket on the base lets you mount it on a microphone stand. The airSynth is priced under $300 and provides an innovative way to include electronic sounds and sound effects in the studio, classroom, or performance ensemble.

Electronic Performance Ensembles

Combine a group of performers playing MIDI controllers and MIDI keyboards and you have an exciting performance medium that can support the instrumental curriculum. These ensembles carry a variety of names including synthesizer ensemble, MIDI ensembles, and electro-acoustic ensembles.

Teaching Strategy 44

Start a MIDI ensemble in your school to attract students who are not currently involved in the traditional school performing groups: band, orchestra, and chorus.

(Listen to an audio example of the Hilltop HS MIDI Ensemble on the companion CD-ROM.)

From elementary school to university, schools are finding that an electronic ensemble adds a new dimension to the existing instrumental music program. Dennis Mauricio, director of the Hilltop High School MIDI Ensemble in Chula Vista, California, has had wonderful success over 16 years directing a MIDI ensemble.[4] At the college level, Rocky Reuter of Capital University and George Hess of Central Michigan State University both agree that the MIDI ensemble offers new and exiting performance options for students.[5]

Figure 5.13: The Capital University MIDI Band directed by Dr. Rocky Reuter

In Dennis Mauricio's article "Starting a Synth Ensemble" he states, "A synthesizer ensemble is an excellent way to attract and involve students in your music program who may not otherwise be in a traditional music group."[6] Schools that have formed electronic ensembles (MIDI ensembles, synth ensembles or electro-acoustic ensembles) are finding that the students who play keyboard now have an avenue of expression in a performing ensemble.

Starting a MIDI Ensemble

To get started, all you need are some electronic keyboards and a mixer and sound system. Consider also adding some of the MIDI controllers described in this chapter to include those who do not play keyboard. If your school does not own multiple keyboards, invite students to bring their own instruments in to school.

Drummers can play MIDI instruments and other alternative MIDI controllers can be added to the group. Mauricio also encourages students who play acoustic instruments to join his ensemble. Using signal processing gear and pitch-to MIDI converters allows virtually any instrumentalist to participate in the electronic experience. Lynn Purse advocates electro-acoustic ensembles, where both electronic and acoustic instruments are combined in the same ensemble.[7]

Music for MIDI Ensembles

The challenge is to select the music for the MIDI ensemble. Currently, there are only a few publishers of music written specifically for the MIDI ensemble. For the most part, directors create their own custom arrangements as MIDI ensemble size and configuration varies greatly from school to school. Dr. Rocky Reuter writes many of his arrangements himself. He also encourages his students to create music.

For those who want to purchase music, there are some options. Don Muro has composed a series of trios and quartets for synthesizers. Joy Cardin also has several performance books in print. Refer to the list of publishers and web sites in Appendix A.

Summary

Electronic instruments have had a tremendous impact on the entire music industry. Most notably, they have brought musical instruments into the home and school at a relatively low cost. It is, of course, up to the music educator to devise ways to incorporate these new instruments. As the price of MIDI wind instruments becomes more affordable for parents of school children, these instruments may have an increased mass appeal. Wouldn't it be terrific if the instrumental drop-out rate would decrease to less than 10% using electronic instruments? Possibly, students would find practicing more enjoyable if the instruments did not require hours of practice just to make a pleasing sound. Students could concentrate on fingering and note reading from the outset and achieve success much more rapidly.

This is not to imply that traditional acoustic instruments will disappear. I recently attended a drum and bugle corps competition and it reaffirmed my feeling that the warmth and presence of acoustic instruments can never be replaced (I can't image seeing the strongest kid in the percussion section carrying a computer central processing unit (CPU) onto the field rather than a bass drum!). However, electronic instruments surely will find their own niche in education, just as they have in professional performance and the recording industry.

Investigate the technologies described in this chapter and search for ways that they can assist with the existing music program either by using electronic instruments to supplement existing ensembles and classroom activates or by creating new electro-acoustic ensembles.

Review Questions

1. List the five categories of alternate MIDI controllers.
2. What is the advantage of using a drum machine?
3. What are the advantages of using MIDI percussion controllers instead of an acoustic drum set with an instrumental ensemble? What are the limitations and potential problems?
4. What are the limitations of MIDI wind controllers?
5. There are several electronic instruments designed for the music classroom. What are the advantages and disadvantages of using electronic instruments in the music classroom?

6. What is a pitch-to-MIDI converter? How can it be used to generate electronic sounds and sound effects?

7. What is an unconventional MIDI Controller? Examples include the airSynth and the SoundBeam (http://www.soundbeam.co.uk).

8. What is a theramin and how can be used in performance or in the classroom?

9. What do MIDI ensembles, technology ensembles, and synth ensembles all have in common?

10. MIDI ensembles can serve students who are often not involved with school bands, choruses, and orchestras. With this in mind, list the benefits of non-traditional ensembles.

11. List two or three options for selecting music for a technology ensemble.

12. Some music educators both predict and fear that electronic instruments will someday displace the traditional, acoustic instruments such as the violin and trumpet. Pick a stance and support your opinion.

CD-ROM Activities

- Project 5.1: Explore the Chapter 5 Web links: Review the sites you visit.
- Project 5.2: Project 5.2: Write an arrangement of Amazing Grace for four electronic instruments. The melody and chords are on the files linked below. In your arrangement, be sure to include the sounds to be used and other expressive characteristics such as pitch bend, vibrato, and volume changes.
- Project 5.3: print out Don Muro's trio, "On a Joyous Morning," and perform it with three synthesizers.
- Project 5.4: Prepare a list of what would be needed to start a school MIDI ensemble. Read the articles on the CD-ROM by Rocky Reuter and Dennis Mauricio.

Reference

Abeles, H.& Van Scoyoc. (1990). *wind controllers, new options for music teachers. Music Educators Journal,* Technology for Teaching, October, pp. 14-18.

Mahin, Bruce (1994). *Advances in electronic instruments.The Instrumentalist,* September. pp. 62-72.

Muro, Don (1993) *An Overview of Electronic Musical Instruments Video.* J.D. Wall Publishing Co., Box 297, Smithtown, NY

Oppenheimer, L. (1993). *Big bang boom. Electronic Musician,* December, 1993. pp. 60-69.

Purse, Lynn and Rudolph, T. *TI:ME 2A Electronic Instruments.* Technology Institute for Music Educators, 2000.

Rudolph, T. (1989) *Using synthesizers in the instrumental program. New Ways,* Volume 5, Number 2, Winter. Yamaha Corporation of America. pp. 8-9.

Smith, G. editor (1995-96) *Hi-tech kids and electronic percussion. A Music Technology Resource Guide for Educators,* Advanced Technologies, South Bend, IN. pp. 112-114.

Chapter 6

Instructional Software (Computer-Assisted Instruction)

National Standards that can be addressed: 1, 2, 4, 5, 6, 7, 8, 9
NETS (National Education Technology Standards): 1, 2, 3, 5, 6

In Chapter 1, the concept of using technology as a tutor, tool, or tutee was introduced. The objective of this chapter is review the oldest and perhaps the most popular use of technology in music education: technology as tutor. Robert Taylor summarizes this approach as follows:

> To function as a tutor in some subject, the computer must be programmed by ("experts") in programming and in that subject. The student is then tutored by the computer executing the program(s). The computer presents some subject material, the student responds, the computer evaluates the response, and, from the results of the evaluation, determines what to present next. At its best, the computer tutor keeps complete records on each student being tutored; it has at its disposal a wide range of subject detail it can present; and it has an extensive and flexible way to test and then lead the student through the material. With appropriate well-designed software, the computer tutor can easily and swiftly tailor its presentation to accommodate a wide range of student differences.[1]

Computer-assisted instruction software, often referred to as CAI, can be used to introduce and reinforce musical concepts in music theory, ear training, piano instruction, and instrument fingerings. Please note that there is no universal term for computer applications in music education. Computer-assisted instruction serves as an umbrella for several interchangeable terms including computer-assisted instruction in music and computer-based music instruction.[2] Another common CAI term is courseware. Courseware is software designed to be used in an educational environment. Courseware is sometimes a series of sequential programs designed for a specific subject such as music courseware or math courseware. Two advantages of using CAI are:

- Computer-assisted instruction is easy to use and very little training is needed for either the student or teacher. CAI software is designed for novice computer users.

- It is easy to align CAI software with the existing music curriculum. For instance, if you are teaching the names of the white and black keys on the piano keyboard, there are programs to help students practice this concept.

The disadvantages of using instructional software are that it can become tedious and boring. CAI doesn't, in most cases, involve higher level thinking skills such as creating and composing. However, as you will find in this chapter, there can be some very effective applications of CAI software for music instruction.

History of CAI in Music

Technology and computers are not new to the field of music education. Music educators have utilized computers in the instructional environment since the 1960s. Music theory and ear-training exercises were originally presented on large computers at some colleges and universities. In the 1960s an expensive mainframe computer was required to store and generate the exercises. These programs were the result of college research efforts and were not geared to general or public education. Such instruction was not available to elementary and secondary schools, as they did not have the facilities for these expensive computers and terminals.

In the late 1970s, the microcomputer revolutionized the role of computers everywhere, especially in education. Self-contained computers became available at a fraction of the cost of a mainframe computer. With the creation of personal computers, software began to be written for a variety of education, business, and entertainment uses. The first microcomputer programs for music, like the mainframe applications that preceded them, were in the field of music theory and ear-training. Later, as microcomputers became more powerful, programs were developed to include sequencing and printing.

David Peters[3] describes the evolution of CAI as occurring in four separate generations. The first generation was in the 1960s and early '70s when college mainframes were all that existed. The second generation came in the late '70s as these mainframe programs, mostly geared toward college level music theory and ear-training, were rewritten to take advantage of the new microcomputers. The Apple II, Commodore 64, and other affordable computers became popular in schools. The third generation occurred in the early '80s with the introduction of MIDI. With MIDI, the sound quality produced was no longer limited to the built-in speaker inside the computer. Also, now users could input information through a musical instrument rather than by typing on a typewriter keyboard. The introduction of the mouse as a pointing device was another important step. With a mouse, young children could operate a computer.

The fourth generation, the generation we are currently in, takes advantage of many new and exciting technologies. Digital audio samples can be played by the computer and students can listen to compact disc recordings while learning about various aspects of a piece. Some fourth generation software also allows students to input information by singing or by playing an acoustic instrument. One thing is certain, as computers continue to become more powerful and less expensive, applications for music education will continue to expand.

Hardware Configurations

One of the main advantages of CAI is that some programs can be used with off-the-shelf computers without electronic keyboards or other musical devices. Other CAI software requires MIDI instruments, sound cards, or a CD-ROM.

> **Teaching Strategy 45**
>
> Use software that runs on stand-alone computers. This is an inexpensive way to introduce computer applications at all levels.

With some CAI programs, sounds are produced by the computer's built-in sound capabilities. Today's Macintosh and Windows computers come with good quality built-in sound. If computers are available in your school, then the only cost involved is the software purchase. This offers a relatively inexpensive way to incorporate computers into the music curriculum.

> **Teaching Strategy 46**
>
> Connect a computer to a MIDI keyboard or device to allow for better sound quality and for input from a music keyboard.

The next level, beyond using just a computer, is purchasing software that takes advantage of MIDI. The sounds of MIDI keyboards and MIDI sound modules are superior to those of most computers. However, it also means that a MIDI capable instrument and a MIDI connector or interface must be purchased.

> **Teaching Strategy 47**
>
> Use a computer with a CD drive to access compact disc quality sound, pictures, text, and video.

Some programs include audio CDs that are used with the software. There is an advantage to this as the sounds used can be both acoustic and synthesized.

PDAs and CAI

PDAs, or Personal Digital Assistants, such as the Palm, can also be used for CAI and other music applications. Although the power of these tools is far inferior to computers, they can be a viable way for students to access some applications and for portable instruction in music.

> ### Teaching Strategy 48
> PDAs (such as a Palm) can be equipped with music software for students to drill musical concepts.

There are a variety of available programs including theory and ear training. For more detailed information review the article on this topic from the December, 2001, issue of *Electronic Musician*. The article can be viewed at: http://emusician.com/ar/emusic_music_palm_hand/index.htm.

Categories of CAI or Instructional Software

There are dozens of music CAI programs designed to be used in an instructional setting.

> ### Teaching Strategy 49
> Use existing resource guides published by various organizations and authors to help sort through the vast array of music software.

With such a large quantity of software, it can be overwhelming when trying to select the best application for a specific need. The first step is to understand the various categories of instructional software available. There are many variations of software. Some titles are designed for one basic application and others include many in the same program.

The basic content areas include:

- theory
- aural skills
- history
- instrument instruction

There are several places I to turn when I want to review the latest CAI offerings. My first stop is the *Technology Directory*, published by the Association for Technology in Music Instruction.[4] This directory, published annually, contains the most complete listing of information about all types of software, hardware, and printed materials. The 2001 catalog lists more than 300 titles of CAI. Simply join ATMI and you will receive a copy of their comprehensive directory. The cost of membership is worthwhile even if you only use the directory. Another benefit of membership is an informative quarterly newsletter. I also refer to catalogs published by companies that serve the music education community. Companies including Lentine's Music, McCormicks, SoundTree, Brook Mays, The MIDI Workshop, AABACA, J.W. Pepper, and Kelly's Computers are all excellent places to start. A complete listing of their addresses and web sites can be found at the end of this chapter. By referencing one or more of the above mentioned sources, you can select the best CAI program for a particular lesson or teaching situation.

Instructional Software Formats

Essentially, for each subject area (theory, aural skills, math, etc.) there are four types of instructional software. Each is examined in a section below. They are:

- drill and practice
- games
- tutorials
- simulations

Drill and Practice

One of the oldest instructional applications of technology is referred to as drill and practice. Patrick Suppes describes drill and practice programs as:

> ...Meant to supplement the regular teaching process. After the teacher has introduced new concepts and ideas in the standard fashion the computer provides regular review and practice of basic concepts and skills...These would be automatically presented, evaluated, and scored by the computer program without any effort by the classroom teacher.[5]

An example of drill and practice software used in a music theory class would be to drill intervals and chords. The teacher would introduce the concept in class and then provide students with the opportunity to practice these skills outside of class using the software.

Games

Today's students have grown up with video games. They are accustomed to the fast action and challenges. Educators can capture and take advantage of this enthusiasm by using the music games geared to keep interest high and provide an interactive setting for students. In addition to applying skills and concepts in a game environment, these music programs have other benefits as well. To master a game, a student must acquire a working knowledge of the rules. Games also provide pupils with healthy peer competition and can be a fun classroom activity.

Tutorials

Tutorial software teaches musical concepts. It presents concepts to the student in a sequential manner with built-in assessment along the way. These programs are designed to teach specific skills and/or content, e.g. the names of the lines and spaces or notes on a piano keyboard.

Simulations

A simulation offers choices to the student. They can click on a variety of options and explore the software in their own, personal way. The most popular simulation is the flight simulator where the software imitates the act of flying. In music, simulations offer the student experiences in a variety of musical areas from classical to contemporary.

Suggested CAI Titles for Music

The software list mentioned in the following section is not all-inclusive, nor does it identify only the best programs. Final selection of software should include evaluating software and using it with students, which will be addressed at the end of this chapter.

Alfred Essentials of Music Theory

Theory drill and practice programs are available for elementary through college level. An excellent option is Alfred's Essentials of Music Theory, available for Macintosh and Windows. It includes tutorial and drill and practice exercises from beginner to advanced levels.

Teaching Strategy 50

Use CAI software as a supplement to music theory classes.

Their program has three levels appropriate for grades 4–12. The software presents basic-to-complex theory concepts in a logical, sequential manner.

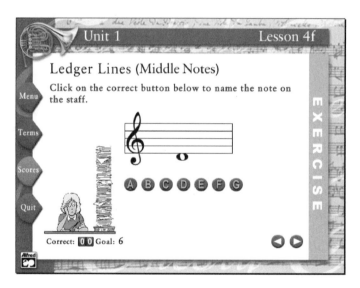

Figure 6.1: Alfred Essentials of Music Theory Software
(www.alfred.com)

There are also corresponding textbooks that can be purchased for students to reinforce the content of the software. The feature I like most is that the sounds produced by the program include digital audio recordings of acoustic instruments. There are 75 lessons divided into three volumes that can be purchased separately.

The Music Ace Series

Another excellent program that includes both theory and aural concepts is Music Ace by Harmonic-Vision. There are two programs from which to choose: Music Ace and Music Ace 2. Both programs include tutorials on musical concepts and fun, interactive games to test the student's knowledge. Harmonic-Vision, the publisher of the program, offers the software in two versions: software only or an educational version. The educational version comes with a binder full of lesson plans, activities, and worksheets that can be copied for classroom use.

Figure 6.2: Music Ace (www.harmonicvision.com)

Once the student completes the tutorial portion of the lesson, they are instructed to go to the game. Here they receive a score for correct answers. This program can be used at all levels elementary through high school and is presented in an enjoyable and engaging manner.

Practica Musica

An excellent example of aural training software for the secondary level is Practica Musica, published by Ars Nova (Macintosh and Windows). This program includes a variety of exercises.

> **Teaching Strategy 51**
>
> Assign computer exercises for ear-training and theory students to complete outside of class.

At Gettysburg College, Dr. John Jones uses Practica Musica with his music theory/ear training classes. Because Practica Musica has a variety of exercises including intervals, chords, melodic and rhythmic dictation, and note reading, students can practice a wide range of skills. Students are given individual disks to store their scores and Dr. Jones periodically checks their progress. Dr. Jones finds that software helps his students to internalize many ear training concepts.

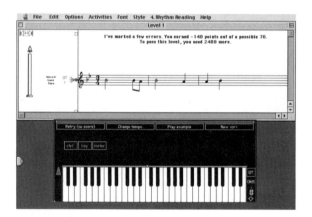

Figure 6.3: Sample exercise in Practica Musica
(www.ars-nova.com)

Auralia and Musition are companion programs that are designed to address theory and ear-training. Auralia focuses on ear-training and Musition on theory.

> ### Teaching Strategy 52
> Use software that allows for aural input to help students improve their singing voices.

Auralia allows users to input responses using a microphone connected to the computer. It has hundreds of exercises from beginning to advanced levels, covering 26 topics, with exercises that ask the students to:

- identify and sing intervals and notes from chords
- take melodic and rhythmic dictation
- identify cadences
- recognize and correct poor tuning
- sing upper or lower part of a two-part phrase
- write down chord progressions

The assessments are designed for classical, jazz, and rock/pop students, with special exercises for jazz/contemporary scales, chords, and progressions.

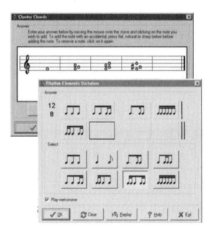

Figure 6.4: Auralia by Sibelius
(www.sibelius.com)

Musition, on the other hand, focuses on the theory part so the two programs go well together. Musition covers all levels from beginner to advanced, and have activities such as:

- tapping a rhythm with the space bar
- identifying pitches on treble, bass, and C-clefs
- identifying key signatures, chords, and inversions
- identifying scales and modes, and correcting wrong notes
- identifying range and transposition of instruments

MiBac Music Lessons

Another option in the theory/ear-training software is Music Lessons I and II from MiBac. These programs include a customizable function where the instructor can pre-determine the exercises. It also features an extensive tutorial help mode.

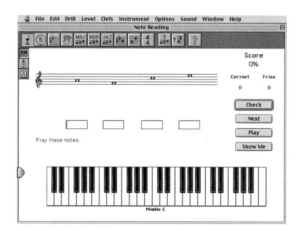

Figure 6.5: MiBac Music Lessons
(www.mibac.com)

Which one to choose? Download a demo copy from the publisher's web site and check out the software. Better yet, let your students use it. Speak with other educators and see what they are using. Making your software selections should involve a good deal of hands-on review.

Music Theory for Younger Students

For the elementary level, there are some excellent choices including Pianomouse Meets Theory FUNdamentals. Designed for students ages 6-12, the program includes an introduction to keyboard basics, pitch, and the musical alphabet and other theory basics. The use of interesting and engaging graphics and games helps capture young students' interest.

Figure 6.6: Music Theory FUNdamentals
(www.pianomouse.com)

Music Games

Music games provide students with a game centered on music concepts.

Teaching Strategy 53

Use computer games to develop skills and create an interactive, healthy competitive atmosphere.

A delightful game is Musicus, by Electronic Courseware Systems for Macintosh and Windows. The game is modeled after the one time popular game Tetris, by Andromedia Software LTD. In Tetris, different shapes fall from the top of the computer screen and the user must try to stack them together into rows. In Musicus, the program lowers musical durations and the student must identify the durations and move them to the correct beat. The goal of the game is to give students an opportunity to review note durations and to quickly recognize them. It can help students understand note values and time signatures and have some fun at the same time.

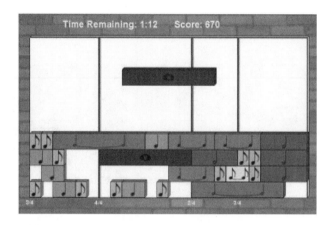

Figure 6.7: Musicus by Electronic Courseware Systems (www.escmedia.com)

Adventures in Musicland, published by Electronic Courseware Systems for Macintosh and Windows, is a series of games based on Alice's adventures in Wonderland. The four games include Music Match, a concentration-style game for matching music symbols and names; Melody Mixup, a melody memory game; Picture Perfect, where students attempt to guess the identity of a composer, instrument, or musical symbol; and Sound Concentration, where the student tries to match sounds or musical tones. This excellent set of activities appeals to preschool through middle school students.

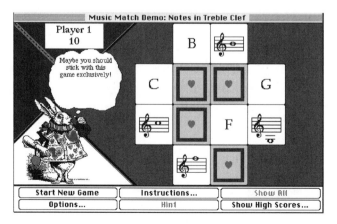

Figure 6.8: Adventures in Musicland (www.ecsmedia.com)

Game Strategies

Computer games work best when the teacher designs a structure to help motivate and encourage the students. Ken Peters, an elementary classroom teacher in Havertown, Pennsylvania, has developed a unique approach to computer games. First, he selected a music game that relates to his curriculum. Then he devised a system to help motivate the students to use the software.

> ### Teaching Strategy 54
> Use the "Hall of Fame" concept to motivate students to play music computer games and compete for the top ten highest scores.

When you play an arcade video game, the top 10 scores are usually displayed on the screen, referred to as the "Hall of Fame." When a player achieves a score in the top ten for that machine, he or she enters their initials or name. This is a big deal with video game users. I remember playing my first video game as an adult and when I finally made it into the hall of fame, or top ten scores, it was very exciting! Ken Peters has successfully introduced the concept of the Hall of Fame into his classes.

Ken calls his the Wall of Fame. He places a poster in the music classroom for each class he teaches, with spaces numbered 1 through 10. Students are taught to use the game and are permitted to play the computer game before and after school, during recess, and, in some cases, during music class on a rotating basis. These elementary students are highly motivated to use the game and compete for a spot on the Wall of Fame. Of course, they also become more proficient with the musical skills and concepts that the game reinforces. When using computer games, it is wise to establish a score to beat or some other goal for students. For example, you might post a score of 1000 as the goal for the class. Students then have a target to shoot for.

> ### Teaching Strategy 55
> Divide a general music class into two teams and have them compete for the best score using a computer game.

A cooperative learning strategy is to divide the class into teams, with each team competing for the highest score. Teams take turns using the computer and the team with the highest score at the end wins. First, give each member of the team a number. When round 1 begins, student number 1 uses the computer for the first question or round. Then the second team gets a turn. In this way, one computer can be used with an entire class and every student gets an opportunity to try their hand at the computer game. Elementary and middle school students find this type of activity especially motivating, and it simultaneously improves musical skills.

Some educational institutions do not permit computer games to be played on school computers. Many school districts feel that computers should be focused on instructional areas and goals and should not be used for students to merely play video games. With this in mind, I use the prefix "educational" when referring to the use of games with administrators and parents. For example, the Educational Computer Game, Adventures in Musicland, can be a motivating experience for students of all ages.

Music History Software

Computer software can be used to review knowledge about music history. An excellent program is Music History Review published by Electronic Courseware Systems for Macintosh and Windows.

Teaching Strategy 56

Use music history programs as a review and for independent study.

This program features information on composers from the Renaissance to the twentieth century. The program can be used by high school and college students as it is coordinated with Grout's A *History of Western Music*. Questions are presented in multiple choice format.

Music History Review: Composers

Quiz Index

- ⦿ Medieval
- ○ Baroque - 1
- ○ Baroque - 2
- ○ Classical
- ○ Renaissance - 1
- ○ Renaissance - 2
- ○ Romantic - 1
- ○ Romantic - 2
- ○ Twentieth Century - 1
- ○ Twentieth Century - 2

[OK]   [ESCAPE]

Figure 6.9: Music History Review
(www.ecsmedia.com)

An excellent option for elementary and middle school students is Pianomouse Meets the Great Composers. This CD-ROM has an introduction to the lives and music of eight composers from the Baroque, Classical, and Romantic periods. Each composer biography is followed by fun, interactive games that test your knowledge. The composers are J.S Bach, Handel, Haydn, Mozart, Beethoven, Schubert, Brahms, and Tchaikovsky. The games are Meet the Composer, Puzzle Challenge, Composer Creations, The Traveling Composer, Composer Concentration, and 3D Mouse Maze.

Figure 6.10: Pianomouse Meets the Great Composers
(www.pianomouse.com)

131

The same company that produced filmstrips and videos on a variety of music topics, now offers an extensive line of music history computer software titles that have been specifically designed to supplement and enhance core topics.

Teaching Strategy 57

Use music history software as a lecture assistant in the classroom, to pinpoint examples, and reference materials on screen.

The CD-ROMs feature complete multimedia presentations with text linked to a full 24-volume, concise student encyclopedia and a customized glossary. Each disc is compatible with both Macintosh and Windows. There is a complete list of titles covering every major era of music history as well as jazz and music and culture.

Figure 6.11: The History of Music (www.clearvue.com)

The Bach Chorales

Bach Chorales is a musical simulation by PGMusic. It is a professional, fully featured music program containing inspiring performances of Bach's famous chorales. You can listen to a professional choral ensemble sing some of Bach's most enchanting compositions, complete with a detailed multimedia history of the life and times of Johann Sebastian Bach. Each voice (soprano, alto, tenor, and bass) has been recorded on a separate track, so the parts can be isolated and listened to separately. Powerful features let you study the arrangements, hear the music, and sing along with a top chamber ensemble.

This interactive program contains nearly an hour of high quality vocal music, a fascinating history of J.S. Bach, and a timeline of his life—all with seamlessly integrated multitrack audio, MIDI, chord symbols, lyrics, and music notation.

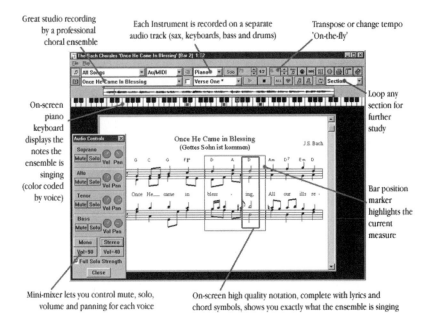

Figure 6.12: Bach Chorales for Macintosh and Windows (www.pgmusic.com)

In addition to the Bach Chorales, other titles include blues, rock, barber shop, and others.

Instrumental Instruction

Another area of CAI software is designed to help students learn to play an instrument or to sing. These programs are excellent supplementary materials for classes and group or private lessons. They can also be excellent for adults who want to learn to play an instrument in their spare time.

Piano Pedagogy

Piano pedagogy programs are written with the objective of teaching piano via the computer. Typically, these programs have tutorial lessons and drill and practice modules that provide feedback on student performance. Some programs also have games and other options, such as notation and recording. There are several excellent publishers of piano software including eMedia, Adventus, and Alfred.

> ### Teaching Strategy 58
> Use piano pedagogy software to help students learn to play the piano.

The eMedia piano and keyboard course comes with a CD-ROM featuring video of the on-screen instructor, Irma Irene Justicia, M.A., a popular piano teacher who has taught at the renowned Juilliard School of Music. Skills covered include sight-reading and playing familiar songs. The method is song-based, including songs from eMedia's guitar method, so students can play together as they learn. MIDI accompaniments help make practicing with simple songs exciting, and quizzes reinforce skills. Throughout, custom interactive technology offers feedback to help students correct any mistakes made while playing. With approximately 250 lessons, this is a comprehensive and easy to use beginning course.

Figure 6.13: eMedia Keyboard course (www.emediamusic.com)

Teach Yourself to Play Piano CD-ROM

Alfred's piano course comes with an interactive CD-ROM that teaches piano from the very beginning. It includes a song player feature that lets you see exactly how each song should be played.

Figure 6.14: Teach Yourself to Play Piano (www.alfred.com)

Guitar Instruction

There are several excellent tutorial programs for guitar instruction. These programs can be used individually or to supplement a group guitar instruction class.

> **Teaching Strategy 59**
> Use software to assist individual and classroom guitar instruction.

eMedia Guitar

eMedia Guitar is a complete, comprehensive approach with videos on CD-ROM to support the learning process. It includes 155 lessons covering basics, chord strumming, playing melodies, and finger picking. Learning guitar is made fun with more than 70 songs including hits from artists such as Bob Dylan, The Grateful Dead, and Steve Miller. The program features videos and over three hours of audio from guitar instructor/national performer Kevin Garry, Ph.D. You can learn songs in either guitar tablature or standard music notation, as the notes on the screen highlight and fingering is displayed on the animated fretboard. A built-in automatic tuner allows you to interactively tune your guitar. In addition, the program includes a digital metronome, recorder with playback, Internet song guide, and 250-chord dictionary.

Figure 6.15: eMedia Guitar (www.emediamusic.com)

Teach Yourself to Play Guitar CD-ROM

This easy-to-use CD-ROM uses the same great teaching approach as the best-selling book in a fun, interactive, audio/visual format. Beginners of all ages can learn to read standard music notation and tablature, perform songs in a variety of styles, and play chords, scales, and cool licks on either acoustic or electric guitar. Exercises reinforce your technique as you follow along with the music on-screen. Interactive song player lets you change tempos, adjust audio levels, and record your performance. Videos of an instructor teaching and clearly demonstrating lessons help you start playing right away. Bonus games reinforce concepts taught in the method. The customizable ear training program gives you the tools to play any song you hear. The new, interactive guitar tuner helps you keep in tune.

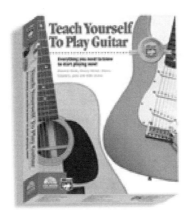

Figure 6.16: Teach Yourself to Play Guitar (www.alfred.com)

Voice Instruction Software

Teach Yourself to Sing covers all the basics of singing, including breathing, posture, warming up, and more. It focuses on the mind/body connection to singing and presents a comprehensive approach to reading music. Styles include rock, jazz, blues, and others. Accompaniments can be transposed to any key, allowing you the comfort of singing within your own range.

Figure 6.17: Teach Yourself to Sing (www.alfred.com)

Band and Strings

There are very few programs dedicated to teaching band and orchestra instruments. However, there is an area of software that can be used by students who play an instrument—tuning software.

> **Teaching Strategy 60**
> Use a tuning program to help students improve their pitch awareness.

Some instrumental teachers find using a tuning program to be an effective application of computers and technology. The program Tune-It II, published by Electronic Courseware Systems for Macintosh and Windows, is a simple program to operate. The objective is to tune two pitches to unison. It offers both visual and aural modes and various levels of difficulty. Instrumental teachers can use this program to help students become aware of the tuning process.

Figure 6.18: Tune-it II (www.ecsmedia.com)

Designed primarily for band students, Intonation Trainer is the most complete tuning software currently available. The software teaches woodwind and brass students how to listen for and eliminate intonation beats. They learn how to play in Just Intonation and why an E in a C major chord has to be played lower than the same E in a C-sharp minor chord. Students learn which notes on their instrument are flat and which are sharp to anticipate pitch problems and how to solve them quickly. Students can experiment with the computer playing intervals or chords and move the pitch of one note in and out of tune to hear the beats. Pulsating graphic shows beats as you hear them.

Figure 6.19: Intonation Trainer (www.finalemusic.com)

Instruments of the Orchestra

Some teachers may remember the wonderful program Microsoft Musical Instruments that unfortunately has been out of print for several years. This void has been filled by a new program, Sibelius Instruments. It is a unique interactive encyclopedia of instruments, bands, orchestras, and ensembles. It includes complete information on every orchestral and band instrument, with full details of their characteristics, how to write for them, and hundreds of high-quality recordings.

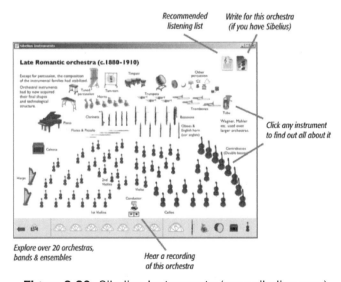

Figure 6.20: Sibelius Instruments (www.sibelius.com)

Teacher Resources

Sibelius Starclass software is designed to offer a wealth of resource material for music lessons. It guides the teacher through 180 ready-to-use lesson plans that support the National Standards for Music Education. Starclass includes full explanations of musical concepts for non-specialist teachers. It has hundreds of music clips and printable pictures, and an audio CD to play in class. This software is designed for teacher use. It contains a wealth of information including many cross-curricular lessons and applications. With over 180 ready-made lesson plans, a 99 track audio CD for playback in class, and hundreds of sound-clips and printable pictures, it can be used as a resource or as a multimedia presentation tool for classes.

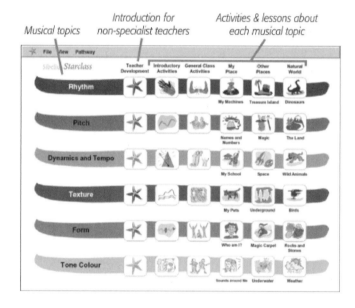

Figure 6.21: Starclass (www.sibelius.com)

Curriculum Integration

Teachers need to think through the process of integrating software into their music curriculum. Use programs that will assist you in your existing classes. Choose software that will supplement what you are currently teaching. Initially, avoid programs that require a great deal of time to learn.

Teaching Strategy 61

Select instructional software that supports or aligns with your existing curriculum.

Strive to align software with your existing music curriculum. Look for ways that the computer can assist with a particular goal within your music program. In other words, try to find ways that the computer can reinforce what is already being taught.

Teaching Strategy 62

Use 1-3 computers in the classroom for drill and practice.

Some music teachers have success using 1-3 computers in the music room for instructional software. Computer software can challenge gifted students or assist mainstreamed students. Many classroom teachers employ a rotating schedule so that many students have an opportunity to use the classroom computer(s). Students take turns using the computer throughout their class period.

Teaching Strategy 63

Take the general music class to the school computer lab and practice theory drills.

If, as in many schools, your school has a computer lab, consider taking music classes into the lab to use drill and practice, theory/ear training, and game software. Consider taking the music students to the school computer lab for a 2-4 week unit using music software as a supplement to the concepts presented in the classroom. In a lab setting each student typically has their own computer and therefore can work at his or her own pace. Be sure to review the copyright restrictions discussed in Chapter 16.

> ## Teaching Strategy 64
> Use a large screen monitor to display the computer screen to an entire class.

Another approach for using software in the classroom is to connect the computer to a large monitor or use a computer projection unit. In this way the computer image can be displayed large enough for an entire class or ensemble to see. The software can be used as a presentation tool eliciting student responses to questions as part of a group activity.

> ## Teaching Strategy 65
> Use computer software to enrich independent study.

Some schools permit students to take music classes on an independent study basis. In this case, students can work independently using computer music software.

> ## Teaching Strategy 66
> Allow students to sign-out software for home use overnight and during the summer.

Music teachers can take advantage of the millions of computers owned in homes. Students could be permitted to sign-out out software over weekends and during the summer.

Developing a Plan and Course of Study

This chapter focused on selecting efficient software. The next step is to develop a plan and course of study for integrating instructional software into the music curriculum. There are three important steps to follow:

1. Select the instructional software.
2. Use the suggested lesson sequence, if available, or devise your own custom sequence.
3. Devise a method for student record keeping and evaluation.

Selecting the Software

Music software should be carefully scrutinized before purchasing in order to determine which of the many available programs fulfills the demands of each particular situation. It is important to invest time in reviewing software before purchasing. Some software publishers and vendors offer demos that can be downloaded for free. Others offer demonstration disks for free or at a nominal cost. I have found it helpful to pilot software with students. Sometimes a program that looks interesting to me bores my students.

Think of selecting software like selecting printed music for performance ensembles. The catalog description can be helpful, but the best advice is to get the music on approval to peruse the score and perhaps try it with your students. Use the same approach with software. Get a chance to try a program before purchasing. When selecting software, weigh the following information:

- **Program information:** Publisher, title, author, cost.
- **Program requirements:** What must the student know or understand to use the program? What class or course could use the program? Can it be used with more than one course?
- **Program format:** Is the program drill and practice, tutorial, testing, or a game?
- **Hardware requirements:** Is a MIDI device required or can the software be used on stand-alone computers such as those in the school computer lab?
- **Written documentation:** What directions does the program provide, either in print or on disk? Are there suggested lessons or other information of benefit to the user?
- **Program customization:** Any program allowing the teacher to customize the sequence can be very helpful.
- **Student record keeping:** Some software records the student's progress so it can be later viewed by the teacher. This can be a time-saving feature.

Choosing a Vendor

There are two ways to purchase software: you can buy directly from the publisher or through a third party vendor. Both are effective ways to procure programs. Many music stores and mail order houses offer discounts on software, but always check directly with the publisher because sometimes they offer special educator discounts. Actually, many companies offer an educational discount. The advantage of working with a third party company is that you gain access to their assistance. Personally, I purchase all of my software from third party music education and technology companies. There are many to choose from. See the list at the end of this chapter.

Selecting the Best Hardware

If you have the option of choosing the computer hardware, be sure to decide the appropriate software applications first. Most of the programs today are offered for Macintosh and Windows computers. However, there are some titles that are only offered for one computer platform. My advice for finding the best computer is to ask yourself what software is best for your needs? After the software is selected, what computer platform does it run on? If it runs on both Macintosh and Windows, then what platform does your school support?

Instructional Software and the Internet

The most comprehensive and interactive instructional software offerings are software-based. However, there is a growing number of internet sites that offer lessons and CAI-like experiences. An Internet connection is required to access these programs.

Teaching Strategy 67
Use Internet sources for on-line versions of CAI. Students can use many of these sites free of charge and from any computer so long as it is connected to the Internet.

An excellent source for lessons on theory and basic piano skills is Piano on the Net from www.pianonanny.com. There are three levels of lessons on music theory and related topics.

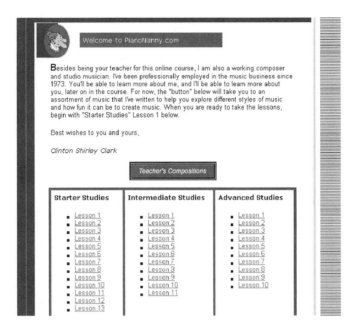

Figure 6.22: Music Lessons Online (www.pianonanny.com)

The site MySheetMusic.com (Fig. 6.23), also includes a set of free lessons. Piano lessons on hand position, music theory, and other basics are included.

Other sites offer interactive instructional software. These sites use Flash, QuickTime, and other multimedia formats. When you visit the site for the first time, it will tell you what plugins you need. These may have to be downloaded. So if you are using web sites with a class, be sure to check the computers prior to the first class to be sure the necessary plugins are installed (see Chapter 2 for more information on web plugins).

Morton Sobotnik's site, www.creatingmusic.com (Fig. 6.24), includes games, puzzles, and creativity exercises. The software versions of these activities are described in detail in Chapter 10.

Figure 6.23: Piano lessons at http://www.mysheetmusic.com/lesson1.asp

Figure 6.24: Creating Music Web site www.creatingmusic.com

Want to test your skill at identifying intervals? Many of the software packages listed in this chapter include interval drill and practice, but there is an online option that can be used for free, The Original Online Ear Trainer, www.ossmann.com/bigears. You can check the intervals you want to practice. Then click on the big ears to play those intervals. Make your guess and continue.

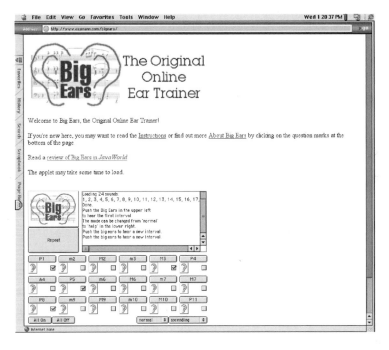

Figure 6.25: Online Ear Trainer (www.ossmann.com/bigears)

Summary

Instructional, or computer-assisted instruction, software is the oldest and one of the most popular software applications for music education. A variety of program formats including drill and practice, tutorials, games, and simulations. However, all software needs to be evaluated prior to implementing it. Taking time to review software before purchase is a must and the best way to use software is to integrate it into the existing music curriculum.

Dealers of Education Music Software and Hardware

(these links are on the companion CD-ROM).

AaBaCa . . . . .www.aabaca.Com

Brook Mays . . . . .www.brookmays.com

Kelly's Music & Computers . . .www.KellysMusicAndComputers.com

Lentine's Music . . . . .www.lentine.com

McCormicks . . . . .www.mccormicksnet.com/

The MIDI Workshop . . . . .www.midiworkshop.com

J.W. Pepper . . . . .www.jwpepper.com

SoundTree . . . . .www.soundtree.com

Sweetwater . . . . .www.sweetwater.com

Review Questions

1. List two or more advantages and disadvantages of using drill and practice software.
2. Describe the four generations of change in the field of computer-assisted instruction software.
3. List several ways computer games can be used in the general music class. Be sure to include at least one cooperative learning example (students working together in groups).
4. Describe the options for sound output when using instructional software.
5. There are four categories of instructional software. The categories include drill and practice, games, tutorials, and simulations. Define each and give an example of a representative software program.
6. What is a PDA?
7. How can you locate music software for a PDA?
8. List two or more music instructional programs that are available for PDAs.
9. Select one of the game strategies and describe its application in the music classroom or rehearsal room.
10. List a software title that is designed to teach piano, guitar, and other instruments.

11. What are the three steps to follow when developing a course of study with instructional software?

12. What are the advantages and disadvantages to using Internet web sites for instructional purposes?

CD-ROM Activities

- Project 6.1 Visit the ATMI on-line music technology directory:
  - http://www.music.org/atmi/Directory/Directory2002.html
  - Click on the CAI link. Find titles mentioned in this chapter and review their respective home page. Search for additional titles and download a demo.

- Project 6.2 Evaluate a music CAI software title using the supplied form on the CD-ROM. Select a title that is relevant to your area of specialization (instrumental, choral, classroom). If you do not have access to CAI software, refer to the web links to download a demonstration copy.

- Project 6.3 Configure the sound output for sound using instructional software. Diagram the signal flow of the sound generated by the software.
  - Computer output to speakers
  - Computer output to headphones
  - MIDI keyboard output to speakers
  - MIDI output to headphones

- Project 6.4 Search the World Wide Web for lessons on music education and technology. Visit web sites with testimonials such as http://www.harmonicvision.com/successes.htm. Select one lesson plan and revise it to fit a specific application or need.

CD-ROM Lesson Plans

- Lesson 6.1: CAI in the elementary school
- Lesson 6.2: CAI in the middle school
- Lesson 6.3: CAI in the high school

Reference

Booty, Charles, Editor (1990). *TIPS: Technology for music educators.* Music Educators National Conference, Reston, VA.

Carpenter, Robert A. (MCMXCI) *Technology in the music classroom.* Alfred Publishing, Van Nuys, CA

Haugland, S. W., & Wright, J. L. (1997). *Young children and technology: A world of discovery.* New York: Allyn & Bacon.

Idea Bank (1986). Idea bank: does CAI really work? *Music Educators Journal,* December.

Murphy, Barbara, Editor. (2002) *Technology directory.* Association for Technology in Music Instruction. http://www.music.org/atmi/Directory/Directory2002.html

Peters, G. David (1992) Music software and emerging technology, *Music Educators Journal,* November pp. 22-25.

Pontif, E. (2003). *Spotlight on technology in the music classroom.* MENC The National Association for Music Education, Reston, VA.

Resse S., McCord, K, & Walls K. (2001) *Strategies for teaching technology.* MENC The National Association for Music Education, Reston, VA.

Richmond, Floyd (2002). *Interactive internet lessons in music.* Pennsylvania Music Educators News. Spring.

Rudolph, Thomas, et al (1997) *Technology strategies for music education.* Hal Leonard Corporation, Milwaukee, WI.

Rudolph, Thomas (1985). Computer music games - exciting and educational. *Pennsylvania Music Educator News,* March pp. 10-11.

Shields, J. & Poftak, A. (2002) A report card on handheld computing. *Technology & Learning,* Volume 22, Number 7, 24-36.

Taylor, C. (2001) Music in the palm of your hand. *Electronic Musician,* December, 42-58.

Taylor, Robert, P. Editor (1980) *The Computer in the school: tutor, tool, tutee.* Teachers College Press, New York.

Williams, D. B. & Webster, P. (1999) *Experiencing music technology: Software, data, and hardware, Second edition.* Schirmer Books, NY.

Wilkinson, Scott. (1994) Teach your children. *Electronic Musician.* April. pp 70-81.

Chapter 7

Notation Software

Music Education National Standards: 1, 2, 4, 5, 6, 7
NETS (National Education Technology Standards): 1, 2, 3

Since MIDI is able to tell computers about notes being played, what their value is, what the tempo is, and divide the music into individual channels, the next logical step in the process is for computers to translate that information into notes, key signatures, time signatures, beats per measure, and specific staff and part information.[1]

I remember watching a demonstration of one of the first music printing computer programs, Polywriter, in 1984. While I watched the clinician play music on a MIDI keyboard, the notation instantly appeared on the computer screen—I just about fainted! However, as I soon discovered, the first generation of music printing programs had their problems. Like many early notation software efforts, Polywriter took longer to input and edit the notes than it would take to write them out by hand. After years of software development and the advent of more powerful personal computers such as the Macintosh and Windows PC, notation software has become not only a worthwhile investment but also an invaluable teaching and composition tool. In the 1990s and early 2000s significant improvements in the field of music notation software have made it an indispensable teaching and teacher's tool. And what became of Polywriter? It quickly became obsolete, and is no longer published.

In the old days before microcomputers (1978!), anyone who composed music had to be well versed in music theory, notation, and transcription, not to mention have access to performers who could realize the composition. I vividly remember taking an orchestration class during my undergraduate days and after spending hours creating my project the only feedback I received was the red ink markings written on the score by my instructor. This does not have to be the case today. Computers and software have placed composition capabilities within everyone's reach. No longer must one be a Mozart to compose music (of course, composing like Mozart is a different story). The computer acts as a musical palette providing both paint and canvas. Using notation software, a student can experiment and literally paint music onto the staff, then connect the computer to a MIDI device, and the entire orchestration can be played and heard.

What's in a Name?

Programs that print out musical notation are known by several names. In their excellent book, *Experiencing Music Technology*, Williams and Webster call it "music notation software." In the Lentine's Music Catalog it is called notation and scoring software. Other companies, including J.W. Pepper, SoundTree, and Brook Mays call it "notation software." Some people use the term "printing software." All of the various names used for printing notation—notation, scoring, or printing—have one thing in common: their *main* objective is to produce traditional music notation for musicians to read and/or play. Throughout this chapter and the rest of the book I will refer to software for printing out music as notation software.

Please note that there are other programs that are designed to enhance creativity and use non-traditional notation. These programs will be described in detail in Chapter 10.

Notation Software = Tool

When considered as a part of the tutor, tool, tutee model described in Chapter 1, notation software most definitely falls into the tool category. It is a tool designed for entering, editing, transposing, and transcribing music notation. Notation software is the musician's version of a word processor.

With a word processor, text can be entered, edited, copied, and corrected on the computer screen. Music notation software does the same with notes and rests: notation can be entered, edited, transposed, and adjusted in many ways before printing. Notation software is not designed to teach the user about music or music notation. It gives a blank slate for writing and printing music just as the word processor provides a way to write and edit text. Of course, it is possible for an educator to design student lessons for notation software just as an English teacher creates student assignments to be completed using a word processor.

When should a notation program be used? Simple. When the main objective is to print out a part or score for someone to read. Remember the "n" rule: if notes are required, then use a notation program.

Notes = Notation Software

Advantages of Notation Software

Notation software can be used for many applications. One of the most popular is producing printed parts and arrangements. Just about every professional composer, arranger, copyist, and publisher now uses notation software. Vince Leonard, a professional copyist who used to copy music by hand, now exclusively uses a computer to print scores and parts. The reason? Vince finds that with the computer he can enter music with a MIDI keyboard faster than he can write. Also, once the score has been entered, the parts are simply extracted one at a time. Before computers, Vince had to create a score and parts separately. Now he only creates the score and then lets the computer automatically extract the individual parts. In Vince's words, "The parts are an afterthought."

For music teachers, the most obvious reasons for learning to use a notation program are to save time and produce more readable pieces of music. I am a middle school band director. No matter which arrangement I purchase, minor revisions are needed to match the abilities of my students, so I often re-write some of the parts. In the dark ages before notation software, I would often re-write parts by hand. Even in the best of circumstances my left-handed scrawl is barely legible. Hence, questions such as, "Is the first note an E, F, or G?" or, "Isn't my part missing 10 measures?" were commonplace. Now, with the help of notation software, I hand out music that looks professionally typeset. Students are able to read my revisions as well as they read their professionally printed music. Another advantage of using notation software is the way it helps find mistakes. Simply play back the composition and "proof listen" to the piece. It is often easier to find mistakes while listening than solely by inspecting the printed score. Wrong notes can be edited with the click of a mouse.

Music educators agree that notation software can be a valuable, time saving tool. Mark Ely, in his article "Software for Classroom Music Making"[4] identifies several benefits of using notation software:

Benefits to teachers:
- develop composing and arranging skills
- write out exercises or create a complete method book
- create lead sheets with lyrics and chords
- rewrite parts to meet the demands of the ensemble
- further listening skills via immediate feedback

Benefits to students:
- develop composition and arranging skills
- develop listening skills
- use and apply musical concepts including harmony, rhythm, transposition, key signatures, etc.

Obviously, the benefits of using notation software are many. However, notation software can be initially time consuming and difficult to master. There certainly is a definite time investment required to learn to use it. A warning regarding notation software: unlike computer-assisted instruction, it does require some time to learn. You may even have to read the manual!!

Sound = Sequencer; Notes = Notation Software

As stated above, notation software has one main purpose: printing out music notation for musicians to read. This simple comment bears repeating. I know of many musicians who became very frustrated because they sat down with a notation program when their goal was to produce an accompaniment arrangement. Sequencers are designed for sound recordings. Notation software is designed to print notes. Remember this simple, yet essential, advice:

> If you want SOUND —
> use a SEQUENCER
> If you want PRINTED NOTATION —
> use a NOTATION PROGRAM

Types of Notation Software

Notation programs, like all software, are published with a specific audience in mind. Some notation programs are written for the musical novice while others are written for the professional composer or educator. The key question is: who was the software designed for? It is important to get a proper fit by selecting the best program for the desired application. For example, a teacher may choose a more powerful and complex program than one selected for student use.

Warning! Many programs print out notation, some of which are not specifically for notation. These will be discussed in later chapters. Be sure to select a program with the features you need for printing. In most cases, this means choosing a notation program similar to those described below.

Notation software can be grouped into five categories: notation software for printing out scores and parts; sequencers designed for recording or sequencing music; integrated notation and sequencing software; music scanning; and creativity applications. The first four types of software are the most common and are covered in this chapter. Creativity applications are discussed in Chapter 10.

Notation Software

Notation software is designed to print out scores and parts. I recommend choosing one of these programs for both teacher and student use. They are the easiest to learn of the notation-capable programs and several options are available. A notation package is an excellent program for the teacher, student, and computer lab. The steps for selecting a program and how to evaluate notation software follow.

Sequencing Software with Notation

In Chapter 3, sequencers were introduced. Sequencers are used primarily to create sound recordings, similar to a tape recorder, however, almost every software sequencer also offers notation printing. Notation printing in these programs is not the primary focus. Sequencers that have some notation options can be used to print notation. However, they typically do not have the notation editing capabilities found in programs written primarily to print scores and parts. Purchasing a sequencer with notation capabilities can be helpful if you just want to print a composite of a sequence, produce a leadsheet, or edit the sequence using notation. However, for most notation printing applications, consider a notation program.

I tell music teachers at my workshops that if they see notes on the computer screen they are most likely using a notation program and if the screen looks like a tape recorder it is most likely a sequencer. Generally, this is an accurate way to evaluate notation and sequencing software although today most sequencers do offer the option of viewing and printing music notation. For example, Cakewalk Home Studio (by Cakewalk for Windows), PowerTracks Pro (by PG Music for Windows), and Performer (by Mark of the Unicorn for Macintosh) are primarily sequencers that offer a printing option. However, they are first and foremost sequencers and should not be thought of as complete notation programs. A review of sequencing software is found in Chapter 8.

If simple printing is all you require, then a sequencer with notation options can be used and will save the expense. If you plan to do a lot of part printing and/or arranging, consider one of the options that follow.

Integrated Notation and Sequencers

Almost every notation program offers at least some sound (sequencing) options and, as mentioned above, many sequencers allow for some limited printing options. There are some programs that totally integrate both worlds: notation and sequencing. Cubase SX, (by Steinberg for Macintosh/Windows) and Logic Gold (by Emagic for Macintosh) are programs that offer integrated sequencing and notation capabilities. These programs offer most of the essential editing and printing features. However, because they have so much in one package, they are very complex and hence can be difficult to learn.

They are also quite expensive since they combine two powerful programs into one. George Litterst, in his article "The EM Guide to Notation Software," states:

> Sometimes, the line between these two types of programs (sequencers and notation) is quite blurred...In general, however, sequencing programs do not excel at notation, so many people opt to use both types of programs.[3]

My experience using sequencers and notation software leads me to agree with George Litterst and to recommend using separate sequencing and notation programs. However, integrated sequencer/notation programs are a viable option if your budget only allows for the purchase of one program and if your printing requirements are not complex.

Scanning Music

After you have selected a notation program, you will want to take advantage of scanning music to save time inputting notes. Dr. John Kuzmich[4] calls music scanning capabilities ". ..a milestone in computer music applications." Some notation programs include free music scanning software and there are also programs specifically designed to scan music. In order to scan music, you will need a flatbed scanner. The vast majority of scanners made today will work with music scanning software.

Figure 7.1: Flatbed scanner

Some notation programs come with scanning built-in and others require that you use two separate programs for scanning. Scanning options are reviewed later in this chapter.

Selecting a Notation Program

If printing notation is your primary concern, then select a program designed to help you accomplish this task: notation software. The challenge is that there is a wide variety of programs available and selecting the best one for your needs is essential. Some notation programs are written for the occasional user or music novice while other programs are highly sophisticated and designed to professionally typeset music. The ATMI 2000 directory (see references at the end of the chapter) lists 31 music notation titles. How to sort through 31 programs and select the one that best suits your needs? Some specific steps should be followed to make the best selection.

I am often asked the question, "Which notation program is the best?" I give the same answer when someone asks me which is the best electronic keyboard or the best computer, "What are your goals and what support do you have?" Your goals and specific needs are the first consideration. Then you can begin to sort through the available notation software.

Selecting a notation program is similar to purchasing any commodity like a car or a microwave. There are various models from which to choose. Do you need a microwave with all of the bells and whistles and a manual that takes a few hours to read, or do you want an easy-to-use, heat-up-your-coffee type of microwave, where all of the commands and controls are written on the front panel? One type of microwave is not better than the other, they simply meet different needs. Notation software also comes in various versions designed for specific applications. First, begin with three main questions:

- Are my needs entry-level or advanced ? (selecting the level)
- Considering my level, which software program is best for my situation? (review software options)
- What computer brand support do I have? (select the computer)

I find it helpful to try to group notation software into entry-level, or easy to learn and use programs, and advanced, or complex, programs.

Following is a list of what I consider to be basic and advanced notation programs based on my own personal experience. These programs were evaluated as of the publishing date of this book. Programs are constantly upgraded and new ones enter the market all of the time. So be your own judge. Use the above criteria as your guide to select the best program for your own personal and professional needs.

Entry-Level Notation Applications

Programs in the basic category are relatively easy to learn. These programs don't require hours and hours of practice. Also, a basic notation program typically doesn't require constant reference to the manual or help menu. The cost is also typically under $100 for a single copy. Some basic notation applications include:

- Students in grades 3–12 can compose, arrange, and orchestrate music.
- Teachers can create notation examples for students, copy a practice sheet, or simplify a piece of music.
- Teachers can create music examples for tests, handouts, overheads, classroom posters, and so forth.

Advanced Notation Spplications

The advanced user requires a powerful notation program that offers complete control over the printed page, the ability to automatically extract parts, and other features. Speed is an important issue. Usually, advanced programs give more options for music input and are therefore take longer to learn. The advanced user composes frequently and needs software that can finesse the printed page. Advanced applications include:

- Composing band, orchestra, or jazz band scores.
- For composition projects.
- For composers and music theorists who require non-traditional notation, mixed meters, and other esoteric notation.

Basic and Advanced Applications:
General Considerations

Now comes the difficult part: putting the software into the entry-level (basic) or advanced category. Not every expert in the field will agree with my placements. Furthermore, due to constant updating of software, placements may change over time. Some notation programs are in the "gray" area. I use the following criteria when trying to label a notation program as entry-level or advanced.

- **Weigh the manual!** If it weighs more than two pounds and if there are two or more manuals, it definitely is in the advanced category. If you drop the box the software comes in on your foot and it hurts a lot, it is in the advanced category. I say this only slightly tongue-in-cheek, because it is true!
- **Does the program come with a video tape or DVD for instruction?** If so, you can be fairly sure it is for the advanced user.
- **When you start up the program on your computer are all of the commands on the screen?** In other words, are the commands available from the menus or windows on screen? If so, then it is most likely designed for basic use. If you have to keep a list of commands open next to the computer or memorize multiple tools then the software may be in the advanced category.
- **Strangely enough, cost can be a deceiving factor.** Generally, however, advanced programs are more costly than basic ones.

Entry-Level vs. Advanced: Technical Considerations

There are many technical aspects to consider when selecting a notation program. George Litterst[5] suggests looking at the following categories:

- **Number of staves**
  Basic applications: 1-16 staves is usually sufficient.
- **Viewing modes**
  Basic applications: seeing the music as it will be printed on the page, referred to as page view, is usually sufficient. Advanced: it is best if the program can reduce and enlarge music to many different percentages.
- **Keys, meters, and clefs**
  Basic use: standard key signatures and meters (3/4, 4/4, etc.) and basic clefs such as treble and bass are usually sufficient. Advanced: mixed meter, uncommon clefs, and non-standard key signatures are often a necessity.

- **Alternate notation**
  Basic: requires only standard music note heads. Advanced: requires a variety of note heads.
- **Lyrics**
  For both basic and advanced applications, lyrics should be available.
- **Transposition**
  Basic: transposition from one key to another. Advanced: chromatic and diatonic transposition should be available.

Some additional criteria I look for in a quality notation program are:

- **Ease of note entry.** Are there several ways to enter notation both one note at a time and playing on a MIDI keyboard?
- **Part extraction.** Can parts can be automatically extracted from the score?
- **Outside support:** Does the company have on-line support? Do you know of someone on your faculty or at your institution who is an expert in a particular program? If so, this is a major asset. Good technical support is important for advanced users.

"Different strokes for different folks" definitely applies to notation software. Programs are written for a specific audience and it is important to consider this when selecting a program for your needs. For example, when I go to a school district for a one day in-service training on notation, I always use a basic program such as NotePad, PrintMusic, or G7 by Sibelius. The reason for choosing a basic program is that it can be learned in a few hours. These programs are also excellent for student use.

When I teach a week-long course on music notation, I select an advanced program such as Finale or Sibelius. In most cases, the time investment required to learn an advanced notation program pays off in the end.

Notation Software Selection Chart

The following chart represents the majority of popular music notation programs. With software titles changing frequently, be sure to check for updates and changes. This is not a comprehensive list of music notation software. Rather, it is the list of software that I recommend considering for your use.

As of this writing, I recommend two options for educational use: either the Finale or Sibelius family of products. Both companies include free scanning software and have a wealth of educational additions not found in the other programs listed here or the others available on the market.

Notation Program	Web Site	Entry Level	Advanced Use	Free Scanning	Guitar	Mac/Win
Finale Products:						
NotePad	www.finalemusic.com/notepad/	x		no	no	Mac & Win
NotePad Plus	www.finalemusic.com/notepad/	x		no	no	Mac & Win
PrintMusic	www.finalemusic.com/printmusic/	x		yes	no	Mac & Win
Finale Guitar	www.finalemusic.com/finaleguitar/	x		yes	yes	Mac & Win
Finale	www.finalemusic.com/	x	x	yes	yes	Mac & Win
Sibelius Products:						
G7	www.sibelius.com	x		no	yes	Mac & Win
Sibelius 3	www.sibelius.com	x	x	yes	yes	Mac & Win
Gvox Products:						
Encore	www.gvox.com	x		no		Mac & Win
MusicTime	www.gvox.com	x		no		Mac & Win
Geniesoft Products:						
Overture 3	www.geniesoft.com/	x	x	no		Mac & Win
ScoreWriter	www.geniesoft.com/	x		no		Mac & Win
Misc. Products:						
PlayMusic	www.notationtechnologies.com/	x		no	no	Win Only
Mosaic	www.motu.com		x	no	no	Mac Only
GOODFEEL (Braile Music)	www.dancingdots.com/	x				Win Only
Scanning Software:						
Photoscore MIDI	www.neuratron.com/photoscore.htm	x				Mac & Win
Photoscore Professional	www.neuratron.com/photoscore.htm		x			Mac & Win
SmartScore Professional	www.musitek.com/smartscre.html		x			Mac & Win
Sharp Eye	www.visiv.co.uk/		x			Win only

Figure 7.2: Music Notation Software Chart

Entry Level Software

For beginners, there are several options. These include: Finale NotePad, NotePad Plus, PrintMusic, Play Music, MusicTime, and Score Writer 2. Also in the entry level category are two guitar-oriented programs, G7 by Sibelius and FinaleGuitar. These programs cost from free to well under $100. This makes them excellent for school and home use.

Which ones to choose? The things I look for are price, features, and support. Of the above programs, I tend to lean towards the industry leaders: Sibelius and Finale. Both have a line of notation products. It is also possible to use Sibelius and Finale at the entry level. Both can be used by young students and novice computer users. The main reason that I put them in the advanced area is due to the price, which around $250 for educators.

> ### Teaching Strategy 68
>
> Take advantage of educator discounts on software in general and music notation software in particular. Manufacturers and third party vendors often provide this discount to schools, churches, and other institutions.

Finale NotePad: Free Music Notation Software

Finale NotePad is a free program that can be downloaded from www.finale-music.com/notepad or purchased from Finale for $19.95. The parent company, MakeMusic, often gives away free copies at music education conferences. Since it is a free program, it can be put on every computer in the school.

> ### Teaching Strategy 69
>
> Use Finale NotePad, a free entry level music notation program for Mac and Windows. Download a copy and install it on every computer in the school and encourage students to download it at home for their personal use. It's free!

Finale NotePad can be used with all of the other programs in the Finale family. Since Sibelius has the capability of loading Finale format files, NotePad files can be exported over to Sibelius. There are many limitations to the program including no MIDI input or output and very limited entry and editing tools. However, the basics are there and compositions can contain up to eight separate staves.

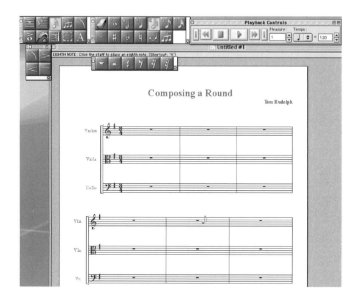

Figure 7.3: Finale NotePad for Macintosh and Windows
(www.finalemusic.com/notepad)

Finale offers NotePad Plus for $12.95. It includes the added features of being able to save files in MIDI format and to import and export MIDI files. This feature is especially important if you are using Sibelius or other advanced programs in addition to NotePad.

The Finale Family

The company MakeMusic (www.makemusic.com) offers a complete line of notation products, starting with its free version, NotePad, mentioned above. Next in line is PrintMusic for under $75. This program is well suited to student use at both the elementary and secondary levels. It includes basic scanning and MIDI input and output. FinaleGuitar is similar to PrintMusic but it has added guitar tab features and improved scanning capability. The high end offering is Finale, with many advanced features for students and teachers. This is the most powerful program in the Finale line.

Guitar Notation Offerings

MakeMusic's FinaleGuitar and G7 by Sibelius can print tablature and includes other features. Both programs are priced in the low-end range and include built-in music scanning features. G7 also includes some excellent guitar instruction features.

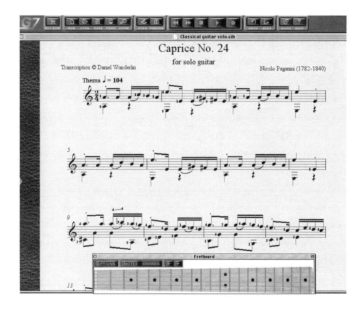

Figure 7.4: G7 by Sibelius

Sibelius

By virtue of its cost, Sibelius is put in the advanced area. However, it is very easy to use and students can quickly learn it. As of this writing, Sibelius only offers the complete version and a guitar program. The advantage of using Sibelius is that there are no tools and everything on the screen can be moved just by clicking on it and dragging it with the mouse. Note entry is also quite simple.

Advanced Notation Software

The two strongest candidates for my money are Finale and Sibelius. Finale and Sibelius support education and their manuals and tech support are excellent. Sibelius and Finale both offer free scanning and their music can be easily saved to be posted on an Internet web page. Also, both programs offer many additional features of interest to teachers and students. Coupled with the fact that both companies have a line of notation products makes them my choice in the end. Others in the running are Mosaic (www.motu.com), which is especially good for Digital Performer users, Overture 3 (www.geniesoft.com), and Encore (www.gvox.com).

Some of my favorite Sibelius features include being able to automatically display brass instrument fingerings and counting or Solfeggio syllables on the music. In Finale, I find the ability to harmonize a melody using a variety of styles to be most helpful. Which one is best? Personal preference does play a role, so download a demo of each and make your own choice.

Figure 7.5: Sibelius Plug-in: automatically numbering beats

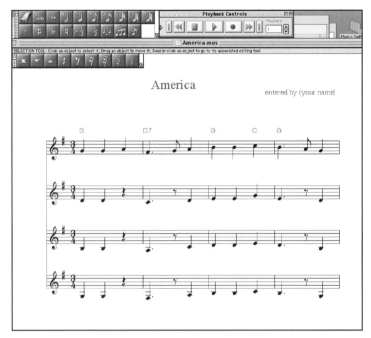

Figure 7.8: Finale using the auto-harmonizing plug-in

Using Notation Software

Templates

One of the best time savers when using a notation program is to use templates. Using a template is similar to using blank score paper as it already contains all the staves, clefs, instrument names, and any other element that you use regularly in a document.

Teaching Strategy 70

Use templates to save time preparing a score each time you start a project.

Templates definitely can save you time. I am a middle school band director and I often want to print out an exercise or melody for the ensemble. For example, I know the parts that I need include a B-flat part for trumpets/clarinet, an E-flat part for alto saxes, and a Bass clef part for tuba and trombone/baritones. The first time I set up a score, I save it and call it "band exercise template." Then each time I want to create an exercise or arrangement, I call up the template. I do not have to create the score, name the parts, or set the transposition.

Most programs include built-in standard templates. Both Finale and Sibelius have a wealth of templates that are made available after you install the program. These range from band and orchestra scores to test and worksheet masters.

Scanning Software

Another compelling reason to lean toward the two heavies in the notation world, Finale and Sibelius, is that they both include free music scanning. Finale, Finale Guitar, and PrintMusic all contain a light version of SmartScore built into the program. Sibelius comes with a light version of Photoscore built-in. The more expensive the version, the more scanning features.

There are limitations to the built-in scanning options. As of this writing both versions will recognize music notation but not text or other graphical elements. No text, graphics, chords, and so forth can be detected. In order to capture all of the notes and graphic information, you will need to upgrade to the full version of SmartScore for Finale and Photoscore Professional for Sibelius.

> **Teaching Strategy 71**
> Use scanning music software to input printed music into notation programs. This can be a big time saver when transposing music and parts.

For users of other notation programs, a version of Photoscore can be used because it converts scanned music to MIDI data. Because all music notation programs can import MIDI, this is the scanning program of choice. For Windows users, there is an additional option, Sharp Eye. To get more information on these programs, visit the company web sites listed in Figure 7.2.

Scanning software is not 100% accurate. With most scanned pages, the converted part must be edited. However, with the latest versions of the above programs, 95-99% accuracy is not uncommon, just be sure to double check the scanned data for errors.

Music scanning is helpful if you are planning to re-score an arrangement (within the copyright guidelines), or change the key of a piece. Of course it could also be useful to scan in music and then import it to your sequencer. Once the music is in the sequencer, an audio recording can be made for accompaniment and demonstration.

I am looking forward to the day when we will put on an electronic hat and simply think the music and it will appear on the computer screen! Don't laugh! It (or something like it) will be here before we know it.

Making the Notation Software Choice

Which program to choose? First, determine your needs as either entry or advanced level. Then, review several notation programs. Lastly, determine the type of support you have and select the program. Really see which program is best suited to you. Get a demonstration at a conference, download a demo, and ask your colleagues what they recommend. Again, from my perspective, the Finale or Sibelius family are the best ways to go. A comprehensive review of Finale and Sibelius has been documented in the book *Music Engraving Today* by Steven Powell. He states:

> ....Finale and Sibelius...have somewhat different strengths. Finale is deeper, more stable, and–for an experienced user–faster. Sibelius has a much shorter learning curve and does more things correctly without significant tweaking. [6]

Be sure to check with your institution to see what type of computers are used there. It is important to determine the support you have before choosing the computer platform. You can't go wrong if you are using a Windows or Macintosh as there is a variety of basic and advanced programs from which to choose.

I know of many music educators who purchased a program that was too advanced for their needs. Someone once wisely said that, "you don't need a bazooka to kill a rabbit." This premise can be applied to notation software.

The opposite is also true, as I know of several music teachers who purchased an entry level notation program and found out that the software was not meant to be used for the complex projects they had in mind. So be sure to take some time, and choose carefully.

Teacher Use of Notation Software

Notation software can be applied to music education in several areas: for the teacher's use to print out parts and arrangements, for students to use to compose, as a class/rehearsal presentation tool, and for both to create music to post on a web site.

Band, choral, and orchestra directors can find many applications for notation software. As a middle school band director, I have often thought, "If I had the time, I would write out exercises for the band to help prepare them for playing specific pieces." With a computer and a notation program, and some practice using it, I now can accomplish this task.

Teaching Strategy 72

Use notation software as a tool to create studies, exercises, and custom parts for students in band, chorus, or orchestra.

Some teaching applications for notation software follow. Use these ideas as a starting point to brainstorm your own needs.

- **Simplify parts for students.** You might need a custom clarinet part for students not yet over the break; or perhaps the range of a particular piece goes above that which is comfortable for your soprano section. Notation software can be used to slightly reduce the difficulty level of the part.

- **Re-orchestrate an existing arrangement.** In my middle school band I now have 18 alto saxes and two trombones. Yet the arrangements I purchase are usually written for three trombones and two alto saxes. I enter the second and third trombone parts and print them out for the alto saxes. Parts for all ensembles can be re-orchestrated in this manner.

- **Create warm-ups and practice exercises.** Suppose you have developed some of your own favorite warm-up exercises. Notation software can help you to quickly print out your exercises. A notation program works like a word processor. Notes can easily be copied and pasted into other parts of the music. With practice, a notation software will allow you to create professional-looking parts much faster than you could create them by hand.

- **Create ensemble music such as duets, trios, and quartets.** As long as the music is original or in the public domain, you can create your own chamber music for any instrument combination.

- **Reduce a piano part so students can accompany a chorus or other ensemble.** Many times, the piano accompaniment part is too difficult for student accompanists. Notation software can help the teacher simplify the part.

- **Compose difficult parts, such as descants, to challenge the more advanced students in the ensemble.** How many times have you heard the better students in your ensembles complain that the music is boring or too easy? With notation software, directors can create challenging parts.

- **Write your own compositions, arrangements, or even a method book.** If you have been avoiding writing original compositions or arrangements because of the cost of having parts copied, notation software remedies this problem. Also, once a composition has been entered into the computer, it can be listened to, edited, and revised as often as you like.

- **Use the transpose function to quickly print out parts for various instruments.** Every good notation program has built-in transposition capabilities. Parts can be entered in concert pitch and then automatically transposed and printed out for instruments in other keys (B-flat, E-flat, etc.).

These are some of the many ways music educators can use notation software. Granted, you will need to invest some time to learn the software, but once learned, the benefits will certainly equal the effort expended.

Student Applications

A notation program is a fascinating tool in the hands of students. A notation program will not teach students to compose any more than a word processor will teach them how to write. However, just as a word processor can assist a student with editing, copying and pasting, spell-checking, and so forth, a notation program can assist in the music composition process. Notation software gives students a fast and legible way to enter and print music and then immediately hear what they have written.

Teaching Strategy 73

Teach students to use notation software to create original music and to compose harmonies and rhythms as listed below.

Once the appropriate hardware and software are made available to them, students experience a wide variety of composition activities. Some ideas are listed below to help you get started.

- **Teach student librarians to use notation software.** Many of the applications listed above, such as re-orchestrating parts from an arrangement, could be delegated to students. They can enter the part and then have the computer make the proper transposition(s).

- **Allow students to use a notation program to create original music.** Dave Burkhart, a teacher at Interboro High School, in Interboro, Pennsylvania, has found that the use of computers in his program has increased interest and motivation, especially of his better students. Students use notation software to compose their own arrangements and compositions.

- **Teach students to transcribe melodies, perhaps the parts they are playing in the ensemble.** Through the process of entering notation, students should "discover" many aspects of music such as note values, number of beats per measure, direction of stems, and so forth.

- **Use notation software as a tool for students to apply concepts as they are introduced.** For example, if students are learning about tonality and chord functions such as tonic, dominant, and subdominant, ask them to compose their own variations using the computer.

- **Take classes to the school computer lab and use notation software to compose and arrange music.** Notation software can be used with off-the-shelf computers. If the school has a computer lab, notation software for creating original music and arrangements can be installed.

- **Use notation software for students to create legible theory class assignments.** Students in music theory classes at the high school and college level should have access to computers to create legible exercises and assignments.

- **Use notation software for creativity, higher level thinking skills, and portfolio assessment.** Notation software provides a tool for students to create and printout music. A printed piece of music is a tangible outcome that can be used for assessment.

Create Partially Completed Exercises for Students

So where to begin? I have found that the best way to proceed is for the teacher to create files prior to the start of class and copy them to the hard drive of each computer. This can usually be done over the school's network. Next, the students open the file you created and modify and add to it. This procedure limits the essential skills students need to complete each exercise. This is especially beneficial when dealing with a large class in a computer or MIDI lab.

Following is an example of a notation lesson:

> Lesson description: Students enter a three-part round such as the round "Are You Sleeping?" and add a percussion part. The objective is to learn how to enter notation using notation software, create an arrangement of instruments, and compose a percussion part.

> Teacher preparation: Use your notation software to create a four-staff score with three different instruments and one percussion staff. Enter the entire melody for "Are You Sleeping?"

in the top staff. Include text to provide directions for the lesson.

Are You Sleeping?

Figure 7.9: Sample student lesson using notation software

Student action steps (I usually write these instructions at the top of the page of the file that I have created):

1. Enter the second and third parts of the round by clicking in the notation. Use the mouse or copy and paste.
2. After completing the three-part round, experiment with different instrument timbres for the various parts. Change the instrument timbres and volumes of each part.
3. Compose a percussion part on the fourth staff using quarter and eighth note patterns.
4. Play back often and make changes to your arrangement.
5. Save and print the composition.

For additional exercises, make variations on this format. Create a file and have your students complete the assignment. The key to developing notation lessons is to have a specific goal for students to accomplish and to get them started with a partially completed file.

Supplemental Materials

Looking for lots of ways to use notation software? Two excellent publications can be of assistance. The first one, *Strategies for Teaching Technology*, published by MENC, includes 15 lessons on music notation for all levels. The lesson plans are organized around the national standards. A sample lesson is found on the cCompanion CD-ROM. These lessons cover all areas of technology, but several focus specifically on notation.

The second is a wonderful package called Sibelius Notes (formerly called Sibelius Teaching Tools, www.sibelius.com). I have found this to be a very helpful application and it has given me many new ideas to use with my students. It covers all school levels (K-12) and contains ready-to-use exercises and worksheets on everything from notation to composing, plus dozens of music files and other useful resources on CD-ROM. Students can use Sibelius Notes on computer or with pen and paper, as Sibelius permits photocopying of worksheets.

Vermont MIDI

Another excellent source of information is the Vermont MIDI site at www.vtmidi.org. This web site was created as part of a grant that paired students, teachers, and professional composers. When you log on to the site there is a link for student work. Here you can read the student's comments about their compositions and listen to their finished pieces. The resources on this site helped me to gain many new ideas for my own use with my students.

The following are excerpts from lessons in the publications mentioned above:

- Transcribe a familiar melody by ear into standard notation (*Strategies for Teaching Technology*, page 56)
- Drag or transpose given notes to new locations
- Copy and paste patterns to create a melody
- Add expressive elements to compositions
- Arrange excerpts enhancing the expressive effect of the music (*Strategies for Teaching Technology*, page 135)
- Add chords, such as tonic and dominant, to a given melody
- Transpose tonality of an existing exercise (*Sibelius Notes*, page 102)

- Sibelius Notes:
    - Arrange a piano piece for two instruments (pg. 106)
    - Arrange an SATB score for four instruments
    - Compose a canon for four voices ("Are You Sleeping?")
- Transcribe an instrumental piece for SATB voices (*Strategies for Teaching Technology*, page 116).
- Transcribe a duet or trio for three instruments (*Strategies for Teaching Technology*, page 90).
- Activities with rounds
    - Copy/paste melody "Are You Sleeping?"
    - Add percussion parts
    - Add an original accompaniment
- Question/answer or tension/release activities (*Strategies for Teaching*, page 46).
- Theme and variations projects (Vermont MIDI site).

Notation as a Demonstration/Transcription Tool

A computer connected to a large screen monitor or a computer projector can be used to demonstrate a variety of concepts for a class or ensemble.

Teaching Strategy 74

Ask students to perform a passage on a MIDI keyboard into a notation program. The computer will notate their performance. Then you and the class can compare the notated performance to the original.

- Using notation software with real time entry **students can perform rhythm patterns on the MIDI keyboard** in time with the computer's metronome. After the performance, the program will display the student's performance. Then it can be compared with the original.

- **Use a pitch-to-MIDI converter** (see Chapter 5) and have students play passages on their instrument. The computer will notate the student's performance. Also, jazz solos and other improvisations can be played and instantly notated for the class.

Administrative Applications

Notation software helps instructors to create worksheets, handouts, tests, and the like.

> **Teaching Strategy 75**
>
> Use notation software to create professional-looking tests, examples, and student handouts.

If you are interested in generating music examples for books, tests, and papers, a notation program can be very useful. There are several ways to capture music notation and import it into a word processing document. For serious users who require full pages of musical examples and want the best looking printout, the notation program must be able to export in EPS format files. EPS stands for Encapsulated Postscript and is used for high resolution graphics. Postscript is the language used by the best printers to create high resolution graphics. EPS produces high resolution music notation for a book, dissertation, or publication. Powerful page layout programs like Adobe InDesign or QuarkXpress can import EPS music files for professional looking printouts.

Creating Worksheets

The worksheet rule of thumb that I follow is as follows: if the example I am creating is mostly music, then I create it in the notation program. If it is mostly text with only an occasional musical example (like this book), then I enter the text in a word processor and then export the notation graphic. Sibelius and Finale both have education worksheet templates. These can be a good starting place as the page layout is the most difficult step in the process.

All notation programs allow for text to be typed into the document. If you are preparing a test or other document, you could type in all of the text without leaving the notation program. If your example has more music than text, this is a viable option.

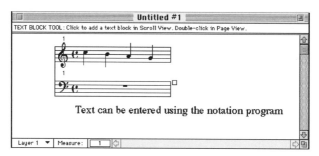

Figure 7.10: An example of text entered

Teaching Strategy 76

Use screen capture as a fast and easy way to import notation and graphics into documents such as tests, papers, and books.

Macintosh and Windows computers can capture the computer's screen display as a graphic. Windows has a print screen command and Macintosh has a key stroke to copy the entire screen. This method is referred to as screen capture and can be used to capture a notation example to be used in another program such as a word processor.

If you do a lot of screen capture then you should consider purchasing a screen capture program so you can grab portions of the screen and the menus. I recommend SnapsPro by Ambrosia software www.AmbrosiaSW.com for Macintosh and Snagit (www.techsmith.com) for Windows. There are others on the market for all major brands of computers.

These programs work very easily. Suppose you are using a notation program (or any program for that matter) and you want to capture a graphic on the screen, perhaps a few measures of music or a menu listing. You press a pre-determined keystroke to capture the screen image, or portion of the screen. Once the information is captured, it is placed on the clipboard, which is a temporary storage place in the computer's memory. Next, go to the word processor and paste in the information. Anything that is displayed on the screen, including text, graphics, and notation, can be captured and pasted into other documents.

Figure 7.11: Menu copied and pasted into this document using a screen capture program.

Every Macintosh computer running system 7.0 or later has screen capture capability built-in. The steps for capturing graphics on a Macintosh are as follows:

1. Go to the notation program and create the desired music or example. Be sure you can see the entire example on the screen.
2. Simultaneously press Command (looks like an outline of an apple), Shift, and the number 3. You will hear a click as the screen is transferred to a file on the desktop called Picture 1. You can take up to 10 pictures.
3. Go to the Finder and open the picture (double click on the icon).
4. Select the exact music you want to copy.
5. Choose copy from the Edit menu.
6. Return to the word processing program and choose paste.

The notation below was created on Finale and the above steps were followed to place it in this text. The music was captured on the screen, sent to the memory of the computer, and then pasted into a word processor. Notice the jagged lines on the eighth notes. With an EPS format file, the graphic would look more professional. However, for most applications, this procedure is sufficient.

Figure 7:12A: Music notation printed using screen-capture technique

For higher quality graphics, consider saving the information in a graphic format that will provide a higher output quality. Sibelius, Finale, Overture, and other high-end programs allow files to be exported in graphic format. This is helpful if you are in need of high quality print or if you want to transfer the files to another program or to post on a web site.

Figure 7.12B: Music notation using EPS format (higher resolution)

The ability to capture graphics from the screen is a tremendous asset for many applications including creating handouts, worksheets, examples for documents, books, and the like.

Notation Software: Internet Applications

The Internet offers many web sites that can be especially useful when combined with the power of music notation software. Sites like Vermont MIDI can be a resource for teachers and students. In addition to education resources, the Internet can be used to search for MIDI files, to find and print out sheet music, and to post notation files on web pages.

Teaching Strategy 77

Become familiar with the common file formats used on the Internet for publishing on the web.

MIDI Files and the Internet

MIDI was introduced and defined in Chapter 3. There are thousands of MIDI files available on the Internet. MIDI files usually can be identified by the suffix used in the file name: .mid. For example: a Bach Chorale might be named: bachchoral136.mid. MIDI files do not contain any sound. They do include information about the musical performance such as the pitch, length, and volume of each note, referred to as an event. MIDI information can also include additional characteristics such as attack and decay time (MIDI is covered in depth in Chapter 8).

MIDI files have several advantages. First, because they only contain performance information, the file size is quite small, usually under 100K per song. Also, they are originally created with some type of MIDI software, so the files can be imported into notation programs such as Finale and Sibelius. It is possible to download a MIDI file from a web site, open it in a notation program, and view the file in music notation. The applications of this technique are endless.

Capturing MIDI Files

There are many web sites that post MIDI files on the Internet. It is possible to play and copy, referred to as download, MIDI files to your computer. MIDI files then can be opened, manipulated, and printed using your notation software. I find this to be a wonderful way to save time and gain access to music.

> **Teaching Strategy 78**
> Take advantage of web sites that offer MIDI files for download. Learn how to download (copy) these files to your hard drive.

Three of my favorite MIDI sites are:

The Classical MIDI Archives . . . . .www.classicalarchives.com

MIDI World . . . . .www.midiworld.com/classic.htm

Choral Public Domain . . . . .www.cpdl.org

These sites allow you to listen to and download MIDI files to your computer. After you listen to a file, return to the page with the name or link of the file. To copy the file to your computer's hard drive:

Windows: Right-click on the link.
Macintosh: Hold down the control key and click on the link.
Then, choose save to disk. You now have a copy of the file on your hard drive.

Figure 7.13: Downloading a MIDI file to the computer's hard drive

The next step is to open the saved MIDI file in your notation program. Follow these steps:

- Open your notation program.
- From the program's File menu, choose open. Select the MIDI file and open it.

You should read the program's documentation on the options for opening MIDI files. Once you become familiar with the steps, you will do this again and again to save time entering notation.

Search Engines for MIDI Files

There is no shortage of web sites that post MIDI files. Simply go to your favorite search engine (see search engine tips in Chapter 2) and type in a composer's name and the word MIDI.

Teaching Strategy 79

Use Internet search engines to locate specific titles of MIDI files. Also consider using special MIDI file search engines.

There are also search engines that only look for MIDI files. These are helpful when trying to locate a specific MIDI file. An example of a MIDI file search engine is www.musicrobot.com. To find more MIDI file search engines, do an Internet search for music search engines. Go to your favorite search engine, such as Google or Yahoo, and type in the words: MIDI file Search Engines. You will find many excellent sites to help you locate MIDI files.

Students and teachers can search for MIDI files, listening to them, and copying files to a computers hard drive. Consider sending students on a scavenger hunt to find files by various composers and to use notation software to analyze, arrange, and print these pieces.

MP3 Files

MP3 files are ubiquitous on the Internet. MP3 files are an extension for MPEG, audio layer 3. Layer 3 is one of three coding schemes (layer 1, layer 2, and layer 3) for the compression of audio files. Layer 3 uses compression to remove information and thus reduce the size of the file without taking away too much of the sound quality. In a nutshell, the MP3 file format takes a CD audio file and reduces (or compresses) its file size to approximately one tenth of its original size.

MP3 files are audio files and cannot be opened in a MIDI program such as notation software. However, the files can be an asset in the music class/rehearsal as a source for listening. Many Internet MIDI sites, such as the Classical MIDI Archives, also offer MP3 files for download. Typically, there is a subscription cost for this service.

PDF Files

PDF, short for Portable Document Format, is a file format developed by Adobe Systems that is now standard on the Internet. PDF captures formatting information from a variety of applications such as word processors and music notation programs, making it possible to send formatted documents that appear on the recipient's computer monitor and can be printed out. To view a file in PDF format, you need Adobe Reader, a free application distributed by Adobe Systems (www.adobe.com/products/acrobat/readermain.html).

Posting Music on the Internet with Scorch and Finale Viewer

A third way to post, view, and print music is using a web browser plugin that will allow site visitors to view, play, control tempo and key, and print music notation. The interesting part of this application is that the plugins required are free to the user. The plugin must initially be downloaded or copied to the user's computer.

The two most common web plugins for music notation are offered by Sibelius and Finale. Sibelius, the most popular of the two, offers Scorch. Finale produces Finale Viewer.

Sibelius Music and Finale Showcase

Finale users can post and view files on the Finale Showcase (hosted by Finale). Sibelius and Finale users can post and view files on www.sibeliusmusic.com, hosted by Sibelius. Sibelius Music also offers a free web page to post your compositions and exercises. This can be done for free and with no web designing experience. You email your files to Sibelius Music and they post them on your very own site.

> ### Teaching Strategy 80
> View notation on web sites using one of the popular music viewer plugins.

Teachers can make music examples interactive by converting them to Scorch (Sibelius) or Finale Viewer (Finale). Students can then interact with these files using any computer in the world for practice, study, and enjoyment. They can view music, change the key and tempo, and print out music. Teachers can also create interactive examples of music notation that can be posted on school and educational web sites.

Viewing Scorch and Finale Viewer Files

To view a file posted by Scorch or Finale Viewer, a plugin must be downloaded to the computer. After the plugin is downloaded, files will open in the web browser.

Creating Your Own Files to Post on a Web Page

It is also possible to create your own files to be posted on a web site in Scorch or Finale Viewer format.

> ### Teaching Strategy 81
> Post your own Finale or Sibelius files on a school or personal web site.

Both Sibelius and Finale offer a "save as web page" or "publish to web page" option. Review the manual and/or online help for instructions. Once files are saved in the proper format, they can be posted on school and personal web sites. In this way, students can view, play, print, and transpose music using a web browser for free.

Many sites listed above use music plugins. As of this writing, Scorch is the most popular format found on music and music education web sites. Sites using web plugins include www.vtmidi.org, www.mysheetmusic.com, www.cdpl.org and others.

Music Web Sites

With the growing popularity of MIDI, PDF, and notation plugins (Scorch and Finale Viewer), many web services and options are becoming available.

> ### Teaching Strategy 82
> Print and capture music from a variety of web sites.

These sites offer both free downloads of music and some that must be purchased. They can be excellent sources of printed music:

My Sheet Music . . . . .www.MySheetMusic.com
Sheet Music Direct . . . . .www.sheetmusicdirect.com
The Choral Public Domain Library . . . . .www.cpdl.org
J.W. Pepper and Son's eprint . . . . .www.jwpepper.com/eprint

Notation Software for Blind Musicians

If you have students with significant visual disabilities, there are special notation program options available for them. Several companies offer software that transforms written notation into Braille music.

> ### Teaching Strategy 83
> Use specialized software to convert traditional notation to Braille music for sight impaired students.

One such company, Dancing Dots, has a variety of programs and applications to assist blind musicians in converting conventional notation into music Braille.

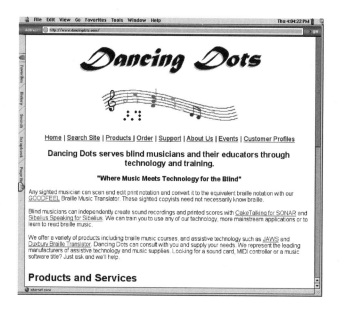

Figure 7:14: Notation software for the blind (www.dancingdots.com)

Copyright Considerations

When using any music software program, it is important to be aware of the legal uses as stipulated by copyright law. See Chapter 16 for a complete discussion of copyright and how teachers and students can abide by its laws and regulations.

Steps for Preparing a Score

Regardless of the package, I have found that there are specific steps to keep in mind when using notation software. The following rules are applicable:

1. If you are entering music from a printed score or handwritten copy, mark in measure numbers throughout the entire piece. This will help you cross-reference with measures on the computer screen.

2. Outline the entire score on the computer before entering any notation: Enter the total number of measures and any meter changes or modulations that may occur.

3. Activate measure numbers on every measure. The computer screen is small and measure numbers help you to pinpoint where you are in the score.

4. Enter the notes, durations, and ties for the entire piece. Add dynamics, slurs, lyrics, etc. after the notes and rests have been entered.

5. Notation programs do not understand polyphony. If the piece contains polyphony, you will have to enter each part separately. Usually this is referred to as layers. The example below is polyphonic. Therefore the soprano and alto part would have to be entered in different layers.

Polyphony example

6. If the piece has lyrics, enter them after the notes and rests.

7. Add chord symbols.

8. Lay out the pages, staves, and staff systems.

9. After the pages have been laid out, enter any dynamic markings, slurs, crescendos, etc.

10. Add slurs, phrase markings, and other score indications.

11. To save paper, view the pages on screen before printing. Most programs have a print preview option. This definitely saves time and paper by allowing you to catch mistakes before printing.

These general guidelines will help make entering a piece a logical process. It takes time to master any notation program. When you are learning a notation program, spend 15-30 minutes per day over a 21 day period. Initially, work on exercises and pieces that you do not immediately need for rehearsal.

Furthermore, consider taking a workshop, buying a training video or a book written on the program. Most notation programs have excellent documentation. Go through the manual's tutorial section to begin to understand the software's operation. It will take time, but once learned notation software will assist you in a wide variety of ways.

Summary

Notation software can be a powerful tool for both teachers and students. There are entry level and advanced programs from which to choose. In addition to printing scores and parts, notation files can be downloaded from the Internet and users can post files on web sites. Be sure to allow time to learn to use the software. Once mastered, notation software can save time and offers new learning activities for students.

Review Questions

1. What is the main goal of notation software?
2. What are the advantages of notation software when compared to writing music by hand?
3. What are the advantages and disadvantages of students learning to use a notation program?
4. List the types of software capable of printing notation.
5. What hardware is needed to scan music notation? How should you select a scanner?
6. There are entry-level and advanced notation programs. List the advantages and disadvantages of each type.
7. Select a notation program that would be suitable for students at the elementary-middle school level. Support your choice.
8. What are templates and how can they be used?
9. What question should be asked when selecting a brand of computer?
10. List 3–5 teacher uses of notation software. Rank them in order from the most to least useful in your opinion.
11. List 3–5 student applications of notation software. Rank them in order from the most to least useful in your opinion.

12. List the three steps for creating a notation lesson for students.
13. List three basic music skills that students can learn using music notation software.
14. What are some supplemental materials that can be used for notation lessons?
15. Name three administrative uses of notation software. Rank them in order of importance in your opinion.
16. Describe two ways to capture graphics from notation software for use in a word processing document.
17. List and define the three most common music notation files found on the Internet.
18. List the name of a search engine for MIDI files.
19. List the steps for posting a notation file on a web site using Sibelius Scorch or Finale Viewer.
20. Describe how students can use free notation software, such as Finale NotePad, on their own home computer to support the skills they are learning in school music classes.
21. Review one of the notation programs listed in this chapter. Spend time using the program and determine if you feel it is an advanced or basic notation program.

CD-ROM Activities

- Project 7.1 Download a demo copy of a notation program such as Finale or Sibelius. Enter and print a single line part.
- Project 7.2 Download a copy of the free software NotePad. Open the tutorials from the help menu and enter the sample song.
- Project 7.3 Prepare a composition lesson plan for students using a notation program such as NotePad, Finale, or Sibelius to compose. Prepare a notation file that students would use to create their composition. Prepare a finished example to illustrate the possibilities to the students.
- Project 7.4 Download a MIDI file from one of the recommended MIDI sites listed in this activity (or use one of the MIDI files on the CD-ROM). After the MIDI file is downloaded open it in a notation program such as Sibelius or Finale. After you open the file, edit it and

print it out. Discuss the editing that was needed in order to make the notation more legible.

- Project 7.5 Go to the web and review samples of Scorch and Finale Viewer postings. Write a summary of how this could be used in your curriculum.

CD-ROM Lesson Plans

Lesson 7.1 Drag notes to create a melody

Lesson 7.2 Drag measures to create a melody

Lesson 7.3 Sample lesson from *Teaching Strategies: Technology* published by MENC.

Reference

Beckstead, D. (2001) Will technology transform music education? *Music Educators Journal*, 87 (6), 44-50.

Booty, Charles, G., editor (1990). *TIPS: Technology for music educators*. Music Educators National Conference, Reston, VA.

Demoline, K. (1999). Choosing a composition program. *Canadian Music Educator*, Spring.

Ely, Mark C. (1993)Software for classroom music making. *Music Educators Journal*, April. pp 41-43.

Hickey, M, editor (2003). *Why and how to teach music composition: A new horizon for music education*. MENC The National Association for Music Education. Reston, VA

Kuzmich, John, Jr. Music reading software: Tomorrow's applications today! *A Music Resource Guide for Educators*, Summer/Fall, 1994. Advanced Technologies, South Bend, IN.

Litterst, George, F. The EM guide to notation software. *Electronic Musician*, August 1993. pp 31-46.

Newquist, H. P. (1989). *Music & Technology*. Billboard Books, New York

Rudolph, Thomas E. & Leonard, Vincent. (2001) *Finale: An easy guide to music notation*. Berklee Press Publications, Boston.

Rudolph, Thomas E., et al (1997) *Technology strategies for music education*. Hal Leonard Corporation, Milwaukee.

Rudolph, Thomas E.. (1999). Notation software: The ultimate tool for the music teacher. *Music Technology Guide*. Lentine's Music, Akron, OH (www.lentine.com/articles/notation_software.htm)

Reese, S. (1998). Music learning in your school computer lab, *Music Educators Journal, 85 (3)* , 31-36.

Reese S., McCord, K, & Walls K. (2001) *Strategies for teaching technology.* MENC The National Association for Music Education, Reston, VA.

Murphy, Barbara, editor. (2002) *Technology directory*. Association for Technology in Music Instruction. http://www.music.org/atmi/Directory/Directory2002.html

Powell, S. (2002) *Music engraving today*. Britchmark Music, New York.

Purse, Bill. (2000). *Mastering the art of music notation with finale*. Backbeat Books.

Williams, D. B. & Webster, P. (1999) *Experiencing music technology: Software, data, and hardware, Second edition*. Schirmer Books, NY.

Chapter 8

MIDI-Sequencing: Overview and Applications

Music Education National Standards: 1, 2, 3, 4, 5, 6
NETS (National Education Technology Standards): 1, 2, 3, 4

The next four chapters will review the various options for recording music. The four areas include MIDI-sequencing, digital audio, loop-based, and creativity. All four of these areas are related, yet distinct in their own right. This chapter will deal with the oldest and most common of the group: MIDI sequencing.

The chapter is in two parts. The first section provides an overview of MIDI sequencers. It is designed for those with little or no experience using sequencers. The second half of the chapter explores educational applications of sequencers, and should be of interest to all music educators.

In the simplest terms, a MIDI sequencer can be thought of as a digital player/recorder. In his book, *The Art of Sequencing*, Don Muro defines a sequencer as:

> ... A device that records and plays back performing information. Sequencers make it possible to change or to edit almost any aspect of this performance information...A sequencer also makes it possible to save or store performance information, usually on a computer disk. This storage capability will allow you to retrieve the data and play back any song at a later time without having to re-record the music. A sequencer, therefore,

is a device that can record, edit, store and play back digital data that represents a musical performance.[1]

There are many similarities between sequencers and their audio counterparts: cassette tape recorders, DAT recorders, and mini-disc recorders. They all have recording and playback capabilities. All can store what is recorded. The enormous advantage of a MIDI sequencer is that the recorded information can be easily altered and edited. For example, if you are recording a live performance on your cassette, DAT, or mini-disc player, and you play one wrong note, it is very difficult—if not impossible—to correct the mistake. Sure, you could try to record just that phrase, but usually, when dealing with traditional analog tape recorders, it is easier to re-record the entire piece or section.

This is not the case with sequencers. A sequencer records information about the musical performance and stores it as digital data. This data can easily be modified. Let's say you recorded a passage using a sequencer and played one wrong note. You can select the incorrect note and type in or re-play the correct note.

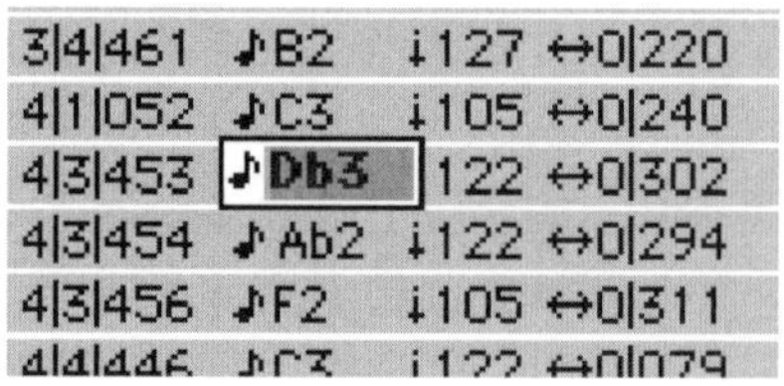

Figure 8.1: Changing one note in a passage

With sequencers, notes, durations, volumes, and just about every aspect of the musical performance can be altered after the performance has taken place.

The History of Sequencers

The analog sequencer was used long before MIDI was created. In the 1960s and 1970s sequencers were built into analog synthesizers produced by Moog, ARP, Roland, and Buchla.[2] The original sequencer could control 8 to 16 events (or notes) at a time and was primarily used for ostinatos.

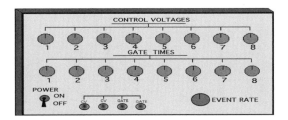

Figure 8.2: Typical 1960s analog sequencer

With the dawn of microprocessor-controlled digital instruments in the 1980s, sequencers could now control thousands of events at a time. It also was possible to record these events on separate tracks, creating a digital multi-track recorder. The original name of sequencer was retained.

Unique Features of Sequencers

Just as a word processor gives the typist an advantage facilitating text editing, a sequencer allows the musician to edit performance information. With sequencers a melody can be transposed without affecting the tempo or speed. This is possible because pitch and tempo are recorded as *separate* pieces of information. Everything that a sequencer records is information *about* the performance.

Sequencers record what note was played; how long it was sustained; what vibrato, if any, was used; the volume played; and other data. A sequencer actually records a stream of data or information one piece at a time, but at an extremely rapid rate. When someone plays a MIDI keyboard, the computer chip inside the keyboard sends a stream of information about the performance—what note was pressed, how quickly it was pressed, how much vibrato was used, etc. Thus, what is recorded is a *sequence* of events. This sequence of events is the information about the performance; hence the term sequence.

Do not confuse the traditional musical meaning of a melodic sequence with digitally created sequences and sequencers. The traditional definition of a melodic sequence is a melodic fragment that moves upward or downward in a like manner.

Figure 8.3: An example of a melodic sequence

197

What does it mean when someone says they are going to *load a sequence?* The sequence is the data or information that has been recorded about the performance and is usually stored on a computer disk. The loading process means moving the data, or information about the performance, from a storage device, such as a disk, into the memory of the computer or sequencer. This is just like putting a tape in your audio cassette deck.

Figure 8.4: Sequencer with tape recorder-like controls

The Sound Connection

A MIDI sequencer does not record the actual timbre or sound being performed. What the sequencer *does* record is the sound number that was played on the MIDI instrument when the music was originally performed. Each sound has a corresponding number, for example, piano = 1. When a sequencer plays back the performance information, it sends the number of the sound to the MIDI instrument or playback device. Therefore, to record and recreate sound you need two items: a sequencer and a MIDI sound source such as a MIDI keyboard or sound module. The sound will only be as good as the MIDI sound source that is producing it. A $300 sound source will not sound as good as a $3,000 one. Think of the sequencer as the device that controls the information about the performance and the MIDI keyboard or sound module is the device that actually supplies the timbre.

The ability to control timbre with a sequencer and MIDI playback device is a distinct advantage over cassette, DAT, and mini-disc recorders. If I turned on my mini-disc recorder and recorded my trumpet playing the melody of Beethoven's Ninth Symphony, I could hear performance playback with a trumpet timbre. With a sequencer and a MIDI sound source, I can select any one of the available instrument sounds—typically 99 to several hundred—to hear the melody played.

Sequencers = Sound

When does someone use a sequencer? A simple way to categorize the sequencer is to use it anytime a *sound* recording is needed. Think S=S or sound = sequencer.

Figure 8.5: Sound = Sequencer

For example, if a recording of a song is required to accompany student practice or to use in the rehearsal or classroom, then a MIDI sequencer is the best tool.

Some of the common uses of sequencers include:

- recording music for classroom demonstration
- creating practice exercises for students and professionals
- composing original music

Tracks

In 1966, the Beatles recorded the Sergeant Pepper album using a four-track, reel-to-reel multi-track tape recorder. Analog tape decks divide the magnetic tape into separate parts, or tracks. Each of these tracks can be separately edited, erased, or changed without affecting the others. The advantage of using separate tracks is control over each part. For example, with a four-track tape recorder the Beatles could record the drums and bass on track 1, come back to the recording studio on another day and record the guitar parts on track 2, and then record the vocals on tracks 3 and 4. Analog tape recorders continued to develop through the 1960s and '70s and eventually were capable of recording 24 separate tracks.

A sequencer can also divide information into separate tracks for independent control over performance information and therefore can function as a multi-track recording device. If a sequencer has 16 tracks, then it can store 16 independent parts. By using multiple tracks, very complex

199

sequences, or pieces, can be created. Information can be stored separately so it can be edited or isolated during playback.

With today's sequencers, one can record from eight to 1,026 or more tracks depending on the type and cost of the sequencer. The cost of an analog multi-track tape deck in the 1960s was in the $10,000 range. Today, thanks to the ever decreasing price of digital technology, schools can purchase digital, multi-track sequencers and sequencing software for $100 to $300, depending on the features.

Tracks vs. Channels

In Chapter 3 we discussed that MIDI is transmitted on 16 separate channels. One of the most confusing concepts when first working with sequencers is trying to distinguish between MIDI channels and sequencer tracks. Each uses the same numbering system (1, 2, 3, 4, etc.), but a MIDI channel is synonymous with timbre. When you record separate parts such as a bass part, chords, and melody, each is placed on a separate track. After information is recorded, you assign the data or track to separate channels for playback. Remember, MIDI channels are each a unique timbre. If you want separate timbres, then you must assign the tracks to separate channels. If you want all the same timbre (a French horn trio for example) then assign the tracks to the same channel.

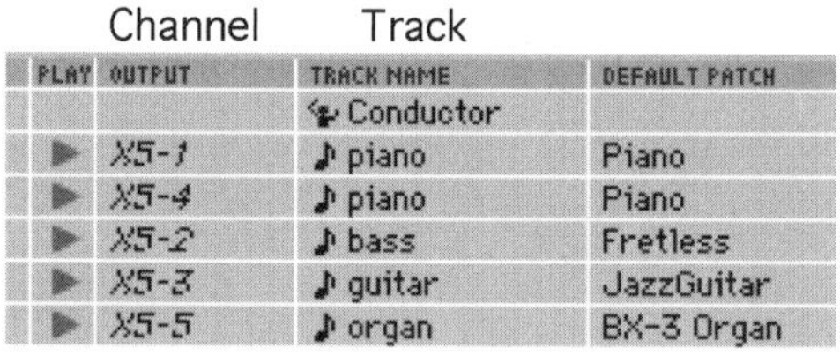

Channel	Track	
PLAY OUTPUT	TRACK NAME	DEFAULT PATCH
	♪ Conductor	
▶ X5-1	♪ piano	Piano
▶ X5-4	♪ piano	Piano
▶ X5-2	♪ bass	Fretless
▶ X5-3	♪ guitar	JazzGuitar
▶ X5-5	♪ organ	BX-3 Organ

Figure 8.6: Track and channel assignments

200

Soloing Tracks

Suppose you would like to make a sound recording for your class so you can demonstrate concepts of rhythm, harmony, and melody. You record the following:

- the drum part on track 1
- the chords on track 2
- the melody on track 3

When you play a recording on a record or CD you might tell the class to "listen to the melody" or "the trumpet is playing the melody." Yet, it is sometimes difficult for students to isolate particular sounds with all of the various instruments playing. With a sequencer, each part can be "soloed," or isolated, for playback. Each track can be played separately or in any combination.

Punching In

Sequencers make it easy to re-record pieces or bits of information. Let's suppose you made one mistake when you recorded a melody. You can simply find the note in the sequence, punch-in at that particular beat, and re-record it. You find the measure and select the beat on which you will begin and the beat on which you will end. When you press record, the sequencer records only the beats or measures you have selected, leaving the rest of the information untouched.

Figure 8.7: Punching in

Step Time and Real Time

Sequencers record music in two ways: real time and step time. Real time refers to music that is recorded in live performance. Analog cassette recorders record only in real time. A real time performance is what we do every time we perform live. Sequencers record in real time if the record button is pressed.

Simply play the MIDI instrument in time with the sequencer's built-in metronome and you are recording in real time.

The other way to record information with sequencers is using step time. With step time, you tell the sequencer the duration and the pitch of each note in the performance, one note at a time. Step time is an excellent way for non-performers to create music. Let's assume you wanted to record the following passage, but were not able to play it in real time.

Figure 8.8: The first three measures of "Ode to Joy"

In step time, you would first select the rhythm value, in the above example, a quarter note, then depress the correct pitch on the MIDI keyboard. Repeat this process note by note, until the entire melody has been entered.

> **Teaching Strategy 84**
> Use step time to record music, especially with students who are non-performers.

Step time is an excellent tool for entering very complex passages and for those who are not trained performers. Students can enter, edit, and play back their own music using step entry.

To Quantize or to Humanize?

Each performance parameter that is controlled by a sequencer is called an event. Events can be a note, volume, program numbers, and more. An additional unique sequencer feature is quantizing. Quantizing is a type of mathematical rounding. If you recorded a melody using a keyboard in real time, there will probably be some timing errors. Some of the notes will be slightly ahead of or behind the beat. Quantizing rounds off the notes to the nearest note value that you select. The best way to choose the note value is to select the smallest duration played. If, for example, you played a melody that had the smallest value of an eighth note, then select this as the quantize value.

Another example of quantizing would be trying to tighten up the sound of a drum part that has been recorded in real time. Suppose the smallest duration in the drum part is a sixteenth note, then this would be selected for the quantize value. Using the quantize command, the sequencer would round off all the notes to the nearest sixteenth note. Quantizing does have a downside as it can turn a musical performance into a very mechanical one since each note will be rounded.

Sequencers are also capable of reversing the process: humanizing. Let's say you entered an entire performance in step time. The final performance will sound very rigid. Because humans don't always play exactly on the beat, the sequencer can take a performance and humanize it by randomly changing the start times of notes to make a piece sound as if it were entered in real time. Consult Don Muro's text, *The Art of Sequencing,* for an in-depth discussion of quantizing, and other sequencing techniques.

Types of Sequencers

Have you ever thought of how many cassette recorders, CD playerss, mini-disc players, and DAT decks are in your possession? You probably have one in your car, one in your home stereo system, a portable "boom box," a Walkman for exercising, and maybe more. Sequencers also come in a variety of sizes and shapes. There are essentially three types of sequencers: software, integrated, and dedicated. In schools, the most popular type of sequencer which runs on a Macintosh or Windows computer, is a software sequencer. The advantage of a software sequencer is that you have access to a large computer screen to use for editing. Software sequencers require a MIDI keyboard and MIDI interface in addition to the computer. The negative side of using a software sequencer is that they are not very portable.

The second type of sequencer is an integrated sequencer, or one that is inside an electronic keyboard. Like the "boom box" approach where the manufacturer includes several components such as cassette player, radio, compact disc all in one unit, there are electronic keyboards that come equipped with a built-in sequencer. The common name given to a keyboard that also has a built-in sequencer is a workstation.

If portability is important and/or you want to go with a less expensive purchase, then choose a hardware or dedicated sequencer. A hardware sequencer is a small box that comes with software permanently installed. Usually these have a small screen for editing and a disk drive for storing the sequences. Sometimes these sequencers are referred to as dedicated sequencers because they are dedicated to one application—sequencing.

Even acoustic pianos can be outfitted with dedicated sequencers. When an acoustic piano is able to record and playback MIDI sequences, it can be thought of as a modern-day player-piano. Instead of using piano rolls, the digital sequencer generates the performance information. Yamaha produces a line of acoustic pianos that have a built-in sequencer to be used for practice and recording. These instruments are called the Disklavier (www.yamahamusicsoft.com/disklavier). The PianoDisc Company (www.pianodisc.com) specializes in adapting and retrofitting acoustic pianos so they can send and receive MIDI data. However, the cost of adding a sequencer to an acoustic piano can be very expensive.

Which type of sequencer is best? There is no one perfect answer. If you do not have a computer or are trying to keep your equipment costs down, then a hardware or integrated sequencer is a good place to start. If portability is important, hardware or integrated might also be the way to go. However, if you own a computer, then software sequencers offer much more on-screen help, making them easier to operate. Each type of sequencer has strengths and weaknesses that make it suitable for various applications.

Choosing a Software Sequencer for Your Computer

If you want to use a sequencer with students, a software sequencer is the best choice. Computers have large screen displays and offer menus and icons that help students quickly learn to use the software. There are many different sequencer programs and selecting the best program for you can be confusing.

Once you have a computer, the first step in selecting a software sequencer is to determine your goals. Then select the best program to support them. After selecting the program, the hardware required to run the software should be purchased.

1. Select the computer—what kind of support do you have?
2. Select the level—are your needs basic or advanced?
3. Review software options—after you identify your level, which software product is best for you?

Sequencer programs are available for both Macintosh and Windows computers. Both of these platforms offer a variety of packages from which to choose. Windows currently has more options and a wider variety than Macintosh.

Which is best for you? First, check with your school and see which computer platform is used. If Macintosh or Windows are already in use, then go with this platform for the simple reason that you will have a built-in support group. Next, decide the level of sophistication required for your needs—basic or advanced, and then select the program with the best options and technical support.

Selecting a Sequencer

When you look through a company catalog selling MIDI sequencers, you will find a myriad of selections from which to choose. (See the list of music technology companies in Appendix A.) After looking at the extensive list, how do you go about selecting a program?

Basic or Advanced

Determine your level of use. Are you going to be an entry-level or advanced user? Programs differ widely in how they operate; some programs were written for music novices and others for the professional recording studio. Remember, a lot of fancy features means a much steeper learning curve, and that means taking more time to learn to use the program.

An entry-level user is someone who mainly records accompaniments and pieces that are not extremely complex. I have been using sequencers for more than 20 years in my teaching and I still consider myself a basic user. I use the sequencer to record accompaniment parts, practice exercises, and the like. I prefer a sequencer with easy to use, easy-to-understand features.

An advanced user is someone who wants to record digital-audio as well as MIDI data, or someone who is going to sync tracks to a videotape or television commercial. Advanced users also are those using sequencers in the recording studio where a high level of control over the sequence is needed.

The cost difference between a basic and advanced program can be several hundred dollars or more. Some basic sequencing programs cost well under $100 while advanced programs can cost several hundred dollars or more.

Questions to Ask Before Purchasing a MIDI Sequencer

- How many tracks do you need? Are you planning on doing complex sequences with more than 30–50 tracks? If so, look for a high end program.
- How easy is the program to learn and teach to students? If your goal is to have students use the sequencer, ease of use is an important criterion.
- Do you want to record acoustic as well as MIDI data with your sequences?
- Do you need to sync your sequences to video?
- Are there support materials such as books available?
- What software are other educators you know using?

Overview of Popular Sequencing Software

For most educational environments, a basic sequencer is sufficient. For high school and college level, an advanced sequencer might be a better choice. For professional sequencing and digital recording, high end *is* the best choice. If both basic and advanced programs are required, it is usually a good idea to stick with one company. The reason for this is that the two programs will use similar commands, so the programs will look alike and work in a similar manner. The coordination makes it easier for students and teachers to go from the less complex version to the high end. Examples of both entry-level and advanced sequencers are listed in the chart below.

MIDI Sequencer	Web site	Entry Level	Advanced Use	Digital Audio	Loop-Based	Mac/Win
Cakewalk Products						
Home Studio	www.cakewalk.com	x		yes	yes	Win
Home Studio XL	www.cakewalk.com	x		yes	yes	Win
Sonar	www.cakewalk.com		x	yes	yes	Win
Sonal XL	www.cakewalk.com	x	x	yes	yes	Win
Mark of the Unicorn						
Performer	www.motu.com	x		yes	no	Mac
Digital Performer	www.motu.com		x	yes	yes	Mac
Emagic						
Logic Education	www.emagic.de	x		yes	no	Mac/Win
Logic Gold	www.emagic.de		x	yes	no	Mac
Logic Platinum	www.emagic.de		x	yes	no	Mac
Propellerheads						
Reason	www.propellerheads.se/		x	yes	yes	Mac/Win
PGMusic						
Power Tracks Pro	www.pgmusic.com	x		yes	no	Win
Steinberg Products						
Cubase SL	www.steinberg.net		x	yes	no	Mac/Win
Cubase SX	www.steinberg.net		x	yes	yes	Mac/Win

Figure 8.9: Listing of popular MIDI sequencing software

Advanced applications have many more features than their basic counterparts. With more options come more commands and a more complicated and difficult to learn program. An entry-level program is easier to learn and use. If you can get by with an entry-level program, then do so! You will spend less time mastering the software and more time making music.

As mentioned in Chapter 7, there are some programs that offer sequencing *and* notation in the same program, referred to as integrated sequencing and notation software. Because these programs are extremely complex and have a steep learning curve, I recommend them only for the high end user. I find it easier to use, teach, and learn separate sequencers and notation software. Examples of integrated sequencer/notation software include Cubase SX and Logic Platinum.

Books, Books, Books

Because sequencing software is extremely popular in all areas of music, there are many helpful books about various sequencers. I frequently purchase third-party books on programs that I want to learn. Start by going to the company's web site and see if it endorses any books. For example, if you are considering one of the Cakewalk programs, its web site has a listing of books that can be purchased to help you and your students.

Another excellent source is to search for books on a web site such as Amazon.com to see what books are available for a specific software package. I have found that third party books can help me and my students learn software faster and they also provide an excellent reference.

Educator Discount

Just like notation software (see Chapter 7), most companies offer significant discounts for teachers, schools, churches, and other non-profit institutions. I suggest that you purchase software from a reputable music technology re-seller. See the listing of companies in Appendix A.

Part II:
Sequencing Applications

Sequencers are everywhere. The last television commercial you heard was probably composed in part or entirely on a sequencer. Not long ago I walked into a fancy hotel in Philadelphia and I heard a $50,000 Steinway grand piano playing. No one was at the bench. Upon inspection, I found a small hardware sequencer that was generating a digital version of a piano roll. Sequencers are also becoming popular in education, providing a wide range of educational applications.

The key to understanding the proper function of sequencers is to think of them as sophisticated, digital, multi-track recorders. As mentioned earlier in this chapter, sequencers should be used when *sound* is the main objective. Sequencer applications can be organized into four distinct categories:

1. Recorded accompaniments for class and rehearsal.
2. Individual practice or "music-minus-one" recordings.
3. A composition tool for the teacher and student.
4. A demonstrator of musical elements to a class or ensemble.

Sequencer = Accompanist

There are many instances when a sequencer can be used to enhance classroom activities, chorus, band, and orchestra rehearsals, and even as a performance instrument. Because sequencers are digital, multi-track recording and playback devices, separate parts can be recorded and isolated for various activities in the classroom and rehearsal hall.

> **Teaching Strategy 85**
>
> Use the sequencer to generate ostinatos and accompaniments for classroom activities.

Ken Peters, an elementary music specialist at Chatham Park Elementary School in Havertown, Pennsylvania, finds a sequencer to be helpful when teaching students to play Orff instruments. He selects a piece for the students to sing and perform on classroom Orff instruments, then records the parts into a sequencer. The pieces he teaches have soprano, alto, and bass parts, so he enters each part separately on a separate track. Then he assigns instrument sounds that resemble those of his acoustic Orff ensemble.

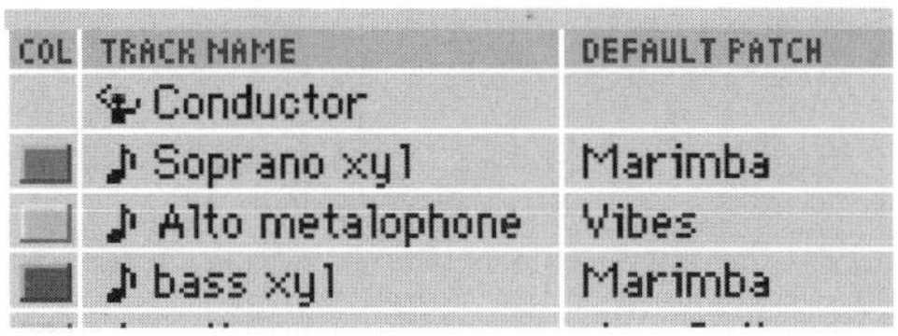

COL	TRACK NAME	DEFAULT PATCH
	🎵 Conductor	
◼	♪ Soprano xyl	Marimba
◻	♪ Alto metalophone	Vibes
◼	♪ bass xyl	Marimba

Figure 8.10: Three-part song record using a sequencer

While the students are learning to sing, move, and play along with the song Ken has selected, he uses a sequencer to play the entire arrangement for the class. While the sequencer is playing the composition, Ken, the instructor, is free to move about the classroom and model and assist students throughout the learning process.

Next, Ken begins to teach students to play the ostinato on Orff bass xylophones and metalophones. Again, he uses the sequencer as an accompanist-assistant. This time he isolates the bass part and plays it alone for the students. The sequencer's ability to isolate separate parts makes it a very helpful tool in the classroom.

It is possible to use a sequencer to enter your own accompaniments and arrangements. However, at the end of this chapter we will review many ways to procure songs in sequencer format. For example, Silver Burdett, McGraw-Hill and other major publishers are offering sequenced versions of the songs in their series. Using pre-recorded sequences can be a helpful idea. This way you do not have to take the time to enter the music into the sequencer.

Teaching Strategy 86

Use your sequencer to provide recorded accompaniments for choral rehearsals and other singing activities.

A sequencer can be an effective tool in the classroom and choral rehearsal. Suppose you are in a rehearsal or class and some students need your direct assistance. It is difficult to help when you are sitting behind the piano playing the accompaniment part. But, if the accompaniment part is entered into the sequencer, you can press the play button and then move about the room to assist students. This technique is especially helpful in choral rehearsals so the teacher is free to conduct while the sequencer generates the accompaniment.

In addition, some choral directors are finding that a sequencer adds a new dimension to their performances. Sequencers can add the impact of a full orchestral accompaniment with brass, woodwind, and string sounds. Suppose the piece you are rehearsing has parts for an optional string quartet. You may not have the budget to hire a professional group to play the accompaniment for a particular piece, but with a sequencer and a General MIDI electronic keyboard, an accompaniment can be entered and used in rehearsal and performance with the appropriate string sounds. Remember that sequencers are digital, so the tempo or key of any piece can easily be altered. Also, because different timbres can be assigned to each part of a sequence, a realistic orchestration can be created for rehearsal and performance.

> **Teaching Strategy 87**
> Create recorded accompaniments for chorus, band, and orchestra warm-ups using the sequencer.

Do you have a set of warm-ups that you use with your students? If so, consider creating accompaniment sequences. The use of a sequencer can free you from sitting at the piano and allow you to move around the class or rehearsal room as students perform warm-up exercises.

> **Teaching Strategy 88**
> Sequence a missing instrument's part to be played in live performance.

Suppose you are getting ready for a spring concert and on the day of the program you find out that the cellist in the string quartet is ill and will not be able to perform. Or perhaps you have two outstanding violinists and a violist but no cello player in the orchestra. Why not sequence the cellist's part and use the computer to play the part live in the concert? Perhaps you have a percussion part that you want played with a choral arrangement. You can use the sequencer to generate the part for rehearsal and performance.

Sequencers = Practice Accompanist

The sequencer is the ultimate practice tool. Everyone is familiar with karaoke, where a recorded accompaniment is used and someone sings or plays along live. A sequencer can be the accompaniment part of a karaoke set-up. Actually, most of the professionally recorded karaoke accompaniments were recorded using a sequencer.

Teaching Strategy 89

Use the sequencer to generate accompaniments for students to use for practice.

Most students own or have access to a cassette tape recorder or CD player, and they enjoy playing with recorded accompaniments. Instrumental teachers can create accompaniments for songs and exercises, transfer these sequences to cassette or CD, and then have their students play along.

Choral directors can record parts from a piece being rehearsed, placing each part on a separate track. Students can then rehearse with the sequencer. A soprano can isolate the soprano part to help learn it. Then, she can mute the soprano part and sing along with the other three parts.

Some teachers, especially piano instructors, find that creating practice sequences helps students improve their performance level. For example, suppose you are teaching a new piece. You could record the first four measures and then leave space for the students to play the second four measures. Or, one version of the sequence could play the right hand while the student plays the left. In this way, the sequencer acts as a rehearsal accompanist.

Every practice room should be equipped with a sequencer for student practice. Anyone who can operate a cassette tape recorder will have very little trouble operating a sequencer. After an accompaniment has been entered into the sequencer, students can slow down the tempo, change the key, and isolate or mute various parts as they learn to sing or play a piece.

Sequencer = Teacher's Tool

If you are interested in creating accompaniments and/or composing your own original pieces, a sequencer can be an invaluable tool.

Teaching Strategy 90

Use the sequencer as a composition tool to compose original compositions and exercises.

Many teachers write their own warm-ups and original pieces for their performance ensembles. A sequencer is an excellent medium for composing music. For example, enter the bass part and record it on track 1. Then have the sequencer play back the bass part while you compose harmony. Continue this process until the entire composition is complete. No longer must you wait until rehearsal to hear how your exercise or composition sounds. With a sequencer you get immediate feedback and can listen to the composition as it develops until you have a completed piece. In this way, teachers can create accompaniments and original compositions and arrangements.

Sequencer = Demonstration Tool

A sequencer can be a teacher's tool in the classroom and rehearsal room with students from the elementary to university level. Sequencers give teachers a blank slate to use for demonstration and for analysis. Another advantage is the ability to save songs to disk. Once each example is saved to disk you will never have to go through the trouble of creating it again.

Classroom specialists and instrumental and choral directors can use a sequencer to demonstrate any musical concept to students. Sequencers are excellent tools for listening and responding to "what do you hear" activities. Once you have created the sequence, listening/responding activities can be developed.

Teaching Strategy 91

Use the solo function of a sequencer to isolate different parts for class demonstration and analysis.

Have you ever played a recording of a piece and said to a class, "listen to the bass part?" I usually get a blank stare when I try this with middle school students. It is difficult for a novice music student to focus on one part while all of the other parts are sounding. Because the sequencer is a digital multi-track recorder/player, each track can be independently controlled. The bass track, or any track can be isolated and played solo. This helps students identify musical concepts such as melody, harmony, and rhythm. Suppose you

213

are trying to demonstrate melody and harmony using a Bach chorale. First record the parts into the sequencer. Now you can isolate the soprano, alto, tenor, and bass parts for class demonstration.

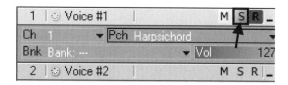

Figure 8.11: Tracks window from Digital Performer with soprano part in solo

In the above example, I entered a Bach chorale and assigned string sounds to each part. In the "Play" column, a blue triangle indicates that the track is play enabled and an orange triangle means a track is muted. In the above example, only the "Soprano xyl" part will play as the other tracks have been muted.

> **Teaching Strategy 92**
>
> Use the sequencer's graphic display to show melodic contour and other musical characteristics.

Most software sequencers use a graphic display to show notation in a piano roll-like manner. This can be an interesting way to demonstrate melodic contour, melodic direction, polyphony, and other musical concepts to a class. However, for the entire class to see the display, the computer will need to be connected to a large-screen display (see Chapter 13).

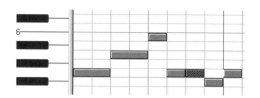

Figure 8.12: Graphic display of a sequencer

Teaching Strategy 93

Create different versions of a piece for same/different analysis.

When I teach my unit on Baroque music in seventh grade general music class, I use a sequencer to demonstrate same/different musical examples. First, I record the theme from Bach's Toccata in D Minor. After recording it, I create a second version in major tonality. This is quickly accomplished by using the transpose feature available with most sequencers.

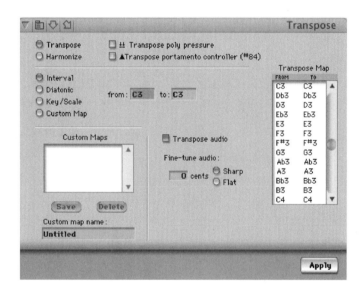

Figure 8.13: Transpose screen from Digital Performer

After transposing the melody from D minor to C major, I now have two versions of the piece which I play for the class and then ask them to identify the difference between the two. Once I have saved the two versions of the piece to disk, I can recall them for later use year after year.

Teaching Strategy 94

Change timbres of each part of a sequence to demonstrate different timbres.

Sequencers play back a musical example using whatever sounds have been selected from the keyboard or MIDI module, regardless of the original instrumentation. All MIDI instruments offer a wide variety of musical timbres. If a General MIDI compatible instrument is used, then Bach's Toccata in D Minor can be played back using any of the more than 100 available sounds. Students enjoy musically "coloring" a piece of music, changing timbres for the various parts. Also, students will listen to a piece of classical music over and over while they experiment with different sounds, volumes, and tempos.

> **Teaching Strategy 95**
>
> With performing groups, create a sequence of a piece to play for the group especially if a recording of the piece is not available.

It is often helpful for performing ensembles to hear a piece of music to get a concept of the composition before learning to play it. If a recording of a composition is not available, then consider recording it into the sequencer part by part from the score. Once entered, the piece can be played for the class providing you with independent control over parts and timbres, tempo, and key. In this manner, a sequencer can be used to expose students to musical characteristics such as instrumentation, form, meter, tempo, accelerando, ritard, dynamics, and every other musical characteristic you choose to include.

Sequencer = Student Composition Tool

In Chapter 1 we discussed Samuel Papert's comments regarding the use of technology in education. Papert sees technology from a:

> ...Vision of an educational system in which technology is used not in the form of machines for processing children but as something the child himself will learn to manipulate, to extend, to apply to projects, thereby gaining a greater knowledge and a self-confidently realistic image of himself as an intellectual agent.[3]

Papert focuses on the technological tools for teaching children mathematical thinking. In music, a sequencer can be used to help students apply musical concepts and to compose and create their own original music. A sequencer can be thought of as a box of musical crayons for students. Brian Moore states: with sequencing "…the focus is not the notation but the sound."[4]

Creativity and Composition

Students can compose original compositions and arrange and orchestrate music using a sequencer to record and playback parts. Students at all levels can learn to use the sequencer as a creative tool. Consider the following activities, all of which can be adapted for elementary, middle, and high school students:

- Manipulate a sequence. The student can control the tempo, insert accelerandos and ritards, and orchestrate a piece by assigning instrument sounds to various parts.

- Add parts to a sequence. The next level is recording additional parts to a pre-existing sequence. I ask students to add a percussion part or harmony line to a piece. In this way, they become familiar with the operation of the sequencer and can begin to compose their own arrangements.

- Improvise rhythms from scratch. Once familiar with the fundamentals of recording, students are ready to compose a drum part consisting of a bass drum, snare, and cymbals.

- Compose original melodies and harmonies using the sequencer.

> **Teaching Strategy 96**
> Allow students to arrange a sequence by inserting tempo changes, volume changes, and timbres.

When I teach my sixth grade general music class a unit on classical music, I use the melody from Haydn's Surprise Symphony, second movement. First,

I create a sequence of the piece by entering the parts one at a time. Next, I break the students into groups so they can work cooperatively to produce their own version of the piece. The students are given a sequencer file of the piece that contains the melody and accompaniment. Each group music decide on the following:

- tempo: choose a starting tempo and determine where to add a ritard at the end.
- timbre: select a starting timbre for the melody.
- volume: mix all the volume levels of each part so the melody predominates at all times.

Each group marks their choices for the above elements on their group copies. Then, each group comes to the front of the room and enters their changes. After all groups have recorded their examples, we play each one for the class and vote on the best, most musical version of Haydn's Surprise Symphony.

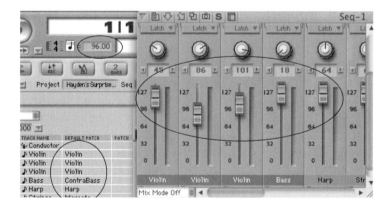

Figure 8.14: Sample of a student file (Digital Performer)
manipulating a sequence of the theme from Haydn's Surprise Symphony.
The students in the group selected the tempo, instruments
(under default patch), and playback volume.

Teaching Strategy 97

Record student-composed melodies using the sequencer.

Many teachers at all levels have their students invent and compose simple melodies. After students have composed a melody and can perform it on the keyboard, they can record the melody with a sequencer. After the melody is recorded, it can be played for the class or recorded on a CD. Used this way, sequencers are fantastic tools to promote creativity and higher level thinking skills.

A sequencer also provides a natural environment for students to work with improvisation.

Teaching Strategy 98
With a teacher-supplied blues progression in E-flat major, students improvise jazz blues melodies using only the black keys on the MIDI keyboard.

Students can record a melody, record a harmony part, and make changes at any time. Also, teachers can produce sequences for students that will help them with the improvisation process. For example, create a 12-bar blues progression and transpose it to the key of E-flat major. Students can then improvise on the black keys of the MIDI keyboard because the black keys become the blues scale (flat 3 and 7) in E-flat major. They can then record their improvisations on various MIDI tracks.

Most advanced MIDI sequencers can import movies in a variety of digital formats. Once these movies have been imported, students can compose music and synchronize the music with the movie.

Teaching Strategy 99
Student records MIDI tracks to accompany a digitized movie.

Ken Simpson, a teacher in Atlanta, Georgia, asks his students to record music for movie tracks. They record a short portion of a film and then record their own music to accompany it. Students learn how to synchronize music to video and compose and create their own movie sound tracks.

Another fun activity for students at all levels is to create a radio commercial and record the voice and background music using a MIDI sequencer.

> ### Teaching Strategy 100
> Students create radio commercials using sequencing software.

Seth Gardner, a teacher in Pennsylvania, asks his middle school general music classes to create original radio commercials. Students collaboratively work in groups. They create the idea, write the copy (words), compose the music, and then they record the spoken part of the commercial using a MIDI sequencer. Finally, they compose the music tracks to accompany the commercial.

> ### Teaching Strategy 101
> Students compose musical examples in a variety of forms: ABA, rondo, theme and variation.

With sequencers, every aspect of the sound can be altered in a variety of ways. Tracks can be copied and pasted, transposed and re-recorded. Students can be assigned the task of creating musical forms such as ABA, rondo, and theme and variations. For example, the teacher could supply the A section, and ask the students to compose a B section and then copy and paste the A section to create ABA form. The recording options are limited only by your imagination.

Teaching Sequencing to Students

In Chapter 7, I stated the key to developing activities and lessons with notation software is for the teacher to provide the students with a file that is partially completed, and assign the students a specific task to complete. This is also the most effective process with sequencing software. The key is to provide the students with partially completed sequencer files along with instructions for them to add to, change, and alter these tracks or add original composed/improvised parts.

Support Materials: Books and Methods

One of the challenges of any new technology is finding a way to integrate it into the curriculum. Sequencers are tremendous tools. However, music teachers are already overworked and developing a complete new curriculum can be an overwhelming task. The best place to start is by using the sequencers owner's manual. Many publishers provide excellent documentation and sample lessons to help students become familiar with recording and manipulating the sequencer.

Teaching Strategy 102

Purchase books and other printed materials to help students learn to create original sequences.

An excellent source for how to teach students to record music using a sequencer is Don Muro's text *The Art of Sequencing*. The book is laid out in a logical, step-by-step manner to teach students how to record a sequence. The book is targeted to the secondary level and can be used with any type of sequencer: hardware, software, or dedicated.

Teaching Strategy 103

Students arrange music in a variety of styles and genres following the advice of professional composers and arrangers.

Corey Allen's book, *Arranging in the Digital World*, is an excellent resource for students who are beginning to create their own MIDI arrangements. He gives excellent, easy-to-understand instructions and tips for beginners. He lists the specific steps he uses to create an arrangement. Included with the text are completed sequences. Throughout the book he describes how he recorded each sequence with instructions such as: Step 1: I turned on the built-in metronome and set it to 104. Step 2: I recorded the hi-hat on beats 2 and 4 on track 5. This book can be very helpful to students who are learning the sequence basics to create arrangements and original compositions.

Students enjoy composing songs. Rick Whitcomb, a high school instrumental music teacher in Havertown, Pennsylvania, teaches classes in a MIDI lab. He designed an elective for high school students called Song Writing by Computer. In this popular course, students learn the basics of music theory and then put together simple songs.

> **Teaching Strategy 104**
> Students learn to compose songs using MIDI sequencing software.

There are many books available from a variety of publishers on how to write songs. These books can provide helpful information for students and teachers. A good one is the book, *You Can Teach Yourself Song Writing*, by Larry McCabe, which covers the basics of song writing. Students can use this book to help them begin to compose original songs.

Curriculum Materials for MIDI Sequencing

Several education companies have produced materials that can be used in the classroom and MIDI lab. These companies include SoundTree, Silver Burdett, and McGraw-Hill.

> **Teaching Strategy 105**
> Teachers review MIDI sequencing methods that are available from educational publishers and adapt lessons for classes and the MIDI lab.

The SoundTree General Music Curriculum

I hesitate to push my own books and methods. In taking many, many graduate courses over the years, I was always suspect when professors required their own books as part of the course and then never assigned a reading from it! I promised myself I would not do this to my students. With this in mind, I only recommend this publication because it is one of the few that offers lesson plans and supporting files for MIDI sequencing activities. A sample lesson is located on the accompanying CD-ROM.

Each of the lessons are organized to include experiences in performance, arranging, and composing. Students use a MIDI sequencer and MIDI keyboard to perform melodies and percussion parts, arrange, create, compose, and improvise. The lessons are designed for secondary students.

MIDI Sequencing and K-8 General Music

Both Silver Burdett and McGraw Hill, the two major music publishers of basal systems for K–8 music, offer MIDI curriculum materials. *Music with MIDI* is closely correlated to McGraw-Hill's *Share the Music* textbook series. Designed for grades K–8, *Music with MIDI* provides professional music technology in an easy-to-use instructional software package. Each grade's package includes 10 songs recorded as MIDI sequences by a professional arranger. *Music with MIDI* allows students and teachers to change elements of the music, isolate parts for study, and create new arrangements. The package includes detailed users' guides; lesson plans that include playalongs, creative activities, and improvisations; and full scores for each arrangement.

Silver Burdett also has a MIDI publication called *Making Music with MIDI* designed to be used with students in grades K–8. There is a separate book for each grade and it comes with ready-made MIDI files allowing you to accompany your students' singing in any key or tempo. The lesson plans can be used by students, individually or in small group. The student worksheet activities include exercises to manipulate music from the program and explore musical concepts in depth. Each book lists technology skills for grades K–8 and correlations with the National Music Standards and the National Education Technology Standards.

Procuring Sequencer Files: Make, Buy, Search

There are many ways to get the sequencer files you need for classroom and rehearsal. One way is to enter the parts one at a time yourself or ask a student to assist. You can play them in on a MIDI keyboard or click in the notation one note at a time. Slow the tempo down when entering on a MIDI keyboard to make it easier to play the correct pitches and rhythms. Remember, tempi can be adjusted after you enter the notes, and once you enter the information into the sequencer and save it to disk, it can be used again and again. I have created dozens of files for my classes in this manner.

It is also possible to purchase MIDI files. There are many sites on the Internet that sell MIDI files. Do a web search using the words, "where to buy MIDI files." Some of the sites that sell high quality MIDI versions of songs include www.midihits.com and www.comtracks.com. The latter bills itself as the largest legal MIDI site on the Internet. There are many others. Buying MIDI files is certainly faster than entering the parts.

The sites mentioned in Chapter 7 (notation), can also be used to download files to play in a MIDI sequencer. The more popular and copyright free pages include www.classicalarchives.com and www.midiworld.com.

Many publishers offer music in standard MIDI format. This means that pre-recorded sequences may be purchased. This saves time and provides teachers and students with a wide range of materials to use for recording, practice, and classroom demonstration. I recently purchased a disk of standard MIDI files to use in a Baroque music unit called Bach MIDI Piano Library published by Music Sales Corporation and available from most music publishers. The package contains a computer disk with 12 complete arrangements of songs: Minuet in G, Musette in D, Prelude in G Minor, and nine others. There also is a booklet containing the notation for each piece. The cost of the disk and booklet is $12.95. The files on the disk are in Standard MIDI file format. Standard MIDI files can be used with software sequencers and hardware sequencers with compatible disk drives.

All types of music are available in Standard MIDI file format: pop, classical, church music, and much more. These files can be purchased through most music dealers and sheet music distributors. Contact your favorite music technology reseller or music store. I did a search at JWPepper.com and entered the words "MIDI disk." The search returned 48 titles of publications that include MIDI files on disk.

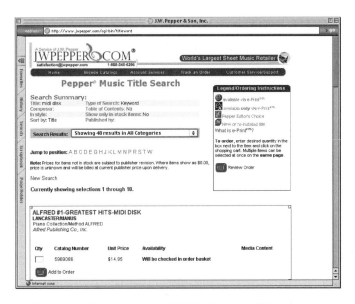

Figure 8.15: Search for "MIDI disk" at JWPepper.com

The Internet can be used to search for MIDI files as mentioned in Chapter 7. It is possible to download files from other computers and music educators around the world. An excellent starting place for MIDI files is the site Standard MIDI Files on the Net (www.manythings.org/midi/). Follow the steps listed in Chapter 7 to download and import MIDI files into your sequencer.

Converting from Notation to a Sequence

Another way to create sequences is by converting notation files to sequencer files. Most notation programs (see Chapter 7) can save music in Standard MIDI file format.

Teaching Strategy 105

After creating a marching band arrangement in notation software, save it as a Standard MIDI file and then open it in a MIDI sequencer. Once imported into the sequencer, make the file sound more like a performance file by entering dynamic changes, ritards, and other sound-related effects.

Scanning

It is also possible to scan music and convert it to MIDI format. This can be done with the software listed in Chapter 7. Once a page of music is scanned and converted to MIDI, it can be opened by a MIDI sequencer.

The Drum Connection

If you are working with popular music, and will need drum parts, there are several ways to get them. The most obvious way is to enter the drum parts using the MIDI keyboard. In order to do this, your MIDI keyboard or sound module must have percussion sounds.

Another option is to purchase Standard MIDI files of drum patterns. Several companies publish MIDI drum tracks. One of the largest is DrumTrax (www.drumtrax.com/). Their patterns were entered by live drummers and they sound much better than patterns clicked in with the mouse or played by non-percussionists. You can use these files to build excellent sounding drum grooves and tracks.

Drum parts can also be transferred from programs that generate drum parts like Band-in-a-Box and Jammer. These programs are explored in detail in Chapter 10.

Converting MIDI Files to Burn to a CD

Once you have created files using your sequencer at some point you will want to convert them to a WAV (Windows format) or AIFF (Macintosh format) file to burn on a CD. To do this, go to your MIDI sequencer manual and check the index. Many programs have this capability built-in. For example, Cakewalk Home Studio (see Figure 8.9) can convert MIDI tracks to WAV for burning to a CD.

If this is not an option with your program, you will need to convert the file using another program. I use QuickTime Pro from Apple to convert MIDI files to WAV on both Macintosh and Windows computers.

Converting WAV Files to MP3

For Macintosh users, iTunes can be used to convert MIDI files to audio format (AIFF on the Mac) and to MP3. See tutorial 4 on the companion CD-ROM for the steps and procedures.

Windows users can consult an excellent article on the Classical MIDI Archives site entitled "MIDI to MP3—How to Produce MP3 Files From MIDI's" by Arthur Sulit.

Check it out at http://www.classicalarchives.com/ faq_mp3.html

Internet Resources for Sequencing

Many web sites offer articles and support on the topic of MIDI sequencing. There are articles on every aspect, lessons posted by other music specialists, and resources for teachers and students. Some of my favorites are:

Articles on keyboards,
    sequencing, and other topics . . . . .www.iaekm.org
Articles on all topics of technology, several
    excellent MIDI sequencing articles . . . . .www.lentine.com
Lesson plans written by
    music educators . . . . .www.ti-me.org/members/lessonplans.html
Sequencing lessons on
    Cakewalk products . . . .www.cakewalk.com/Support/Lessons/Lessons.asp
Sequencing lessons on Cubase and other Steinberg products
    .www.steinberg.net/education/en/education_service/index.phtml_ Online
courses on music technology
    and sequencing .www.berkleemusic.com/school/
MIDI sequencing tutorial . . . www.classicalarchives.com/tutorial/index.html
Articles and curriculum
    integration ideas . . . .www.soundtree.com (click on Teaching Resources)

Summary

The sequencer is a tool that has virtually limitless educational applications. It can be used as a teacher's demonstration tool, as a practice unit and for student composition. Students can learn to use a sequencer to create original arrangements and compositions. Sequences can be created from scratch or purchased in Standard MIDI file format. The sequencer is the ultimate "musical crayon" for both the teacher and student.

Review Questions

1. What is the definition of a sequencer? What does a piano roll, used on a player piano, have in common with a sequence?
2. A sequencer can be thought of as a multi-track MIDI recorder. List the advantages to recording on separate tracks.
3. Name three elements of music that can be controlled by a MIDI sequence.
4. The original synthesizer sequencer was in use during what decade? How many events could it control?
5. Define a melodic sequence not to be confused with a sequencer.
6. The main objective of a sequencer is to produce_____.
7. Define MIDI tracks and MIDI channels. What is the basic function of each?
8. What is the difference between recording in step time and recording in real time?
9. Define the term quantize.
10. How can quantization be used to edit tracks?
11. Describe an educational situation where an entry-level sequencer would be the appropriate choice. Name an educational situation where an advanced sequencer would be the appropriate choice
12. Focusing on either the elementary, secondary, or college level, list three ways that a sequencer could be used as a student's practice tool.
13. Describe an example of when the sequencer could be used by the teacher as an accompanist.
14. Give one example of how a teacher could use the sequencer as a compositional tool.
15. Give one or more examples of how students could use sequencers as a creative tool.
16. List two examples of MIDI publications designed to be used with students.

17. List three ways to procure MIDI files for use in the classroom and/or rehearsal.

CD-ROM Activities

- Project 8.1 Go to a site of one of the major manufacturers of MIDI sequencers and download a demo of the program. Do this with two sites and compare the features and ease of use of the program.
- Project 8.2 Download a MIDI file from the Internet and import it into a MIDI sequencer. After the file is imported, make alterations to the track to include: change the timbre of the tracks, alter the tempo, transpose it up or down, and mute/solo individual tracks.
- Project 8.3 Go to the Vermont MIDI site (www.vtmidi.org) and listen to examples of student compositions. Review the lessons that were developed for these exercises. Use a search engine to look for MIDI sequencing lesson plans for use in an educational setting on other web sites.
- Project 8.4 View the video excerpt from GIA video: The MIDI Sequencer in the Music Classroom. Indicate your reactions to these applications.
- Project 8.5 Design a MIDI sequencing composition lesson for students. Create a finished example of a composition for student reference.

CD-ROM Lesson Plans

1. SoundTree General Music Curriculum lesson sample: lesson number 1.
2. TI:ME Lesson by Pete Pauliks.
3. Komposing Kids by Mike Moniz

Reference

Allen, Cory (2000). *Arranging in the digital world.* Berklee Press, Boston, MA.

Boom, Michael (1987). *Music through MIDI.* Microsoft Press, Redmond, WA.

Deutsch, Herbert A. (1985) *Synthesis An Introduction to the History, Theory & Practice of Electronic Music.* Alfred Publishing, Sherman Oaks, CA.

Emmons, S. et al (2002). *Making Music with MIDI.* Scott Foresman, Glenview, IL.

Faulconer, James (1998). *Music with MIDI.* McGraw-Hill School Division. Farmington, NY.

Freeman, Peter (1994). All for One. *Electronic Musician,* April, 1994. pp. 30-52.

Hickey, M, editor (2003). *Why and How To Teach Music Composition: A New Horizon for Music Education.* MENC The National Association for Music Education. Reston, VA.

Keyboard Magazine, Editors. (2001). *MIDI Sequencing for Musicians.* Hal Leonard, Milwaukee.

Muro, Don (1998) *Sequencing Basics (The Ultimate Beginner Tech Start Series).* Warner Brothers Publications.

Muro, Don (1993). *The Art of Sequencing.* CPP/Belwin, Inc., Miami.

Murphy, Barbara, Editor. (2002) *Technology Directory.* Association for Technology in Music Instruction. http://www.music.org/atmi/Directory/Directory2002.html

Rudolph, Thomas E. (1995) *The General Music Curriculum.* Korg USA, Westbury, N.Y.

Rudolph, Thomas E. (1997) *25 Ways to Use the Sequencer in the Music Classroom.* Lentine's Music www.lentine.com/articles/25%5Fways.htm

Rudolph, T & Peters, K. (1997) Video: *The MIDI Sequencer in the Music Classroom.* GIA Publications, Chicago.

Rudolph, Thomas (1986) Composing and Printing Music by Computer. *Pennsylvania Music Education News.*

Rudolph, Thomas & Leonard, Vincent (2001) *Recording in the Digital World.* Berklee Press, Boston.

Rudolph, Thomas, et al (1997) *Technology Strategies for Music Education.* Hal Leonard Corporation, Milwaukee.

Reese, S. (1995) . MIDI-assisted composing in your classroom. *Music Educators Journal, 81* (4), 37-40.

Reese, S. (2001). Tools for thinking in sound. *Music Educators Journal,* 88 (1), 42-46, 53.

Resse S., McCord, K, & Walls K. (2001) *Strategies for Teaching Technology.* MENC The National Association for Music Education, Reston, VA.

Taylor, Robert, P. Editor. (1980) *The Computer in the School: Tutor, Tool, Tutee.* Teachers College Press, NY.

Williams, D. B. & Webster, P. (1999) *Experiencing Music Technology : Software, Data, and Hardware, Second Edition.* Schirmer Books, NY.

Wilson, D. (2001) Coaching student composers. *Music Educators Journal,* 88 (1), 42-46, 53.

Chapter 9

Digital
Audio

Music Education National Standards: 1, 4, 6, 7, 8
NETS (National Education Technology Standards): 1, 2, 3, 4, 6

The biggest advances in music technology over the last eight years have been in digital audio recording. In the 1996 first edition of this book, digital audio was only mentioned briefly. The reason? In the mid-1990s the cost of digital audio software and hardware was in the thousands of dollars. This put it out of the reach of most schools and educational institutions. However, today the cost has come down dramatically—making this medium and its many applications available to students and teachers at all levels.

The purpose of this chapter is to introduce various options and applications of digital recording and to highlight some of the many ways it can be used in the music curriculum. In this chapter I will explain and explore CD recording, stereo editing software, and multi-track recording. The chapter is arranged from the least to the most complex recording options. Some of the specific applications explained include recording group and individual student practice sessions and rehearsals, recording live concerts, teaching students how to record and manipulate digital audio, developing a recording studio in the school, and students using digital audio as a creative tool for composition to name just a few.

Working Through the Maze of Options

The most difficult part of using digital audio is working through the maze of applications in the digital world to ascertain which ones are best for you and your students. There are dozens and dozens of products and more are introduced seemingly every day.

This chapter will provide you with an overview and hopefully a basis for making decisions regarding the equipment and software that best suits you and your students' needs. This chapter is not intended as a comprehensive guide to digital audio. Review the list of books and materials at the end of the chapter for additional study and reference.

The Big Picture

I find the best way to get a handle on this topic is to put the applications into two distinct categories. First are devices that record digital audio directly onto a disk or magnetic tape. These include CD, mini disc, and DAT (digital audio tape) recorders.

The other category consists of those devices that use a computer hard disk to store digital information, conveniently named hard disk recorders. Computer hard disk recorders are either stand-alone boxes or a combination of software and hardware for Macintosh or Windows computers. All digital recording devices do one of two things: record in stereo or multi-track.

Stereo or Two-track Recording

The easiest equipment to learn and use is designed to record in one pass to make a stereo, or two-track, recording. The options in this area include mini-disc, DAT, CD-R, and CD-RW recorders.

CD Recorders

CD recorders are ubiquitous in today's world. Units can be found on most Macintosh and Windows computers. They also can be purchased in stand-alone units. Because CD recorders are so common, I recommend them for recording in the school or home.

There are two types of CD recorders: CD-R and CD-RW. CD-R, or CD recordable, means the machine can record data and audio on a CD that can then be played in any CD player (audio or computer). A CD-R disc can only be recorded one time. It holds 650–700 megabytes of storage, which is roughly an hour of digital audio. CD-RW stands for compact disc rewritable. Like a cassette tape, CD-RW can be erased and re-recorded multiple times.

Looking for a simple solution for recording CDs? Purchase a CD-R or CD-RW dedicated recorder. With this and a couple of microphones, you are ready to go. Microphone selection will be covered later in this chapter.

Teaching Strategy 107

Use a CD recorder to create CDs of performances and rehearsals, and for individual student assessment.

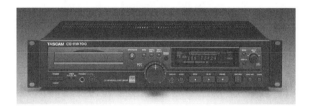

Figure 9.1: Tascam CD-RW 700 recorder

CD recorders include the Tascam CD-RW 700 and the Yamaha CDR-HD1000 CD that start around $500 for the unit. Insert a blank CD-R or CD-RW, plug one or two microphones into the back of the unit, press record, and you're off! It is not much more technical than recording a stereo cassette tape, but you have the added advantage of getting a CD with a superior sound quality as the final product.

The downside of stand-alone CD recorders is they can do very little besides making a direct recording of the signal. If you want to add effects such as reverb and EQ, you will have to take the CD and import the file onto a Macintosh or Windows computer and use stereo two-track software such as Sound Forge for Windows or Peak for Macintosh. More on this software application follows later in this chapter.

CD Recorders with More Bells and Whistles

Several companies including Superscore and Marantz produce advanced CD recorders that may be of interest to music educators. These units cost more (around $1,000) but they include many additional features designed for use in the practice and rehearsal room. They also have CD recording capabilities. One of these all-in-one machines might be all you need for your digital recording options.

Figure 9.2: Superscope PD300 from www.superscopetechnologies.com

The Superscope PD300 serves a wealth of educational applications, and the real value is that all of the features are built into one unit. The Superscope has two CD drives and can duplicate CDs. It has inputs for microphones or instruments on the front panel and boasts a built-in microphone and speaker. Plug in two microphones, insert a blank CD-R, and record practices, recitals, and concerts. Each time you press the stop button, a new track is created.

Teaching Strategy 108

Use the Superscope or Marantz all-in-one CD recorder, duplicator, and practice unit to record CDs for practice and transcription.

Features Unique to the Superscope

The Superscope unit has many neat features in addition to stereo recording capabilities. It is possible to control a CD's pitch and speed independently of one another. Perhaps you would like to play a commercial CD, but slow it down for practice. No problem! You can also adjust the key by half steps; all with the touch of a button.

If you would like to transcribe something from a CD recording, the PD300 has a special conversion halfspeed mode that copies tracks you select at double speed. When you play them back at normal speed, they sound half as fast and down an octave. This can make transcribing from a recording much easier.

Another helpful feature is the capability of removing vocals from a CD. This makes it possible to create practice tracks for vocalists. The technical term for this is center cancel. What actually happens is the signal in the center of the stereo mix, which is usually the lead vocals, is cancelled. Center cancel does not work with every commercial recording.

Want to create a recording of someone performing along with a CD? This is also possible with the Superscope. Put a commercial disk in the upper drive and then a blank, recordable disc in the other drive. Plug in a microphone or use the built-in mic to record an instrument or voice performing along with the CD.

Phantom power is required for some types of high-end microphones (see the microphone section later in this chapter). Currently, the Superscope ships without phantom power. Educational institutions can add it for an additional $99.

Stereo Two-Track Editing Software

So, you have recorded some tracks using one of the CD recorders mentioned above and you want to make some edits. For example, you would like to eliminate the talking in between numbers or you want to fade out the endings. Or, perhaps you did several takes of a particular piece and you want to combine the first section from take one and the second section from take two.

The best way to accomplish these goals is with a stereo or two-track editor. They are available in both Windows and Macintosh computers.

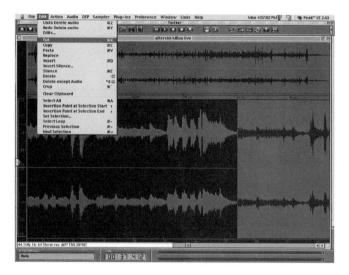

Figure 9.3: Cutting a portion of a track using Peak LE Waveform editor

Stereo editing software works as follows. First, purchase the stereo editor software. The most popular program for Windows is Sound Forge Studio, a light version of the high-end Sound Forge for Windows (www.mediasoftware.sonypictures.com). For Macintosh, I recommend Peak LE (www.bias-inc.com), which is a light version of the professional offering, Peak. Both Sound Forge Studio and Peak LE cost less than $100 per copy. The full versions are designed for high-end applications and come with lots of bells and whistles. They are also more expensive, around $250. The light versions pack enough power for most academic applications.

Teaching Strategy 109

Use stereo waveform editing software to cut and paste, fade-in, fade-out, and add sonic effects to CD tracks.

After purchasing, install Sound Forge Studio or Peak LE, open or import tracks previously recorded by your CD recorder. Once imported, the files can be edited using features such as cut, paste, fade-in, fade-out, and other tools.

Digital information can also be processed using DSP (digital signal processing). Things like EQ (equalization) can be added. Adjusting the EQ is similar to adjusting the bass and treble knobs on your home stereo. It is also possible to add sonic processing, called plugins, and include delay, echo, and reverb. It does take some time to master, but the manuals are clear and tutorials cover the basics. If you get stuck, ask one of your students to lend a hand. Frequently students as young as third and fourth grade have experience editing digital audio using similar software.

Teaching Strategy 110
Create custom listening lessons by editing tracks from commercial CDs using stereo editing software.

I often find that a stereo editor such as Sound Forge (Windows) and Peak (Macintosh) is a wonderful tool to create custom CDs for listening examples. Perhaps you have purchased several CDs with music examples you want to play for your class or ensemble. You can use editing software to import the tracks, edit them, and then burn a custom CD for your use. I have used this method to create a series of examples of jazz licks played by a variety of performers. It is also helpful to extract parts of songs to demonstrate music form such as ABA. Once the files are imported and edited they can be saved in a variety of formats. See Chapter 11 for more specific information on file formats.

Recording and Archiving Old Recordings: Cassette and Vinyl Records

Both CD recorders and stereo editors can be used to import your old cassettes and vinyl records. Simply plug the output of the turntable or cassette deck into the inputs of the CD recorder, or, if you are using a computer, to the microphone input. Press record on the device and play on the turntable or cassette.

Hard Disk Multi-Track Recording

The combination of CD recording and stereo editors is sufficient for most live recording and editing applications. The next level is to consider one of the options for recording digital audio with more than two-tracks, referred to as multi-track recording. Multi-track refers to software or hardware units that are capable of recording more than two tracks of information. In other words, it is possible to record part of the final piece such as the piano and bass and then go back and record other instruments on separate tracks. After all the parts are recorded on separate tracks, they are mixed together as part of the final mixing process.

Today, the majority of multi-track recording is accomplished using a computer hard disk, hence the term hard disk recording. In its simplest form, the process can be thought of as follows: A microphone picks up sound vibrations, the information is converted into digital data, and then stored on a hard disk. After the audio information is digitized and stored on a hard disk, software is used to edit and manipulate the data. The final step is to then copy, or bounce, this information onto a medium that can be shared with others. Currently, that medium is the CD and DVD.

There are many advantages to using a computer to store the digital audio information. Because the audio signal is converted to a list of numbers, it can be edited, changed, and manipulated. Older technologies such as magnetic tape and vinyl records cannot be easily edited once the information has been recorded.

The advantage of multi-track recording is that you can separate the finished performance into parts and re-record solos. You have control over these independent tracks with regard to volume (mixing), sonic placement left and right—referred to as pan or panning—and much more. The disadvantage is that the mixing process takes time. You can end up spending a lot of time recording and mixing, especially when compared with hanging a couple of microphones to make a stereo recording.

Stand-Alone and Computer-Based Hard Disk Recording

There are two distinct ways to accomplish hard disk recording: using software that runs on a Macintosh or Windows computer or by using stand-alone hard disk recording devices. There are advantages and disadvantages to each. If you are new to digital audio recording, review the options below and make the choice that is best for you.

Stand-Alone Hard Disk Recorders

So, you want to record a performance in mono or stereo, and you would like to add more tracks at a later time. You want a simple, cheap way to record multiple tracks. Multi-track recording is useful when you have a soloist on a number and you would like to record the ensemble and then add the soloist later. It also helps when you are recording a live jazz band and you want to have a group of mics that can be controlled independently. You place one mic on the trumpets, another over the trombones and two for the saxes. You do this so you can control the volume of each of these sections in the final mixdown. Doing this requires a multi-track recording device.

> ### Teaching Strategy 111
> Use a stand-alone multi-track digital audio recorder to make CDs of student performances and practice sessions.

Multi-track recorders come in two categories: computer-based and stand-alone. The stand-alone units have everything in one neat package. Microphones plug directly into the unit. Tracks are recorded independently and the final version can be burned to a CD. Most units have a built-in CD burner and software, so there is no need for a computer or any additional equipment besides microphones. Stand-alone recorders are quite portable and stable. By stable, I mean they rarely will crash and are quite reliable when moved from one location to another.

Figure 9.4: Roland VS-1824CD

241

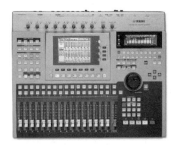

Figure 9.5: Korg D1600   **Figure 9.6:** Yamaha AW4416

Teaching Strategy 112

Use a stand-alone multi-track digital audio recorder to make practice CDs for students.

There definitely is a learning curve for these devices. You will not be able to open the box and start recording in seconds, as is possible with the CD recorders mentioned above. When I purchased my unit, it came with a training DVD. I played it in my DVD movie player to learn basic operation of the unit.

Which model to buy? Korg, Roland, Yamaha, and others make multi-track recorders. They run the gamut from under a thousand to several thousand dollars. Of course, the more you pay, the more features you get. The price points can usually be grouped by the number of inputs or microphones and instruments you can plug in at any one time. Expect to pay more for more inputs.

Back to Stereo Editing (Sound Forge and Peak)

The one downside of self-contained multi-track recording units is that editing on their small screens can be difficult. Some of the more expensive models ($2000+) have an output for a computer monitor, but the ones most likely to fit in school budgets have very small screens for editing.

I recommend that if you go with a stand-alone multi-track unit you also purchase a digital audio editor such as Sound Forge Studio (Windows) or Peak LE (Macintosh). After you record and burn the final CD on the unit,

242

you can the open your digital editing software on your computer and import the tracks. It takes seconds to delete unwanted talking and noise at the beginning or end of the performance and to save the file in a variety of formats for a variety of applications.

Computer-Based Multi-Track Digital Audio

The other option is to record multi-track digital audio using software that runs on a computer. The main advantage of using a computer to record digital audio is that there are many more options and the systems can be expanded. Also, if you own a fairly new computer, it is cheaper to purchase low-end digital audio software than to buy a stand-alone unit.

The disadvantage of using a computer is that setting-up and configuring the system can be complex and confusing. It can take longer to learn a computer system than modular and portable digital recording equipment. You also have the added problems of system conflicts and computer instability such as crashing. I recommend that you use the computer as the central part of the studio if you are fairly comfortable using software and have a newer (within the last 1-2 years) model computer.

Remember, if you are going to use the computer to record digital audio you will need a powerful computer and you will need to transport the computer to the recording area. Purchase the newest, fastest computer you can afford for digital audio.

Selecting Digital Audio Software

Of course, as you might imagine, there is a variety of recording software from which to choose. The different types include the stereo software mentioned earlier in this chapter, multi-track software for recording multiple tracks of audio, MIDI/digital audio software for recording MIDI and audio, and digital audio software with limited MIDI support.

Digital audio can be recorded using almost all of the MIDI sequencer programs on the market today (see Chapter 8). If you are comfortable using MIDI sequencing software, such as Digital Performer for the Macintosh or Sonar for Windows, then consider using this software to record digital audio. These programs can record multiple tracks of digital audio.

243

If you are going to do a lot of sequencing and also digital audio, then go with a program that excels in MIDI such as Digital Performer, Login, Cubase, or Sonar. If you are primarily going to work with digital audio and plan to do some or no MIDI, then consider one of the programs that excel in digital audio such as the ProTools family or Steinberg's Nuendo.

The following chart is designed to give you an idea of the types and titles of software in the various categories. Software versions and titles change frequently, so consult with one of the music education and technology vendors in Appendix A to find the latest versions.

Publisher	Title	Web Address	Platform
Stereo (2-track) Editing Software			
Bias, Inc.	Peak	www.bias-inc.com/	Mac
	Peak LE	www.bias-inc.com/	Mac
Sonic Foundry	Sound Forge	www.sonicfoundry.com/index.html	Win
	Sound Forge Studio	www.sonicfoundry.com/index.html	Win
Free Software	Audicity	http://audacity.sourceforge.net/	Mac/Win
Multi-Track Digital Audio Software			
Bias, Inc.	Deck	www.bias-inc.com	Mac
Syntrillium	Adobe Audition	www.adobe.com	Win
MOTU	AudioDesk	www.motu.com	Mac
Multi-Track Digital Audio and MIDI			
Digidesign	ProTools FREE	www.digidesign.com/	Mac/Win
	Pro Tools Mbox	www.digidesign.com/	Mac/Win
	Pro Tools Digi001	www.digidesign.com/	Mac/Win
	Pro Tools Digi002	www.digidesign.com/	Mac/Win
Emagic	Logic Education	www.emagic.com/	Mac/Win
	Logic Gold	www.emagic.com/	Mac
	Logic Platinum	www.emagic.com/	Mac
Steinberg	Cubase SL	www.steinbergaudio.com/	Mac/Win
	Cubase SX	www.steinbergaudio.com/	
	Nuendo	www.steinbergaudio.com/	Mac/Win
MOTU	Digital Performer	http://www.motu.com/	Mac
Cakewalk	Home Studio	www.cakewalk.com	Win
	Home Studio XL	www.cakewalk.com	Win
	Sonar	www.cakewalk.com	Win
	Sonal XL	www.cakewalk.com	Win

Figure 9.7: Digital Audio Software Chart

If you choose your computer as your multi-track digital recorder, I strongly suggest you purchase a program that supports multiple tracks—see the multi-track digital audio options above.

You will want to have digital editing software for the final mixdown of your projects, so also consider purchasing Sound Forge Studio (Windows) or Peak LE (Macintosh).

Which Software to Choose?

With so many options, where to begin? If you already own one of the programs listed above, and you are familiar with it, you might consider using that for your digital audio recordings. If you are interested in digital audio recording and have no previous software experience, then go with a program that has lots of flexibility and support. When a program was chosen for my school district, we decided to go with the ProTools family. The reasons included a free version of the software that could be loaded on all computers, a family of options from $400 to $10,000, and it is one of the most popular programs in the digital world with lots of books, videos, and support.

ProTools has MIDI sequencing built-in, but that is not the focus of the program. Digital audio is the main focus in terms of features, editing, and so forth. Another excellent test for a program is to do a book search for it. I suggest going to www.amazon.com and entering the title of the software and see how many books come up. The more there are, the more support you and your students will have in learning the software.

Getting Audio into Your Computer (the I/O options)

If you are going to give it a go with your computer, there is one other major area to tackle: how to get the audio signals into your computer. Most Macintosh and Windows computers have some audio input capability in the form of a microphone input directly into the computer. But the standard Windows Sound Card and the built-in microphone inputs of the Macintosh are only acceptable for speech and reference recordings of digital audio. When you record directly into the computer without adding any additional hardware, the sound quality is poor. You will hear distortion similar to and sometimes worse than cassette tape analog recordings.

Built-in I/O (Input/Output)

The advantage of using the built-in hardware is cost. It is the least expensive—you don't need any hardware! For example, if you are going to work in a MIDI lab with students doing digital audio, then you might want to use the built-in hardware to save money. The teacher station in the room, or several student stations, might be equipped with better I/O equipment.

The disadvantage is the sound quality. It is not the quality of sound you would consider for CD projects. I only recommend using the built-in mic for student use in a lab or for reference recordings.

Low Cost Windows I/O Upgrade

Say your budget is tight and you have less than $100 to spend on a digital audio I/O upgrade. For Windows, purchasing and installing a sound card upgrade is the best option. Sound Blaster, M-Audio, and Turtle Beach make high quality soundcards for Windows computers. Purchasing even a low-end card will give much improved audio. They are also a great choice if you (or your students) are into playing video games. The microphone will plug into the mic input on the back of the sound card.

Figure 9.8: M-Audio Revolution sound card (www.m-audio.com)

Low-Cost Macintosh I/O Upgrade

For Macintosh, the under $100 option is to purchase a device that connects to the computer via USB. One such product is iMic from Griffin Technology. This option allows you to plug in a microphone or line input. The device connects to the USB port on the computer. The sound quality is much better than the built-in mic, and some Macintosh iBooks (laptops) do not have a mic input at all. For under $50, the iMic is an inexpensive way to improve the quality of sound input for recording. Be sure to check that the software you are using will work with the iMic. I have experienced times when software did not recognize USB devices.

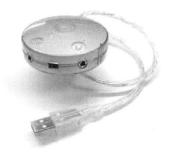

Figure 9.9: iMic from Griffin Technology (www.griffintechnology.com)

Recommended I/O for Digital Audio

If you want the best possible sound quality, I recommend spending more money on the I/O device. You can spend anywhere from $400 to several thousand dollars for a higher quality I/O device that connects to your computer. The more you spend, the more inputs for microphones and other instruments that will be available to you.

Many digital audio software companies also produce digital I/O devices. These companies include Digidesign (ProTools), Emagic (Logic), and Mark of the Unicorn (Digital Performer). There are also companies who make audio I/O interfaces that work with almost any software. For example, M-Audio produces a variety of audio I/O products that can be used with programs made by many companies such as Cakewalk and Cubase. First select your software and then select a compatible audio I/O that suits your needs.

The Family Approach

When I am thinking about curriculum integration and technology, I like to lean towards a product line that has a family of offerings from low-to high-end. This enables a school to use simpler, less-expensive products at lower grade levels and more sophisticated, expensive products later in the academic sequence. Many companies offer this family approach including Cakewalk, ProTools, Emagic, and Cubase. Refer to the above chart for specific titles.

> **Teaching Strategy 113**
> Purchase digital audio software from a publisher offering a family or range of options from low-end to high-end.

For example, ProTools offers a range of products from $400 to several thousand dollars. The $400 option is called Mbox and is a small device that plugs into the USB port on the Macintosh or Windows computer. It is limited to two mic inputs, so only two tracks of audio can be recorded simultaneously. Because ProTools is multi-track software, additional audio tracks can be added. It also can record separate tracks of MIDI.

Figure 9.10: ProTools Mbox ($500 range)

Control Surfaces

A control surface is a physical piece of hardware that includes real sliders and knobs that you can manipulate with your hands. Mackie, Emagic, ProTools, and M-Audio are examples of companies offering the option of control surfaces as part of the I/O device. For example, the ProTools Digi001 is larger than Mbox and permits up to four microphones or inputs. Digit002 is an even larger interface and allows up to eight microphones or inputs.

Figure 9.11: ProTools Digi002 ($2,500 range)

The top of the line ProTools choice is the TDM option where a card is plugged into the computer's expansion slot. It also comes with a control surface that has more knobs and sliders on it. The TDM costs several thousand dollars.

Figure 9.12: ProTools HD systems ($10,000 range)

Other companies including M-Audio and MOTU offer hardware for digital audio recording.

Select the Software First

It is best to select the digital audio software you want to use and then select an I/O option. Check the software company's web site to see the options your software supports. Some have their own I/O devices and some also support other, third party devices.

The more powerful the software, the longer it will take to learn. Digital audio is complicated, so any digital audio program will take some time to master. If you select high end software, it will be very complex. Keep this in mind when choosing the best product for your needs.

Portable Digital Audio Devices

There may be times when you will want a hand-held digital audio recorder to record concerts or for a playback device. There are several options. I recommend these devices only if you don't have the funds to purchase a CD recorder or a computer recording device as listed above.

MiniDisc

MiniDisc is a medium designed by Sony as a portable replacement for music CDs (compact discs). These recorders use a disc format that is smaller than a CD. However, MiniDiscs cannot be played in most CD players. The advantage of a MiniDisc player/recorder is its small size and portability. I recommend MiniDisc if portability is the main concern. One can be purchased in the $100–$200 range, making them affordable for schools, teachers, and students.

> **Teaching Strategy 114**
> Use a MiniDisc portable recorder to record and playback music for classroom activities and rehearsals.

Ken Peters uses a MiniDisc recorder as a portable way to play music for students. He uses it in class and rehearsals/performances so he doesn't need to carry equipment from his classroom to the auditorium. Because a MiniDisc can record from any audio source, it can make copies of CDs and other recordings.

The downside of MiniDisc is that the quality of the sound is not as good as compact discs. It is better than cassette tape and very similar to FM radio music broadcasts. The reason is the sampling rate of the unit. Sampling rate refers to how often the audio signal is sampled per second. The more samples, the higher the accuracy and hence quality of the sound. Compact discs use a 44,000 sampling rate. MiniDisc uses 22,000 sampling rate—so the quality is not quite as good.

MiniDisc players are a good replacement for a portable cassette tape recorder, and for transferring music to a medium that is very transportable.

DAT (Digital Audio Tape)

DAT is an acronym for "digital audio tape." It uses a type of magnetic tape that looks like a smaller version of traditional cassette tape. Because DAT is a tape that is recorded, information cannot be searched as easily as CDs, mini discs, and DVDs; so it takes a while to locate certain tracks.

DAT recorders are quite expensive ($900 and up) and DAT tapes cost much more than CD-R and CD-RWs. I do not recommend DAT recorders for schools. Rather, I recommend using a CD recording device and, if portability is an issue, consider mini disc.

MP3 Players

Another popular device for storing digital files is an MP3 player. MP3 players cannot record live music, rather they store digital music to play back from an extremely portable device small enough to fit in a shirt pocket.

Many companies including Apple Computer, Rio, and Creative Labs make a variety of players from $50 to $500 dollars depending on features and storage capacity. Visit a local computer/technology store to get a demonstration of these devices or consult your students.

iTunes and MusicMatch JukeBox

Looking for a computer program to organize all of the CD tracks on your computer? There are indispensable programs designed to do this for you. For Apple and Windows users, iTunes is highly recommended. It is a free download from www.apple.com/itunes. For Windows users the most popular player is MusicMatch Jukebox available at www.musicmatch.com. It is $19.95 and worth every penny. Organize your CD tracks and files on your computer. Plug the output of your computer to a sound system and you have a versatile playback system for the music classroom or rehearsal room.

Microphone Primer

If you want to have high quality recordings, selection of microphones is of primary importance. There are entire books and courses dedicated to microphone technology and terminology. This section will serve as an overview of the basics to get you started and to help you make an informed choice about the best microphones for your set-up.

Two types of microphones, or mics, are recommended for school. These are dynamic and condenser mics.

Dynamic Microphones

Dynamic mics are designed to be used close to the instrument or voice. They work best when placed in close proximity to the sound source. When you place a mic close to the sound source it is referred to as close miking. Not too technical, yet! Dynamic mics are rugged and capable of handling loud sounds such as drums, brass, and vocals. They are not ideal for subtle nuances or for capturing sounds with a wide dynamic range.

The most popular dynamic mics are the classic Shure SM58 and SM57. The SM58 is best for vocals and the SM57 for instruments. Expect to pay around $100 a piece. You should have at least two dynamic microphones for your recording needs.

> **Teaching Strategy 115**
> Purchase two or more dynamic microphones for recording loud signals such as solo vocals, instruments, and drums. You can use these same mics with your sound system to amplify your soloist or instrument.

Figure 9.13: Shure SM58 dynamic microphone

These same mics can be used with a sound system to amplify the jazz band, chorus, or any ensemble. Purchasing mics that can meet several needs is a good thing.

Condenser Microphones

Condenser mics are an excellent choice for all around recording in the educational environment and in the recording studio. Sound reproduction is clear and detailed and they are perfect for a noiseless digital recording. They are not as rugged as dynamic microphones, so they must be handled with extreme care.

You should always purchase a pair of condenser mics. Ideally they should be placed together to capture an ensemble's entire performance. Experiment with placement to get the best overall sound of your band, orchestra, or chorus. For quality condenser mics, expect to pay in the $200 to $300 range per mic. Some popular brands include the AKG C1000S and the Shure KSM32.

Condenser microphones require a power source supplied by the mixer or recording device via the microphone cable called phantom power. Be sure that the computer I/O that you use has phantom power, otherwise the mic will not work.

Figure 9.14: Shure KSM32 condenser microphone

Stereo Condenser Microphones

Another excellent option is to purchase an all-in-one stereo condenser microphone. This looks like a single microphone but is actually a stereo pair built into the same mic body. There are two cables, one for the left side and one for the right. This is a good choice to put in the rehearsal room or for making recordings of ensembles. This one microphone may be all that you need. An example is the Audio Technica AT825.

Figure 9.15: Stereo condenser mic—Audio Technica AT825

Training and More Training

There are many books on microphone techniques; consult the reference section at the end of this chapter for some excellent ones. In addition, there are excellent materials on manufacturers' web sites. I have learned a lot from Shure's web site (www.shure.com). There is a link to education and many materials that can be downloaded and printed on microphone placement and related techniques. Check them out at:

http://164.109.27.207/booklets/techpubs.html.

Microphone Stands

Microphone stands are also an important part of your recording gear. Be sure to purchase a solid, well built stand, especially for expensive condenser mics. I recommend getting a sturdy stand with wheels that can be elevated high into the air to get the best overall recording. Atlas makes a good quality stand. My favorite is the Qwuick Lok A50 stand. It is not cheap, about $200. However, it will give you many options and will secure your investment in your microphones.

Mixers

Another piece of gear that you may want is a mixer. If you are going to record multi-track via computer software, you will have a built-in mixer as part of the software. However, a physical mixer should also be available to you. In the class or rehearsal room a mixer allows you to plug in several audio inputs and control the volume and EQ (equalization) of each input while recording. Mixers are also a good idea if you are going into a CD recorder or a recording device that has a limited number of inputs, such as two or four. The mixer can take 4–8 or more inputs including microphones.

In the classroom, a mixer can help you to route the outputs of a variety of sound producing devices such as CD players, video/DVD, microphones, electronic instruments, and any other device.

Many companies make excellent mixers. Yamaha and Mackie are two of the best, each with units costing under $200. They allow you to connect up to eight devices.

Figure 9.16: Yamaha MG-4 mixer

Student Applications of Digital Audio

Digital audio recording has come of age for music education. It can be a most productive tool in the hands of students. Digital audio recording and MIDI sequencing (Chapter 8) can be used as creative tools for composition. Many of the MIDI sequencing strategies listed in Chapter 8 can also be applied to digital audio. Brian Moore states:

> …Digital audio assumes that the user is more comfortable with recording studio metaphors than with musical metaphors.

255

Digital-audio software has the look and feel of an engineer's console where the sound is viewed as a waveform—what would be seen on the screen of an oscilloscope...digital audio technology is best used with an understanding of the science of sound.[1]

With the explosion of affordable digital audio software and hardware, students are exploring digital recording at home. They are excited by the prospect of producing their own digital audio projects and CDs. Digital audio software can be used to enhance many of the national standards for music. A few ways follow:

- Standard 8 – Understanding the relationships between music, the arts, and disciplines outside of the arts. The science of sound helps students make connections between science and music.
- Standard 7 – Evaluating music and music performances–students engage in recording, editing, and producing digital audio projects.
- Standard 4 – Composing and arranging music within specified guidelines

---

Teaching Strategy 116

Teach your students to run the digital audio equipment for rehearsals and concerts. Let them become your recording engineers.

After you have purchased a CD recording system, teach your students to use it. Consider rotating the students so everyone gets a chance to record rehearsals and performances. Use CD-RW discs so they can be reused from day to day. Ask your students who would like to be your recording engineers and find time before or after school to teach them the basics of setting up mics, setting recording levels, and making digital recordings of rehearsals and performances.

Teaching Strategy 117

Using digital audio software in a computer lab setting, offer digital audio electives to students.

As soon as software has been installed in the MIDI or computer lab, students can work with digital audio projects. Considering forming an after school club or elective in digital audio recording. You may be surprised how many students are interested in this area.

Teaching Strategy 118

Record student concerts with the students acting at engineer and producer. Sell the CDs to parents and turn a profit for your organization or school. (Be sure to get the proper copyright clearance—see Chapter 8)!

Work collaboratively with your students to record your winter and/or spring concerts. After the concert has been recorded, students can mix and master it. The final CD can then be sent to a CD duplicating company to make the necessary copies. Students can assist with the production of the graphics and CD label. Then sell the CD to parents and the community realizing a profit. The money generated from this activity can help purchase equipment, microphones, mixers, and the like. Need funds for the equipment? Hire a local recording engineer or a parent to record the concert. Sell the CDs and use the profits to purchase your own digital audio equipment for future use.

There are copyright considerations when selling CDs of copyrighted music. See Chapter 16 for an in-depth review of the necessary steps to take in this regard.

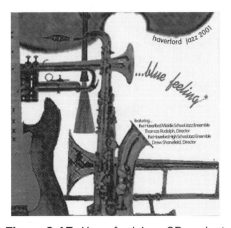

Figure 9.17: Haverford Jazz CD project

> **Teaching Strategy 119**
>
> Create a school recording studio club or elective. Create student-produced CD recordings.

Joe Cantaffa, a high school music teacher at Howell High School in New Jersey has taken digital recording to an extremely high level. He formed an after school club for students calling it 5*Star Records at the middle school and Next2Records at the high school. He created a fully functioning, student-operated record label. He states:

> All of the departments that belong in a recording company are staffed by students in this 'company.' Examples of such departments are A&R, accounting, promotion, marketing and advertising, production, publishing, legal, art, video, artist relations, travel, talent, human resources, media relations, and others. Each year the label can take on several projects from "signing," recording, and distributing a local "garage band," singer, or DJ, to producing recordings of school activities and performances for various purposes.[2]

Students are excited about digital audio recording and this excitement can be transferred to a variety of activities.

> **Teaching Strategy 120**
>
> Have students manipulate (edit) a digital audio file using a stereo editor. Students can cut and paste sections of the piece, create fade-ins, and process sonic effects such as reverb.

Give students the opportunity to work with stereo software by manipulating the wave forms. They can create new music by editing portions of the wave form. Teachers can supply recordings for students to manipulate.

Teaching Strategy 121

Students create a soundscape composition using environmental sounds.

Students can use digital audio software to record environmental sounds and create a soundscape composition. Dennis Mauricio and Steve Adams, in their text *FUNdamentals of Music Technology* suggest that students can create sounds from electronic and traditional instruments and environmental sounds. Using the digital audio software they can combine these into original soundscape compositions.

Teaching Strategy 122

Students create digital audio sound tracks to accompany a movie or film.

As mentioned in Chapter 8 using MIDI sequencing software, students can compose digital audio sound tracks to accompany movies. Most digital audio software allows the importing of digital movies. Students can then compose the music tracks using digital audio software and sync it to the movie.

Teaching Strategy 123

Have your students listen to and evaluate a multi-track recording of a performance. Have them manipulate the digital audio file making changes to the balance, sonic effects, equalization, panning, and so forth.

In the book *Strategies for Teaching Technology*, published by MENC, there is a lesson plan that begins by making a recording of a rehearsal or performance. Students listen to and analyze the recording. They then edit the file by adjusting the balance, blend, and sonic effects.[3]

> **Teaching Strategy 124**
>
> Students import audio files and loops of sounds from the Internet. They use these sounds to create an original composition.

Many audio files available can be purchased or downloaded free from the Internet (see Chapter 10 for a discussion of loop-based software). Students can download audio loops and manipulate them to create original compositions.

> **Teaching Strategy 125**
>
> Students convert digital audio files to MP3 and import them into a report or presentation using presentation software such as PowerPoint.

Once students are comfortable working with digital audio, they can convert the file formats to incorporate them into web sites and multimedia software (more on this in Chapter 11).

Education, Training and Support

Digital audio is a vast topic and cannot be learned without study. Consider purchasing books and methods designed to help teachers and students master the science of sound.

> **Teaching Strategy 126**
>
> Consider using method books and free online courses to teach students the science of sound.

Some excellent books are *FUNdamentals of Music Technology* by Mauricio and Adams and *The Audio Pro Home Recording Course* by Bill Gibson. These books are designed to be used with students.

In addition, I co-authored a book entitled *Recording in the Digital World* that gives extensive descriptions of digital recording. There are other excellent books, some of which are mentioned at the end of this chapter.

Many organizations offer digital audio courses. Check out the summer offerings for music teachers by TI:ME (the Technology Institute for Music Educators) www.ti-me.org. Online courses are also offered; look for Berklee School of Music choices at www.berkleemusic.com.

For support and when purchasing equipment, I recommend using one of the companies listed in Appendix A. Support is very important, especially if you are new to the field of digital audio.

Summary

Digital audio has arrived. Low-cost products including software and hardware put the world of digital audio recording and editing in the hands of teachers and students. It is possible to create high-quality digital recordings using hardware and software applications. Software ranging from under $100 to many thousands of dollars can be purchased. Students can learn the science of sound and get involved in digital audio activities. The possibilities are endless.

Review Questions

1. Define stereo or two-track recording.
2. What is the difference between CD-R and CD-RW?
3. What are the drawbacks of CD recorders?
4. List two or more educational applications using the Superscope PD300.
5. What is the difference between stereo and multitrack recording?
6. What is a stand-alone hard disk recorder? Name a company that makes these devices.
7. What questions should be answered when selecting a digital audio software program?
8. Why is it advantageous to use digital audio software that belongs to a family of software products from entry-level to high end?
9. What is digital I/O?
10. What are the low-cost I/O options for Macintosh and Windows?
11. What I/O options are there for professional or high-end digital audio recording?

12. What is a control surface and why is it helpful?
13. What is MiniDisc and how can it be used in education?
14. Define a dynamic microphone. List one appropriate application of a dynamic mic.
15. What is a condenser mic? List one appropriate application using a condenser mic.
16. What is the function of a mixer?
17. List one or more of the national standards that can be addressed when students are taught to use digital audio software and explain how the students would implement the activity.
18. List two or more sources for training and support in the field of digital audio.

CD-ROM Activities

- Project 9.1 Explore the Chapter 9 web links. Review the sites you visit.
- Project 9.2 Using a freeware, shareware, or published software program such as iTunes or MusicMatch, create a custom play list of songs for use in the music classroom using several audio CDs.
- Project 9.3 Use the Excel spreadsheet to create a budget for digital audio.
- Project 9.4 Find, download, or create a MIDI file and convert it to an audio format such as AIFF (Mac) or WAV (Windows). After converting the file to audio format, burn an audio CD.
- Project 9.5 Using digital audio wave editing software such as Peak LE (Mac) or SoundForge (Win), import an audio track from a CD. Use editing software to create a custom sound clip with fade-ins and/or fade-outs.

CD-ROM Lesson Plans

Lesson Plan 9.1: Using a digital audio editing program or stand-alone hard disk recorder, record your voice counting from 1 to 10. Use cut and paste to convert the original file into a countdown from 10 to 1.

Lesson Plan 9.2: Digital Audio Mad Libs.

CD-ROM Digital Audio Resource Materials

- Shure Educator Guide for microphone placement
- Microphone Recommendations for Education PowerPoint Presentation
- Digital Audio Budget Planner (referenced in project 9.3)

Reference:

Chambers, Mark. *CD and DVD recording for dummies*. Hungry Minds, Inc., New York.

Gibson, Bill. (1996). *The audio pro home recording course*. MIX Books, Vallegio, CA.

Gibson, Bill (1966). AudioPro Recording Courses (free – online). www.artistpro.com/CourseList.cfm. ArtistPro, Vallejo, CA.

Keating, C. and Anderton, C, Editors. (1998). *Digital home recording–Tips, techniques, and tools for home studio production*. Backbeat Books, San Francisco.

Mauricio, D. & Adams, S. (1992). *FUNdamentals of music technology*. Consultant Help Software, Agoura, CA.

Mauricio, D. (2003) *Music Mentor Volume2: An easy approach to recording in the classroom*. RolandUS.

Milstead, Bill. (2001) *Home recording power!* Muska & Lipman Publishing, Boston.

Reese S., McCord, K, & Walls K. (2001) *Strategies for teaching technology*. MENC, Reston, VA.

Robach, Steven. (2002). *Pro Tools for Macintosh and Windows*. Peachpit Press, Berkeley, CA.

Rudolph, Thomas & Leonard, Vincent (2001) *Recording in the digital world*. Berklee Press, Boston.

Rudolph, Thomas, et al (1997) *Technology strategies for music education*. Hal Leonard Corporation, Milwaukee.

Richmond, F., Rudolph, T., Klotz, J., Leonard, V. (2003) *TI:ME 2A digital audio course student workbook*. Technology Institute for Music Educators, Wyncote, PA.

Chapter 10

Creative, Practice, and Performance

National Standards 1, 2, 3, 4, 5, 6, 7
NETS (National Education Technology Standards): 1, 2, 3, 4

This chapter focuses on software and hardware that can be used by students at all levels to create and compose music. Creative applications are a bit difficult to narrow down. Many programs described in earlier previous chapters such as notation software, MIDI sequencing, and digital audio can be used for creativity. However, the software in this chapter is different. The software discussed here offers a bridge to creativity and can be used by students with little or no music theory knowledge. By my definition, a program is dubbed creative if it offers features to assist naive students with music creation. The main focus is technology that will help students creatively explore the world of sound. There are no restrictions of bar lines, meter, and measures. The last section includes a review of accompaniment and practice software that can be used by teachers and students alike.

In the 2000 Association for Technology in Music Instruction *Technology Directory*,[1] creative software is listed as composition software. Other commercial catalogs use the term creativity or creative software. Some just list all of the titles featured in this chapter under CAI (computer-assisted instruction), sequencing, or notation.

Some creative devices and programs are designed for the home user or novice music student. Others are geared to the experienced musician or composer. Given this wide range, it is important to select a product that will meet your specific needs. To select the best creative software/hardware you must first know what is available, and be sure it is compatible with your computer. Most of the applications in this chapter are available for both Macintosh and Windows.

Creativity

Remember painting and coloring in elementary school? I'm sure you enjoyed the paint-by-number approach where an artist's painting was copied and coded then you paint in each color. I still remember the first paint-by-number horse I painted as a kid that my parents hung on our basement wall. It was an exciting experience! Granted, this is not a high form of art, but the process helped me to experience art in a new and personal way. And although I don't have an extremely high aptitude for art (you should see my hand writing!), paint-by-number was a way to "hook" me into the world of art.

I have always been envious of the art teachers. They have so many tools—crayons, colored paper, modeling clay—for students to use in creative, hands-on ways. Walk past the art room in school and student's work can be seen. I've often thought student's work should be displayed outside of the music room, such as music that the students have composed. Now, with technology, students at all levels can delve more deeply into the world of creativity.

Music Crayons

I mentioned in Chapter 1 that technology can be thought of as the crayons for music education. Music software and hardware can enhance music composition and creativity. The difficulty in teaching students to compose music has always been the lack of tools to make composition accessible to the average student. Traditionally, students could not learn to compose until they had acquired a background in music theory. Now, with an appropriate computer music program or hardware device, students of all ages can begin to experiment with making music.

My initial reaction to the idea of teaching composition was, how can kids compose if they don't understand music theory? So I tried to emphasize music theory and found that most students were confused at best and turned off at worst. Shortly thereafter, I visited an elementary art class and found that the art teacher allowed students to experiment and create without first introducing theory concepts. I now use this approach in music composition. Thanks to technology, students can create music with minimal formal training in music theory.

Creative Tools for Music

Technology has made musical "paint-by-numbers" applications possible. These programs let you type or play in some chords, pick a style such as rock, Latin, or jazz; then drag and drop musical patterns to create a phrase, and the technology realizes a piece of music. I think of these "paint-by-number" musical devices as having a degree of musical intelligence. Specific creative software and hardware applications can be used by novices to professional composers.

Creativity/Composition Software

Many programs in the creativity/composition category strive to use the power of the computer to assist the student or music novice to create and compose music. The programs featured in this section include Doodle Pad (www.harmonicvision.com), Making Music and Making More Music (www.creatingmusic.com), Songworks (www.ars-nova.com), Band-in-a-Box (www.pgmusic.com), and Storm (www.arturia.com/en/studio.lasso). There are others on the market. I am focusing on these because I personally know they have a good track record and have been used successfully in the classroom.

Making Music and Making More Music
by Morton Sobotnik

Two wonderful programs for younger students are Morton Sobotnik's Making Music and Making More Music. These programs are designed for pre-K through high school and use graphic, non-traditional notation.

Teaching Strategy 127

Making Music by Morton Sobotnik offers students several creative activities that introduce music composition to pre-K and primary students.

The program uses art education metaphors such as painting musical phrases with a paintbrush tool. Students can listen to the sounds they create with the paint bush and assign an instrument. They can then save and organize melodies and themes into entire compositions. Tools such as retrograde and inversion are available through graphic icons.

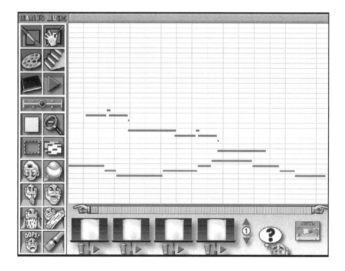

Figure 10.1: Making Music by Morton Sobotnik (www.creatingmusic.com)

The program also includes a unique way to combine melody and rhythm using non-standard notation. The melody is represented by birds that are dragged or clicked onto a note in the scale. Next, the rhythm is selected by clicking on the birds in the eggshells at the bottom of the screen. It takes a while to get used to this interface, but it is be a fun way to introduce composition to younger students.

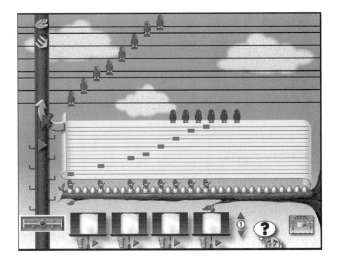

Figure 10.2: Melody Maker from Making Music by Morton Sobotnik
(www.creatingmusic.com)

The music basal series publisher Silver Burdett-Ginn also recommends Making Music as a way to enhance creative activities for young students. They offer suggestions for integrating the software into their basal series for grades K-8 (www.sbgmusic.com).

Making More Music

A more advanced version of Making Music is Making More Music. The program is by the same author for students ages 8 and older. It includes standard music notation and several programs with more advanced applications such as theme and variation.

Making More Music includes several games and interactive activities. Both for creativity and computer-assisted instruction, Making Music and Making More Music have a lot to offer. Making Music and Making More Music are wonderful additions to the elementary music curriculum.

Making Music Online

In addition to the software, Morton Sobotnik has made many of the activities available on a web site. Go to www.creatingmusic.com. There are online versions of several of the modules from both Making Music and Making More Music.

Figure 10.3: Online music software at www.creatingmusic.com

Teaching Strategy 128

Take your class to the computer lab and experiment with creating music online at www.creatingmusic.com.

The site requires the use of QuickTime and Flash. These programs are web browser helpers (see Chapter 2). The web site has some excellent programs, however, students cannot save their work. Therefore, you will want to purchase copies of the software version so students can save and re-open their work. The web site is an excellent way to introduce the program to students and they can experiment with the programs on the site at home for free.

Doodle Pad

Two of the most popular CAI programs are Music Ace and Music Ace 2 (see Chapter 6). When you purchase Music Ace, you will also receive another program built-in for free called Doodle Pad. It is an easy-to-use program for the K-5 level to compose and experiment with music composition.

> ### Teaching Strategy 129
>
> Using Doodle Pad, instruct students to load a song from the Jukebox. Have them drag the notes to new locations to make their own arrangement and change the timbres of the instruments.

There are countless ways to use this program with students. It comes with pre-recorded songs that can be loaded and played. Students can drag the notes to new locations to make their own renditions of existing pieces.

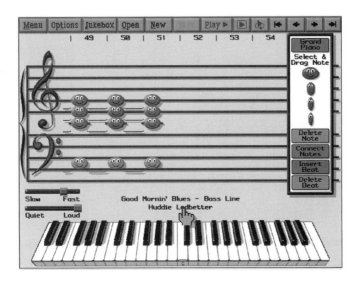

Figure 10.4: Music Ace's Doodle Pad by www.harmonicvision.com

Students can also compose music from scratch. One of the lessons in the accompanying *Music Ace Teachers' Guide* includes a name game for students to learn the names of the lines and spaces. This is a familiar game music educators have been using for decades. Ask students to come up with words spelled only from the letters of the musical alphabet. Examples include bad, dad, and cabbage.

> **Teaching Strategy 130**
> Use Doodle Pad to compose short melodies.

Using Doodle Pad, students can place their words on the proper line or space and select rhythm and instrument sounds for their musical word. Once students learn how easy is to drag notes onto the staff, they can begin composing their own melodies.

As was described in the notation chapter, the key is to create a partially completed file and assign the students to complete specific sections. For example, there are several blues pieces already in the Jukebox. Use these examples or create your own, then compose a melody using specific notes from the blues scale and listen to it played back by Doodle Pad.

> **Teaching Strategy 131**
> Use Doodle Pad as a fun way to introduce younger students to the world of music composition.

Doodle Pad can be used as an introduction to music notation and composition. It uses a non-standard notation set. The duration of a note is represented by its size. Instruments can be selected and polyphonic music can be composed.

Consider contacting Harmonic-Vision directly to purchase a site license for Doodle Pad so that you can have it on every computer in the school.

Songworks

An example of an excellent creativity/composition program that uses traditional music notation is Songworks 2 by Ars Nova Publishing for Windows and Macintosh. Songworks looks like a notation program (see Chapter 7), but its goal is to assist in the music composition process. Notes can be entered by clicking them into the score with the computer's mouse or by playing a MIDI keyboard. After a melody is entered, Songworks offers many options such as composing harmony, creating a counter line, or composing a variation based on the original melody.

Teaching Strategy 132

Use Songworks (Win/Mac) to help students experience composing songs, harmonies, and melodic variations.

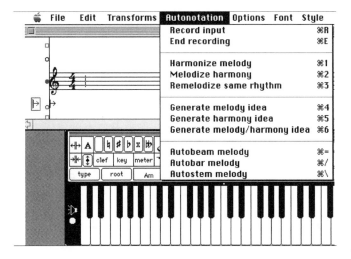

Figure 10.5: Songworks auto-notation options (www.ars-nova.com)

Songworks can be used to help students experience compositional techniques such as retrograde and inversion. In addition, it includes a collection of automatic accompaniment styles. A student can notate a melody and the computer will automatically harmonize and embellish the piece. The final product can be printed out. Songworks is not the program to use for full band and orchestra scores. Rather, it is a specialized piece of software that offers an amazing array of instant compositional tools with the option of printing out the final product.

Teaching Strategy 133

Use Songworks to assist students with adding harmony and melodic variations into their musical compositions.

Many of Songworks' functions can be used to enhance the composition process. A high degree of musical intelligence is built into the program. For example, the program can guess a harmony based on the notes in the melody.

In the following example, I entered the melody and then asked the computer to generate the harmony. Songworks automatically added the chord symbols above the notation.

Figure 10.6: An example of Songworks automatically
generating harmony chords.

In addition, the program can generate a variety of accompaniment patterns such as alberti-bass.

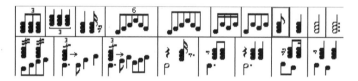

Figure 10.7: Palette of variations possible using Songworks

Songworks is notation-based, and therefore requires some understanding of music notation. An advantage to using Songworks is that it can be used on Macintosh and Windows computers without any additional MIDI equipment. The sound plays through the built-in speaker. Of course, adding a MIDI instrument or sound module is preferable because the sound quality will be much better than that produced by the Macintosh speaker.

Band-in-a-Box: Creative Applications

Band-in-a-Box by PGMusic is one of the most versatile and fascinating programs on the market today. It has been around for years and continues to grow and add new features. It is a wonderful practice/accompaniment tool and will be reviewed in that light later in this chapter. The program has many creativity applications for students.

Teaching Strategy 134

Use Band-in-a-Box to generate an original melody and chords or just a melody to a pre-composed chord progression.

With Band-in-a-Box, first you enter chords for a song by playing on a MIDI keyboard or typing them in from the computer keyboard. After the chords are entered, you select one of dozens of pre-made styles. Once the chords are in place, you can ask Band-in-a-Box to create an original melody.

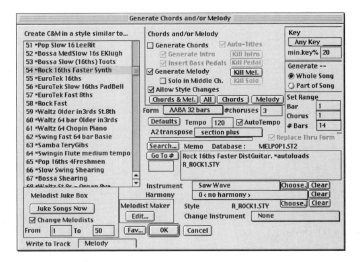

Figure 10.8: Band-in-a-Box Melodist options

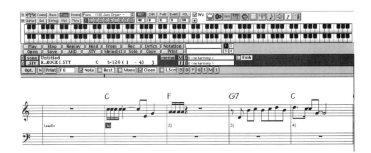

Figure 10.9: Original melody generated by Band-in-a-Box Melodist feature

Another cool Band-in-a-Box feature is the Wizard. Once the Wz box is checked, the computer keyboard comes alive.

> **Teaching Strategy 135**
>
> Use Band-in-a-Box Wizard to record improvised melodies by playing the computer's bottom two rows of keys.

Enter chord symbols and select a style. Then press play. Each key on the bottom row on the computer keyboard becomes a chord tone. Passing tones for each chord tone are available on the second row of the keyboard.

Press record and improvise on the keyboard. The student's melody will be transcribed and notated in traditional music notation.

Improvising with Percussion

Yet another Band-in-a-Box feature is the Drum Window. The percussion sounds can be played by clicking on the pictures of the instruments with the mouse or by striking the corresponding keys on the computer keyboard.

Figure 10.10: The Drum Window in Band-in-a-Box

> ### Teaching Strategy 136
> Use the Band-in-a-Box drum window and ask students to improvise and record drum and percussion sounds.

In Band-in-a-Box, set the melody to MIDI track #10 for drums and you can have your students record their own drum patterns to accompany a song. What fun this can be! What student doesn't want to play the drums? This is just the tip of the iceberg for this valuable program. There is more on Band-in-a-Box as an accompaniment tool later in this chapter.

Loop Software and Hardware

An entirely new category unto itself in the past several years is loop software and hardware. These programs are designed to create musical arrangements and compositions. They are easy to use and take a building block approach to composition. They are used to create soundtracks for movies and background music for web sites and virtually any musical application.

First, let's get a definition of a loop:

> A loop is an audio recording (or section of a recording) that is played repeatedly. Loops are usually short excerpts of instrumental passages or rhythmic patterns that can be used as 'building block' within larger arrangements.[2]

When you combine several loops, it is referred to as a groove. Grooves can be composed and used in a variety of applications. Files can be saved and converted to burn on a CD and import into other programs and applications.

Loop Software

There is a variety of loop software titles. Some are designed for home and school use while some are marketed to the professional musician, DJ, and composer.

Teaching Strategy 137

Use loop-based software with students to create songs in various styles. Students can create complete songs without extensive background in music fundamentals.

Loop software does not require an extensive background in music theory. Simply drag and drop pre-recorded loops to create a song in seconds. High-end loop programs also include sonic effects and control of other devices via MIDI. Windows users have more options in the loop category than Macintosh users.

Rock Rap'N Roll

In music education, the program that got it all started is Rock Rap'N Roll. As of this writing the program is still being marketed and sold by Scott Foresman and many computer software resellers. The program has not been updated and only runs on older operating systems. Windows version runs only on Windows 98 or earlier and the Macintosh model tops out at OS 9.

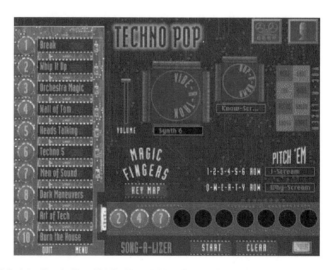

Figure 10.11: Rock Rap'N Roll sold by Silver Burdett (www.sbgmusic.com)

To use Rock Rap'N Roll a student starts with a style such as rock, blues, techno pop, and so forth. Then pre-recorded loops are dragged to create a groove. Users can arrange the loops in song style to create ABA, song form, and so forth. Then they can improvise patterns and record their voice using the computer's microphone input. Rock Rap'N Roll is a wonderful program and hopefully it will be upgraded to run on newer operating systems. If not, there are other options. Fortunately, other publishers see the value of a loop-based program for kids and for schools. Read on!

Super Duper Music Looper

Super Duper Music Looper from Sonic Foundry is only available for Windows. It is a fun and exciting way for kids to create music. Designed for kids ages 6–10 although older children also enjoy it, Super Duper Music Looper can be used at home or in school to explore the fundamental basics of music creation.

> **Teaching Strategy 138**
> Use Super Duper Music Looper with students of all ages to create original music tracks and record their voice or instrument and then save the file to share with others.

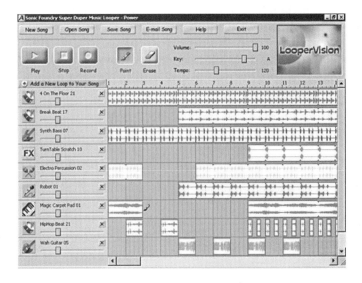

Figure 10.12: Super Duper Music Looper
(www.mediasoftware.sonypictures.com)

Super Duper Music Looper is packed with instrument sounds and amazing sound effects students can put together to create a complete song—literally in minutes. Students can even watch wacky animations as they dance to the music. After all the tracks are created, click the record button and sing or play an instrument. The applications for use in the music classroom are endless.

The Acid Family

Sonic Foundry introduced Acid in 1998. It was the first program to treat loops as interchangeable musical building blocks. The program quickly became the industry standard for looping software. Unfortunately for Mac users, Acid only runs on Windows.

> **Teaching Strategy 139**
>
> Download the free Acid Xpress (Windows only) and put it on every computer in the school. Take students to the computer lab to compose grooves and loops.

Sonic Foundry currently supports a family of Acid products of interest to music educators. Acid Xpress is a free version that provides ten looping tracks and plays MIDI files. It is a great way to introduce these concepts to students. If they have a Windows computer, they can download Acid Xpress at home. Students can even publish their songs at www.acidplanet.com. Acid Techno and Acid DJ are designed to create dance grooves. They also support MP3 file formats. Acid Music costs less then $100 and is primarily a multimedia version for use with video clips and for creating music sound clips. The top of the line is Acid Pro that costs around $350. In addition to handling loops, it also functions as a complete MIDI sequencer (see Chapter 8).

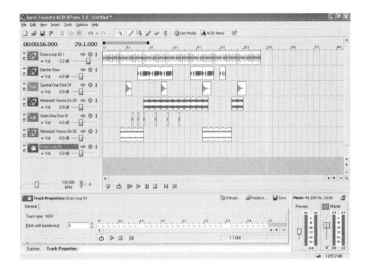

Figure 10.13: Acid XPress (www.mediasoftware.sonypictures.com)

Live

The only loop sequencer that runs on both Macintosh and Windows is Live by Ableton. With their academic pricing a single copy is only about $200. Live is built for live jamming and improvising. It is also possible to record live audio clips that can be included with the loop composition.

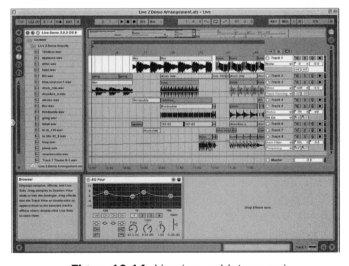

Figure 10.14: Live (www.ableton.com)

After the tracks are assembled, you can record your performance as you click to bring in the various tracks. Also included are many effects processors. Live is not a MIDI sequencer, but it can be synced with another sequencer to run simultaneously.

GarageBand

GarageBand is a Mac OSX application that is part of the Macintosh iLife series. It comes free on all Macs purchased after January, 2004. If you don't have GarageBand on your Mac, you can purchase it for the educator's price of $29.95. The program includes pre-recorded loops, amps, effect, and editing tools. You can also record audio and MIDI using this entry-level program. Find out more at www.apple.com/ilife/garageband.

Sequencers That Support Looping

In addition to the dedicated loop sequencers listed above, many of the sequencers mentioned in Chapter 8 can import and manipulate loops. Programs such as Cakewalk Home Studio and Cubase, as well as others, support loops in songs. The advantage of using a sequencer is cost; doing more than one thing in the same program is cost effective. However, I recommend that you take a close look at loop software, because it fills a need for student composition and improvisation in the music curriculum.

Downloading Loops

Sonic Foundry offers online sound libraries for Acid. Some can be downloaded for free and some must be purchased. There are many web sites that offer loops for purchase. Check out www.soundsonline.com. They advertise themselves as the largest selection of royalty-free loops.

Groove Machines and Samplers

Groove samplers are primarily designed for use in rap and dance styles. The purpose of a groove sampler is to assemble loops of audio into a composition or for live performance. A built-in sampler can record audio samples that are triggered from pads similar to a drum computer. Models have different editing and processing capabilities to alter the samples once they have been recorded. A built-in mixer controls audio output; volume is controlled in real time. It is possible to send the audio signal to a mixer to combine with other MIDI devices and processing.

> **Teaching Strategy 140**
>
> Use a groove sampler to create dance tracks for improvisation and movement exercises.

Some units, like the Roland SP-808, also have a built-in tone generator to add bass or keyboard parts. The Boss SP505, Korg Electribe, and the Yamaha SU200 also have tone generators.

Figure 10.15: Roland SP 808 Groovebox

Figure 10.16: Korg Electribe

Figure 10.17: Yamaha SU200

Instant Accompaniment Software

Several programs are designed just to create chords, bass, and drum parts in various styles such as jazz, rock, pop, and reggae. Students can use this auto-accompaniment software to create and compose their own original chord progressions and melodies. Accompaniment software requires a computer, MIDI interface, and a General MIDI instrument or sound module. Some popular accompaniment programs are:

- **Band-in-a-Box** by PG Music (www.pgmusic.com) for Macintosh and Windows. Band-in-a-Box creates automatic accompaniments from chord symbols including bass, piano, drums, guitar, and strings. The program can also record one single track or melody, jazz solos, and much more.

- **JAMMER Professional** for Windows by SoundTrek (www.soundtrek.com)is a sequencer and auto-accompaniment program. Enter chords on JAMMER's lead sheet, pick a musical style and then press the compose button. JAMMER instantly generates and plays full professional arrangements of the accompaniment in the style you have chosen.

- **Mibac Jazz,** by Mibac Music Software (www.mibac.com) for Macintosh and Windows, is designed to be used for jazz improvisation. It contains multiple jazz styles and lends itself to practicing and improvising jazz.

Auto-accompaniment programs can be used by teachers to create accompaniments for practice and performance and by students to compose and create original music. To determine the best auto-accompaniment program for you, define your specific goal, then review the various programs. Each of the previously listed programs fills a different need. Jammer is best for high end use, when a multi-track sequencer and intelligent accompaniments are needed. Mibac Jazz has the widest selection of jazz styles, and Band-in-a-Box is very easy to use and includes dozens of styles.

> ### Teaching Strategy 141
>
> Use auto-accompaniment programs such as Band-in-a-Box as a teacher's tool to create accompaniment parts for group rehearsal, individual practice, and improvisation.

I find Band-in-a-Box to be my favorite for all-around use. The current version of Band-in-a-Box (12.0) comes with a variety of pop, jazz, and rock styles. In some styles, the program automatically creates string and guitar parts. Band-in-a-Box can also print out a lead sheet in traditional music notation.

To create a song using Band-in-a-Box, type in the chords using the computer's typewriter keyboard. For example: C7, Cmin, and Caug, are entered in the appropriate measure.

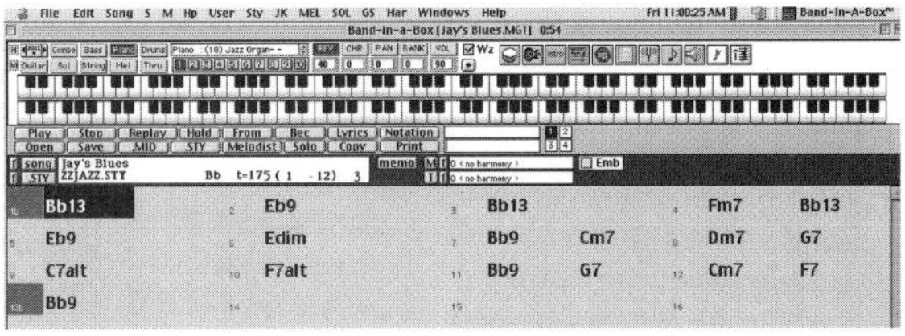

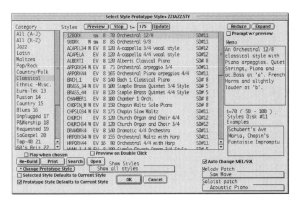

Figure 10.18: Chords entered in Band-in-a-Box

Once the chord symbols have been entered, the next step is to select a style, from choices like jazz, rock, bossa nova, waltz, classical, and many others. Band-in-a-Box has the most incredible selection of styles and hundreds more can be added by purchasing them from the www.pgmusic.com web site.

Figure 10.19: Band-in-a-Box Styles selection window

After entering the chords and selecting the style, press the "play" button and Band-in-a-Box instantly creates an accompaniment including piano, bass, and drums. The styles sound professional, and if played through a quality General MIDI instrument or sound module, the results are truly impressive. Once the chords are entered, a melody can be recorded using Band-in-a-Box's one-track built-in sequencer.

Band-in-a-Box and other intelligent software programs have many other useful features including the ability to transpose a song to any key and the capability of adjusting the tempo.

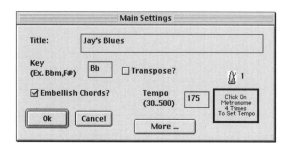

Figure 10.20: Main Settings menu from Band-in-a-Box

Auto-accompaniment software is an excellent practice tool. Students can play melodies and practice improvisation while the computer generates an accompaniment. Intelligent programs are similar to sequencers in many ways. Parts can be individually controlled and muted so it is possible to isolate individual parts such as the bass, piano, and drums, to create practice accompaniments for any instrument. For example, muting the piano part allows for practicing piano in the "minus-one" fashion.

Suppose you would like to create an accompaniment for a song for any class. With Band-in-a-Box it is as easy as typing in the chord symbols and playing the melody.

Once accompaniment parts have been created it is easy to make CD recordings for individual students to take home for practice. The Windows version has a "save as WAV" option. Macintosh users can convert MIDI files and burn a CD using iTunes. A tutorial about converting files to iTunes is on the companion CD-ROM. Another way is to connect the output of the MIDI keyboard to the input of an external CD recorder (see chapter 8).

Teaching Strategy 142

Students can use auto-accompaniment software to compose harmonic progressions.

Auto-accompaniment programs can be excellent creative tools for students. One application is to have students create their own compositions. I usually begin the composition process using tonic, dominant, and subdominant harmony. First students have listened to various compositions using tonic, dominant, and subdominant harmony, then they create their own pieces.

One of my favorite lessons is to introduce several songs that use a twelve-bar blues progression. I usually start with In The Mood. I write the chord progression for the class.

Then I ask the class to analyze the blues progression with the following questions in mind:

1. What are the first and last chords? Answer = tonic
2. What is the most frequently used chord? Answer = tonic
3. What three chords are used in the twelve-bar blues progression? Answer = tonic (I), dominant (V), subdominant (IV).

I then ask the students to compose their own version of the twelve-bar blues following the above three rules. Using these rules, a sixth grade general music student created the following twelve-bar blues progression:

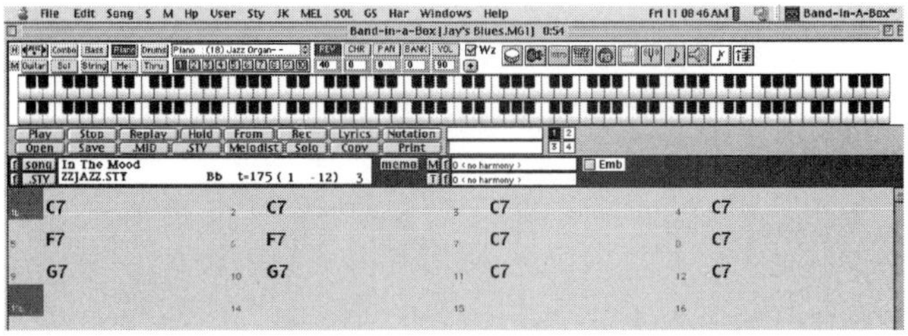

Figure 10.21: Chord progression entered in Band-in-a-Box

After entering their original chord progression, students select a style, adjust the tempo, and improvise an original melody. Band-in-a-Box makes a terrific composition tool as it instantly plays back chord progressions.

Band-in-a-Box also offers a variety of chord types so students can experiment with chords and harmony. Students can enter chords from an existing tune or create their own chord progressions.

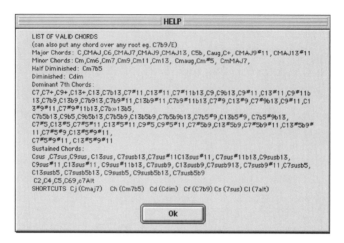

Figure 10.22: List of chords that can be used in Band-in-a-Box

---

Teaching Strategy 143

Use auto-accompaniment software to analyze chord voicings and bass patterns.

Band-in-a-Box will automatically create chord embellishments that are appropriate to the selected style. For example, in the jazz swing style, if a dominant seventh chord such as C7 is entered, the piano part will add altered notes to the chord such as the sixth or ninth scale degree. These altered voicings can be frozen on the screen for analysis. Simply press the appropriate key during playback and the screen will freeze showing the notes that are being played for that chord.

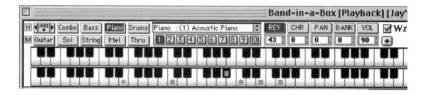

Figure 10.23: Band-in-a-Box piano voicing

More Useful Features

Band-in-a-Box has many more features. These include an automatic jazz soloist function and melody harmonization which are wonderful ways to demonstrate jazz styles. Everything that Band-in-a-Box creates can be printed out or saved as a MIDI file and opened in a notation program (see Chapter 7).

One of its most useful features was added in Band-in-a-Box version 11.0 (and later). This is the ability to open a MIDI file and guess the chord changes. Any Standard MIDI file can be converted including ones created on a MIDI sequencer, downloaded from the Internet, or purchased. Band-in-a-Box will do a good job of realizing the chord symbols.

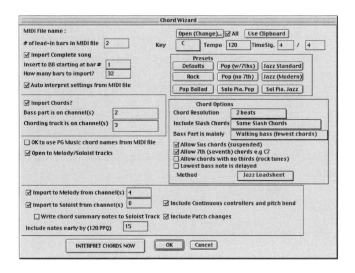

Figure 10.24: Band-in-a-Box chord change analyzer

Sharing Files

Band-in-a-Box is a highly versatile program, but it is not a panacea. One of its limitations is that it can only record one track of music in addition to the automatic accompaniment parts.

> ### Teaching Strategy 144
> Export Band-in-the-Box files as Standard MIDI files, then import these files into a sequencer to add more harmonies, counterlines, etc.

There is a way around this limitation. It is possible to create a file in Band-in-a-Box and then export it as a Standard MIDI file to a sequencer. Once the file is converted to the sequencer, more music tracks for additional harmonies and counter lines can be added.

> ### Teaching Strategy 145
> Export a Standard MIDI file from Band-in-a-Box to a notation program to printout out bass and piano parts.

Band-in-the-Box can print out a lead sheet showing the melody in standard notation. However, if you want to print out the piano, bass, or drum parts that Band-in-a-Box creates, you must export them as a Standard MIDI file and then import them into a notation program such as Finale or Sibelius. For example, if I want to print out a bass line, I type in the chords, select the style and then export the file to my notation software and print out the bass part. This can be faster than entering a bass line one note at a time into a notation program.

The steps for exporting a Standard MIDI file from Band-in-a-Box to a notation or sequencer program are follows:

1. Save the file in Band-in-a-Box as a Standard MIDI file.
2. Open your notation or sequencing program.
3. In the notation or sequencing program, go to the File menu and select, "Import a Standard MIDI File." Some programs do this automatically and if this is the case you simply open the Standard MIDI file. Check your notation/sequencing program manual for the appropriate way to import a Standard MIDI file.

Practice/Accompaniment Software

Technology for practicing and assessment has taken major strides forward in the past few years. If you have been around technology, you have heard about SmartMusic, formerly Vivace. It's been around for some time now. If you have not seen the newest version of SmartMusic, you are in for a treat. I use this wonderful tool in my instrumental rehearsals, MIDI lab, and practice room. If you teach instrumental or vocal music, you will certainly find it useful.

SmartMusic Studio is an interactive, computer-based practice program for woodwind, brass, string, and vocal musicians. You pay for an annual subscription and you then get access to more than 20,000 accompaniments and exercises. Many of the popular elementary band methods are also included. You will find an unbelievable list of solos for every major band instrument and voice. For student practice it is an amazing tool.
SmartMusic features include:

- accompaniments can play at a constant tempo or they can follow the tempo of the performer.
- a chromatic tuner that appears on the computer screen.
- the ability to start anywhere in the music by entering a rehearsal mark.
- the ability to loop any part of the accompaniment to practice difficult passages.
- parts of pieces or repeats can be skipped.
- a music dictionary plus information about every composition and composer.

SmartMusic Teacher Applications

As with all technology applications, SmartMusic can be viewed in one of two ways: as a teacher's tool and as one used by students. I now start my middle school band rehearsals with SmartMusic. I take the output of my computer (the speaker out) and plug it into the room stereo or sound system. Any amplification source will work, such as a guitar or keyboard amplifier.

Figure 10.25: SmartMusic Studio by www.makemusic.com

Teaching Strategy 146

Use SmartMusic as a metronome and tuner for your rehearsals and classroom.

Figure 10.26: SmartMusic Practice Metronome

SmartMusic serves as my accompanying metronome to play during warm-ups and my tuner for checking intonation. Simply click the button on the main screen and you are ready to go. No confusing menus to deal with. All of the buttons are right on the screen.

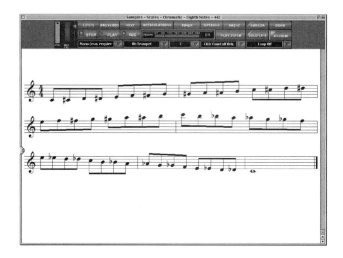

Figure 10.27: SmartMusic automatic exercise creator

Next, create thousands of warm-up exercises for your group in seconds. Click on the desired exercise and print it out. SmartMusic creates a chordal accompaniment that can be muted if preferred. Hit the print button and create your own custom warm-ups for students, sectionals, and entire ensembles. With SmartMusic, you have access to more than 50,000 exercises including thousands of different exercises based on scales, intervals, arpeggios, and twisters. All of these exercises come with accompaniments. You can print an exercise or create an entire lesson plan, create a practice loop for repetition and transpose your exercises to any key and for any instrument.

Importing MIDI Files

I wrote about SmartMusic in the original edition of this book, published back in 1996. The one big drawback at that time was you could not import your own files into the program. Now, this is possible. You will need to have a copy of Finale notation software (see Chapter 7). With it you can create from scratch or import a MIDI file and save it in SmartMusic format. I have used this technique to create accompaniments for my ensembles and sectionals.

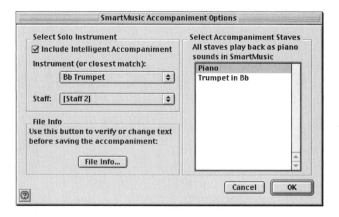

Figure 10.28: Saving Finale files (See Chapter 7) for Smart Music

Now when I begin my rehearsals, I have warm-up files I can open and playback for the group. Want them in a different key? Just click the transpose button, select the interval, and you have access to any key.

SmartMusic in the Hands of Students

Students can use SmartMusic to improve their musical performance by making practicing more fun and having play-along accompaniment to play. SmartMusic is much more than a practice CD. You can change the tempo and key at the touch of a button. SmartMusic can also loop a particular group of measures for practice.

Teaching Strategy 147

Students can use SmartMusic to practice solo repertoire. Choose from 20,000 plus files of many of the common solos for band instruments and voice.

The absolutely amazing thing is access to vast quantities of solo material for band instruments and voice. Most of the popular titles are available. You get them all with an annual subscription. There is nothing else to order.

There are classical, jazz, holiday standards, contest favorites, musical theater and pop, all with professionally arranged backing tracks. The vast amount of music available already recorded makes this a viable practice option. New pieces are released continually, indicating the kind of support that will keep SmartMusic current for years to come.

Teaching Strategy 148

Students can use SmartMusic to record practice sessions. This is an excellent form of assessment. Files can be saved in audio format and burned to disk or attached to an email message.

Using the computer's microphone, students can record practice sessions. They can record and listen to themselves until they get it right. Do your students need to make audition recordings? SmartMusic can be a huge time-saver and help them to self-evaluate.

SmartMusic can also be told to follow your tempo as you play. It will slow down or speed up and to stay with the performer. This is a terrific feature for ritards, accelerandos, and when first learning a solo.

There are even accompaniments for beginning band and string students. Many of the most popular methods, Essential Elements (band and strings), Accent on Achievement, and others are included. Students can practice along with an accompaniment to every exercise in the method book. There is an assessment mode where SmartMusic will evaluate the student's performance. A complete fingering guide is built in. Don't know a fingering? Select the instrument and click on a note.

Teaching Strategy 149

Use SmartMusic as a practice tool for beginning band and string students.

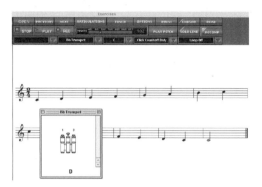

Figure 10.29: SmartMusic exercise showing trumpet fingering

SmartMusic works on a yearly subscription basis. For the price of a couple of pieces of music, you and your students can have all of the above tools. You will have to re-subscribe each year. However, the cost is under $200 for the first computer and with multiple copies, can get as low as $20 per computer.

SmartMusic runs without the need for any external MIDI devices or other gear. All you need is one microphone to record and you're off. Check the system requirements on the www.smartmusic.com web site. It will not run on older computers.

Figure 10.30: SmartMusic band method assessment options

Online Amadeus

Another practice and assessment tool similar to SmartMusic is Online Amadeus from Pyware (www.pyware.com). It is only available for Windows computers. The program costs $499. After purchasing it, you can log on to the web site and open files they have created or you can create your own. The Standard of Excellence band method is available via this service.

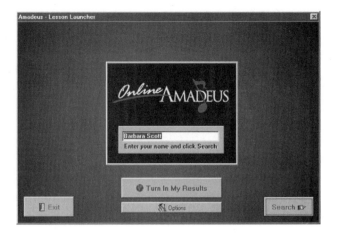

Figure 10.31: Online Amadeus (www.pyware.com)

Once the exercise or passage is selected, the student plays and the computer objectively evaluates the pitch and rhythmic accuracy of that performance. Online Amadeus assigns a numerical grade from 1-100, and displays the results on an easy-to-understand graph. This instant feedback designates problem areas. Now your students have the ability to practice with a purpose.

Creative Software/Hardware and the National Standards

Creative software and hardware can be used to support many of the National Standards for Arts Education.[2] The following section deals with specific areas of the national standards in the area of music. Each application is listed under one of the nine national standards.

#2. **Performing on instruments, alone and with others, a varied repertoire of music**

Teachers can create accompaniment exercises for rehearsal and student practice. Accompaniment software and hardware make it possible to mute individual parts, change tempo and key, making them ideal tools for rehearsal accompaniments and individual practice.

#3. Improvising melodies, harmonies, and accompaniments

Accompaniment software is a natural for practicing improvisation. From a one-chord vamp to a complex composition, accompaniment software can provide a "blank slate" to create exercises for improvisation.

#4. Composing and arranging music

Throughout this text in general and this chapter in particular, I've used the metaphor of technology as musical "crayons." Creative software is an excellent way to help students compose harmonies and melodies. Students can experiment with harmony, styles, and compose original melodies using intelligent software.

#6. Listening to, analyzing, and describing music

Accompaniment software provides teachers with a tool to create an endless number of musical examples to be played and analyzed by students. Students can be asked to identify the meter, tonality, instrumentation, and other musical elements. Also, after creating exercises and saving them to disk, they can be used over and over again year after year.

Summary

Creative software can be used by students to compose and create music at all levels, regardless of students background knowledge in music. Many software titles can be used by students of all ages to enter the world of music via creativity. There are programs that use non-traditional and traditional notation. Accompaniment software is designed for individual practice. It can also become a teacher's tool in the classroom and rehearsal hall.

Review Questions

1. Give two examples of creativity in the visual arts curriculum and make a comparison with how this type of creativity might be accomplished in the music classroom.
2. List two creative enhancing software titles designed for primary grades to enhance creativity.

3. Making Music uses a non-traditional music notation method. List the pros and cons of using non-traditional music notation with students.

4. List a web site where students can go online and create music.

5. What is the advantage of using creative applications with secondary level students?

6. List several ways the program Band-in-a-Box could be used to enhance student creativity.

7. What is loop software?

8. List two applications of loop software and explain the benefits and drawbacks of this application when used with novice music students.

9. What are audio loops and why would you want one?

10. What are groove machines/samplers?

11. What is the role of accompaniment software in the hands of teachers?

12. What are some reasons for students to use accompaniment software and what kinds of music learning activities could they accomplish with it?

13. List several unique applications of SmartMusic practice/accompaniment software.

14. Why would you want to move a music file from one software program to another? What steps are necessary to accomplish this task?

15. List two national standards that can be addressed using creative or accompaniment software.

CD-ROM Activities

- Project 10.1 Explore the Chapter 10 web links. Review the sites you visit.
- Project 10.2 Visit the www.creatingmusic.com web site. Develop a lesson plan for students using one or more computers in a classroom or computer lab.
- Project 10.3 Download a demo or purchase a copy of Band-in-a-Box from www.pgmusic.com. Print out and follow the QuickStart Tutorial for Macintosh and Windows in PDF format. Create an accompaniment for a general, choral, or instrumental classroom activity.

- Project 10.4. Download the demo version of SmartMusic (www.smartmusic.com). Open one of the sample files and change the tempo and key. Next record a melody playing along with the accompaniment. Save the performance to disk in an audio format.

CD-ROM Lesson Plans

- 10.1 Lesson plan using Band-in-a-Box in the music classroom.
- 10.2 Lesson plan using Doodle Pad in the classroom.
- 10.3 Lesson plan using SmartMusic in the classroom.

Reference

Blakeslee, Michael, ed. (1994). *National standards for the arts*. Music Educators National Conference, Reston, VA.

Murphy, Barbara, Editor (2000). *Technology directory*. Association for Technology in Music Instruction, Michigan State University, East Lansing, MI.

Reese, S. (2001). Tools for thinking in sound. *Music Educators Journal, 88* (1), 42-46, 53.

Reese S., McCord, K, & Walls K. (2001) *Strategies for teaching technology*. MENC The National Association for Music Education, Reston, VA.

Rideout, Ernie (July, 2002). Review: PG Music Band-in-a-Box 11: *Keyboard Magazine*.

Rudolph, Thomas, et al. (1997). *Technology strategies for music education*. Hal Leonard Corporation, Milwaukee.

Smith, Greg (2002). Band-in-a-Box: A force in the music classroom. *Music technology guide*. Lentine's Music. Akron, OH.

Souvignier, Todd (June, 2002). Electronic Musician. *Loop-a-palooza!*. PRIMEDIA Inc., NY.

Souvignier, Todd (2003). *Loops and grooves: The musician's guide to groove machines and loop sequencers*. Hal Leonard, Milwaukee.

Wilkinson, Scott April, (1994). Teach your children. *Electronic Musician Magazine*.

Chapter 11

Creating Multimedia
and Internet Applications

Music Education National Standards: 7, 8, 9
NETS (National Education Technology Standards): 1, 2, 4, 5, 6

This chapter is designed to present an overview of the terms and applications of multimedia. It is not intended to be a complete course in multimedia. If you are interested in getting involved in this area, please consult the books at the end of this chapter. There are also many courses on multimedia authoring offered at schools and colleges. Courses for music educators are offered by TI:ME, the Technology Institute for Music Educators (www.ti-me.org), as well as other institutions.

The first part of this chapter deals with creating multimedia. The second part reviews Internet applications. Multimedia and the Internet can be used by teachers and students.

Multimedia

It is difficult to give a simple, one-sentence definition of multimedia. In the purest sense, multimedia is created when two or more media are used simultaneously in a class presentation or lecture. For example, when there is a combination of sound, graphics, text, and/or video.

The term multimedia is often used quite loosely. I recently read an advertisement in a music education magazine for a "multimedia" package designed to be used in the general music class. Further reading revealed that the package consisted of a compact disc recording, printed materials, and a VHS video tape. This is an extremely simple application of multimedia. The passive experience of combining these media is more accurately referred to as "mixed" media.

In the computer world, multimedia "is not a straightforward term like 'word processor' or 'spreadsheet'. It applies to a bunch of applications, lumped together..."[1] Multimedia is the combination of digital media (text, graphics, audio, MIDI, video) in an interactive environment. The variety of media includes text, graphics, photography, virtual reality, animation, video, music, sound effects, narration, and 3-D modeling.[2]

Today's Macintosh and Windows computers are truly multimedia; they are equipped with enhanced audio and video capabilities. If you have access to a computer, there are many educational applications available.

Multimedia Authoring Applications

There are multimedia applications that are commercially produced and designed to be used by students. These programs are described in Chapter 6. This chapter will focus on the software that can be used by teachers and students, often referred to as authoring software. Multimedia authoring software "...helps musicians integrate sounds and images not only for music teaching and learning, but for a variety of musical activities."[3] Think of multimedia authoring applications as a blank canvas on which to paint a picture. They allow the user to create interactive applications from scratch.

Advantages and Disadvantages

There are many advantages to multimedia applications. Both students and teachers can create a wide variety of materials using multimedia authoring software.

> Because multimedia production can involve a variety of resources—music, research, drawing, photography, charts, graphs, layout, video, individual work, and group work—there is a good likelihood that a teacher can use multimedia projects in an attempt to meet each student's learning style.[4]

The disadvantage is that the software takes time to learn. Because the programs are designed to be tools, they require time to become familiar with their operation. Also, because multimedia combines elements from different disciplines, teachers and students alike need to take the time to become familiar with the software tools, the related file types, and other aspects. Even the most basic applications take time to master.

Uses of Multimedia

There are many ways to integrate multimedia into the music curriculum. Like the other areas of technology discussed in this book, multimedia can be a teacher's tool and a productive application in the hands of students.

Teachers can use multimedia tools to prepare materials for class presentations and to create custom software applications for students. They can create interactive web sites for students to use in informational and instructional ways. Students can use multimedia to create projects and materials for reports and presentations. The three general areas of multimedia include:

- presentation (teacher prepared materials)
- instructional materials (teacher prepared materials)
- student produced multimedia projects

Presentation Applications

Teachers can create aural and visual examples for classroom presentations. Notes and examples can be displayed on a computer projector for classes. Teachers can combine text, sound, and graphics. By learning the tools of multimedia, teachers can "...provide students with simultaneous aural and visual examples as they describe and discuss various musical excerpts."[5] Using a variety of the tools described in this chapter, teachers can create customized, interactive presentations.

Custom Instructional Materials

Multimedia authoring tools can be used to create custom computer programs for students. Think of this option as becoming an author of instructional software, similar to the titles presented in Chapter 6. Please note that the creation of custom software applications is no small task. However, in the end, you will have the skills to create your own computer programs for your students, which is a powerful skill to have.

Student Projects

Students can use multimedia authoring programs to create projects, reports, and presentations. In addition, courses that focus on specific multimedia applications such as video production can be offered. A growing number of multimedia courses and electives are finding their way into music departments across the country.[6]

What Is a File Type?

In multimedia, you will encounter a wide range of file types. File type indicates the kind of data or information stored in a file. Macintosh computers store the file type information inside the file itself so you don't have to keep track or indicate it in the file name. Windows operating systems use a three letter suffix to represent the file type. The three letters at the end of the file name are separated by a period, referred to as the file type extension. For example, a text file is indicated by the suffix "txt." A file name could be "myfilename.txt."

The file type tells the computer which application to launch should you open the file by double clicking on the file icon. When working with multimedia, file types are quite important. You will want to use the most appropriate file type for each application and be sure the application you are using can read or interpret the file types you have created in other programs. For an in-depth discussion of file type, consult the books listed in the reference section at the end of this chapter.

Text Files

Text is displayed in a specific typeface, called a font. It can be resized and formatted for use in multimedia. You should have a working knowledge of how to select fonts and change text size and how to copy and paste text within a document and from one application to another.

Graphic Files (Images)

Graphic files include pictures and drawings that can be created from scratch using specialized graphic software. Graphics can also be copied from clip art and from other sources such as web pages, or captured using a digital camera or scanned using a scanner.

The most common graphic file formats include GIF (pronounced JIFF), JPEG (pronounced Jay-Peg), PICT (pronounced pict), Tiff (pronounced tif) and EPS (say each letter). GIF and JPEG are most often used when files need to be small for the Internet or in presentations and when the images are going to be viewed on a computer screen. TIFF is used primarily for printing photographs. EPS is most common when printing music notation at a very high quality.

Teachers need to have a few tools to work with when creating graphics. The basics of editing graphics include:

- cropping or cutting off portions of a picture
- changing the brightness and contrast
- changing the size of the graphic

Most word processors such as Microsoft Word and AppleWorks have graphic editing capability which may suffice for most common applications. If you do a lot of graphic editing, then consider using a graphic editing program to make changes to graphic files. For Macintosh users, I recommend GraphicConverter available from Lemke Software (www.lemkesoft.de). Another excellent advanced application is Adobe Photoshop for Windows and Macintosh. This is an expensive program so consider Photoshop Elements as a lower cost option. Adobe, like other publishers, offers educational discounts, so be sure to ask.

Figure 11.1: Graphic Converter (Mac) by www.lemkesoft.de

Capturing Notation as a Graphic File

There are many times when you will want to incorporate music notation as a graphic file. For example, perhaps you are preparing a presentation for a class on note reading or phrasing. You want to prepare slides in a presentation program such as PowerPoint and you want to include the actual notation created by your notation program (see Chapter 7). Perhaps you are creating a web page and want to include music notation. One way to accomplish this task is to convert the music notation to a graphic file format. For a tutorial on how to accomplish this, see the tutorial on the companion CD-ROM: capturing music notation, Tutorial 11.5.

Digital Video

Digital video can be created using a digital video camera and edited right on the computer screen. Software programs such as iMovie for Macintosh and Movie Maker for Windows have brought the world of digital video to the home and school. These programs can be used for free and come with current Macintosh and Windows computers. They are sufficient for most uses and can accomplish basic editing. At the high-end there are professional programs such as Premiere by Adobe and Final Cut Pro by Apple. These programs can be expensive, costing in the $500 and up range.

As with graphics, there are specific file formats for movies. The most common is QuickTime, a product of Apple Computer that is compatible with both Macintosh and Windows computers. The file extension is .mov for movie. Another popular movie format for Microsoft Windows is AVI, which is short for Audio Video Interleave. QuickTime is the most common format used for displaying digital video on Macintosh and Windows computers. Once the digital video is created and edited, it can be saved in a supported file format and then incorporated into multimedia projects.

Animation

There is a distinct difference between video and animation. Video takes continuous motion and breaks it up into discrete frames. Animation starts with independent pictures and puts them together to form the illusion of continuous motion. The most common program today for creating animation is Macromedia's Flash. Flash is a programming language that creates animations for display on a web browser such as Internet Explorer. Flash requires an Internet plugin in order to function (see Chapter 2). Another popular high-end animation program is Director by Macromedia. Once created, animations can be brought into the multimedia software applications reviewed later in this chapter.

Video Compression

Digital video consumes a lot of memory and the file sizes can be quite large. For this reason, several compression standards have been developed. Compression is used with movies and digital audio sound files to reduce the size of the file without making a significant reduction in quality.

One of the most common compression schemes is MPEG, short for Moving Picture Experts Group, and pronounced em-peg. MPEG refers to the family of digital video compression standards and file formats developed by the motion picture experts. MPEG generally produces better-quality video than competing formats, such as Video for Windows and QuickTime. MPEG files can be decoded by special hardware or by software. There are three major MPEG standards: MPEG-1, MPEG-2, and MPEG-4.

Audio (Sound and MIDI)

There are two types of file formats when working with sound—MIDI and audio. MIDI files can be created using a variety of software (see Chapter 8). Digital audio can also be created with a wide variety of tools as well (see Chapter 9). Both MIDI and digital audio files can be incorporated into multimedia applications.

MIDI files use the suffix "mid." Because MIDI files include only performance information, the file size is relatively small. The upside is the small file size. The downside is the quality of the music cannot be controlled, as the computer or sound source creates the eventual playback. Audio files, on the other hand, are extremely large compared to MIDI. However, unlike MIDI files, you can control the sound quality of audio files. With digital audio, any sound can be recorded, including acoustic instruments, sound effects, speech, acoustic, and electronic (synthesized) sounds.

Audio formats include AIFF (Macintosh) and WAV (Windows). AIFF is a Macintosh format developed by Apple. The file suffix is aif. WAV is a file format for storing sound in files developed jointly by Microsoft and IBM. WAV files end with the extension: wav. It is the most common format used with all Windows applications and operating systems.

> **Teaching Strategy 150**
> When converting file formats for sound, keep in mind the following advice: MIDI = small file size; Digital audio = large.

Audio File Compression

Audio files, like digital video files, are very large in size. One minute of CD quality sound takes up approximately 10 megabytes (MB) of storage. There are compression schemes to reduce the size of audio files without significantly compromising the sound quality. The most common audio file compression format is MP3. MP3 reduces the file size by a factor of 12. MP3 compression removes all superfluous information such as the redundant and irrelevant parts of a sound signal, and hopefully, the stuff the human ear doesn't hear anyway. Because MP3 files are relatively small, they can easily be transferred. The conversion from digital audio to MP3 can be accomplished using the digital audio editing programs discussed in Chapter 10 such as Peak, Sound Forge, iTunes, and Music Match Jukebox.

Converting MIDI Files to Other Formats

MIDI files created on MIDI sequencers (see Chapter 8) or music notation software (see Chapter 7) must be saved in Standard MIDI file format to be used with multimedia software or on the Internet. Each sequencer or notation program accomplishes this a little bit differently, so consult the manual for converting to Standard MIDI file format or SMF. Usually, there is an option in the File menu or the Save As menu. Once the file is saved as a SMF, it can be used in a variety of multimedia applications.

Converting MIDI to QuickTime

When working with MIDI files in multimedia, it is best to convert the MIDI files to QuickTime. The reason for converting to QuickTime is that MIDI files are played on computers using a wide variety of MIDI players and MIDI software. If you or your students are planning to incorporate MIDI in multimedia or Internet web pages, converting to QuickTime will make the file standard no matter what computer operating system is being used.

Converting MIDI to QuickTime can be done for free. Simply download the free QuickTime Movie Player from www.apple.com/quicktime. Launch QuickTime Player. From the File menu choose open. QuickTime will then convert the MIDI file to QuickTime. You will be left with two versions of the file: a MIDI file (with the suffix .mid) and a converted file in QuickTime format with the extension .mov. Once converted, the QuickTime file can be inserted into nearly every multimedia authoring tool.

Converting MIDI to Audio

It is sometimes useful to be able to convert MIDI files into an audio format. This is primarily done when you want to burn a CD of MIDI files that will play in a conventional CD player. To convert a MIDI file to audio, try the following. First, use MIDI or notation software that supports saving files in audio format (AIFF or WAV). Check the program's documentation. A growing list of software programs offer this option, including Finale 2004 or later, Band-in-a-Box 11 or later, Sibelius version 3, and Cakewalk Home Studio. Converting MIDI to audio can be as simple as choosing save as WAV or taking a specified list of steps. When the computer makes the conversion, it accesses the built-in sound synthesis capability of the computer.

Another excellent option is to use a utility program to convert MIDI files to audio. There are several ways to do this. Macintosh and Windows users can use iTunes. See the tutorial on the companion CD-Rom for configuring iTunes to convert MIDI to audio.

Edirol's VSC-MP1 Virtual Sound Canvas can also be used to convert MIDI to audio. It is available for both Macintosh and Windows. Simply open your MIDI file and then press the convert to audio button. The software also allows for adjusting timbres and volumes as well as some effects. The cost of the software is under $50.

QuickTime was mentioned earlier in this chapter. The free version of QuickTime can be used to convert MIDI files to QuickTime. Apple offers an upgraded version of this program called QuickTime Pro for Macintosh and Windows computers. It sells for $29.99. QuickTime Pro can be used to convert MIDI files to WAV and AIFF format. In addition, QuickTime Pro offers a host of other audio and video editing options.

Another option is to use MIDI/digital audio software (see Chapter 9) and re-record the MIDI output as audio. In this case, the output of the MIDI synthesizer is routed to the audio input of the computer. An audio recording is made. After recording the audio, the tracks can be bounced to an AIFF (Mac) or WAV (Windows) file in preparation for burning to CD.

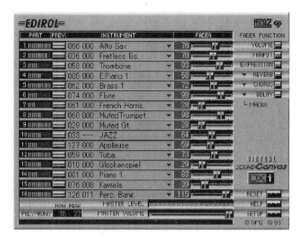

Figure 11.3: Edirol's VSC-MP1 Virtual Sound Canvas

CD Burning Software

The typical way to burn CDs is using a computer equipped with a CD burner. The software comes with the CD burner. For Windows, Easy CD Creator is one of the most popular programs and Toast is a common program on Macintosh. Both are made by Roxio. Using this software, audio files can be assembled into CD tracks and burned to a CD. If you get confused at this stage, just ask one of your students. They are usually experts at CD burning and can walk you though the steps. Be sure to review the copyright restrictions covered in Chapter 16.

Student and Teacher Applications

Once you have acquired the skills to capture and convert graphics, video, and sound, the next step is to select a multimedia application. The areas to consider were mentioned at the beginning of this chapter: word processing, presentation software, and multimedia authoring tools. There is no one right way to go in this regard. Some music specialists start with what they know best. Others check with teachers and colleagues for recommendations. The key is to be sure that the authoring program you choose will suit your needs. Some of the common applications and uses are listed in the following section.

Word Processing

Today's word processors, such as Microsoft Word, AppleWorks, and WordPerfect, can incorporate a variety of media in addition to text. Word processors are on the low end of the spectrum in regard to possible features and applications, but they are a good place to start.

Presentation Software

There are programs that are specifically designed to create presentations that can be used by teachers as a presentation tool. These programs are designed to create multimedia slide shows. Students can use presentation software for creating projects and presentations for classes. Presentation software automatically creates a series of screens that are linked together in a linear fashion. Text, images, sound, and video can be integrated using this software. Popular software includes Microsoft PowerPoint (Mac and Windows) and KeyNote (Macintosh only).

> ### Teaching Strategy 151
> Teachers use presentation software to create professional-looking audio-visual materials for use in lectures and demonstrations.

Presentation software is relatively simple to use. First, enter a text outline for the presentation. It is possible to add graphics either from the several hundred pictures supplied with the program or imported from other graphics files. The final product is a set of professional looking slides. The program also provides a way to easily produce handouts for students. For example, I created the following outline as part of a presentation on technology using PowerPoint by Microsoft.

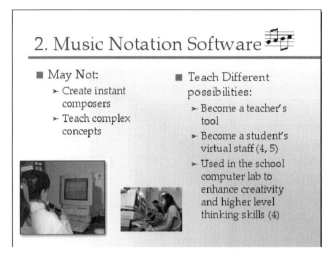

Figure 11.4: Sample PowerPoint slide combining text and graphics

---

Teaching Strategy 152

Students use word processors and presentation software to create multimedia projects containing text, graphics, sound, and video.

Inserting Graphics and Pictures

It is easy to insert a graphic, sound file, or movie file into word processors such as Microsoft Word and in presentation software such as PowerPoint. Simply select the Insert menu and choose the desired file type.

Teachers can add pictures and other graphics such as music notation examples into handouts, worksheets, and tests. Sound files can also be added for class demonstration and analysis. For example, you are studying the Classical period. You want to include some notes and pictures of Mozart. The first step is to obtain or create the picture you want to use. In this case, you may want a picture of Mozart. You could use a variety of methods that include scanning a photo from an existing book or copying a picture from the Internet. Once the picture has been obtained, it can be incorporated into a word processor. Pictures should be saved as JPEG or TIFF files. Check the word processor documentation for the steps to import a picture from a file.

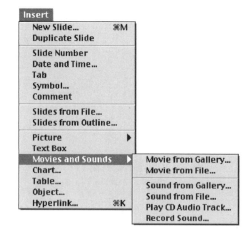
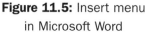

Figure 11.5: Insert menu
in Microsoft Word

Figure 11.6: Inserting
movies, sounds,
and pictures into PowerPoint

Movies can also be incorporated into Microsoft Word and PowerPoint. A video of a performance could be taken and then converted to QuickTime and incorporated into a word processing document.

Teaching Strategy 153

Teachers can create handouts and presentations that include text, graphics, and sound files.

Teaching Strategy 154

Students create multimedia presentations on virtually any topic by combining text, sound, and graphics. They also can use it for portfolio assessment of their work.

Students can use the same skills mentioned above to create reports and materials that include a variety of media types. For example, students could be asked to create a multimedia report or summary about a composer or musical concept being studied. Pictures and sound files could be created from scratch or downloaded from the Internet.

Linking Files

It is possible to link to files from within word processors and presentation software. You are familiar with links when you visit a web site, click on a word and it sends you to another web page or opens a graphic or sound file. This way other documents and files can be linked to text or graphics.

First, put the files you are working with and all media in the same folder. Then link them together. I did not know this little tip the first time I was teaching a multimedia course many years ago. The result was that no one's project worked properly when the files were copied to a disk and taken to another computer.

Save as Web Page

The specifics of creating web pages will be dealt with later in this chapter. However, if you are new to web design or need to create a web page in a hurry, both Microsoft Word and PowerPoint files can be saved in web page format. It is as simple as going to the File menu and choosing "Save as Web page." The software creates the necessary web files. These can then be copied on a disk and given to your school web administrator and posted on the school web site.

Multimedia Authoring Tools

In addition to general purpose applications such as word processors and presentation software, there are specialized multimedia tools that can be used by students and teachers. Multimedia authoring programs include KidPix for younger students, HyperStudio for middle school and up, and web page authoring using HTML (Hypertext Markup Language). High end programs such as Macromedia Director and Flash can also be used.

Authoring Software – Kid Pix

There are programs specifically designed for students to create multimedia. If you want to introduce multimedia to younger students, Kid PiX (www.kidpix.com) is an excellent choice. If you teach in a school district, check with the technology staff and other staff members to see if anyone is already using this program. It is one of the most popular programs used by students grades K-8.

> ### Teaching Strategy 155
> Students in grades K-8 can use Kid Pix as an introduction to multimedia creation.

With Kid Pix, students will discover new ways to express themselves using realistic art tools such as virtual crayons, magic markers, and paintbrushes. There are also 3-D paints and hundreds of stretchable animations and stickers. Students can also import and transform photographs by adding mixer effects, such as warp, spiral, and kaleidoscope. With a microphone connected to a Windows or Macintosh computer, students can add their own sounds to their creations, or even paint with their voice using the Sound Art tools. The Slideshow feature, with many sounds and screen transitions, makes Kid Pix a powerful, easy-to-use multimedia program. With the Slideshow, students can prepare slide shows in every curricular area. There is a free version of the program that is available at www.kidpix.com. If your classroom has an Internet connection, Kid Pix can be experienced using your favorite Internet browser.

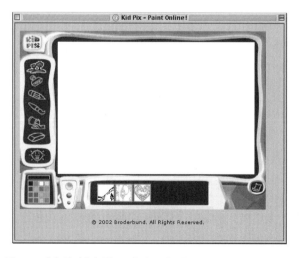

Figure 11.7: Kid Pix – Paint Online (www.kidpix.com)

Authoring Software-HyperStudio

For more than ten years, HyperStudio has been the standard classroom multimedia authoring program, primarily geared for the secondary level. HyperStudio 4, the newest version as of this writing, is a comprehensive desktop and online multimedia communications package for educators and students.

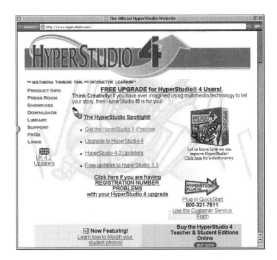

Figure 11.8: HyperStudio 4 (www.hyperstudio.com)

HyperStudio uses the term "cards" in a different manner that we do when we play poker or solitaire. HyperStudio refers to a stack of cards when describing a group of pages created in a project. Each page created in HyperStudio is referred to as a card, a group of cards is referred to as a stack. A project is made up of a stack of cards.

Individual cards may contain pictures, stories, movies, and sound files. They also contain buttons that link media and cards together. Teachers and students can use the program to create multimedia projects. HyperStudio projects can include creating electronic portfolios of student work and creating multimedia projects based on the various topics you are teaching in your classroom such as composers, musical styles, and the like. There are also many HyperStudio resources on the Internet. Visit www.hyperstudio.com for more information.

> **Teaching Strategy 156**
>
> Teachers can use HyperStudio to create multimedia materials for demonstration and student use.

Here is an example of a possible HyperStudio application. The teacher creates a HyperStudio stack to help students study chord progressions. When the student clicks on a chord, a musical example plays while the musical notation appears on the screen. The instructor uses the program as a demonstration tool in rehearsal and leaves the file on the computers in the instrumental room so students can use it independently.

> **Teaching Strategy 157**
>
> Students can create HyperStudio presentations on information they have studied such as the life and history of a musician or comparing two musicians.

HyperStudio can be the basis of music technology electives where students create multimedia projects that contain text, graphics, video, and sound. HyperStudio is an environment that can be used for an endless variety of applications.

Internet Activities and Creating Web Pages

The Internet, by its very nature, is a multimedia environment. Web pages can include text, graphics, sound, and video. With the vast majority of schools connected to the Internet and more and more schools adding connections and labs, music teachers can take advantage of this medium in a variety of ways. These include:

- using the Internet as a discovery and research tool.
- organizing Internet explorations for students, referred to as WebQuests.
- creating and designing web pages for information dissemination and the display of student work.

- students and teachers creating interactive web pages as a multimedia creation tool.

Web Discovery

With an Internet connection teachers can give assignments to students to view web sites that are rich in multimedia.

> **Teaching Strategy 158**
> Organize Internet web searches for students to visit to support the content being presented in class.

For example, if you are studying a particular subject area, take time to search for relevant web sites. Save these sites to your web browser's Favorites (see Chapter 2). With one or more computers in the classroom, students can search for information and explore web pages to support the learning experiences in the music classroom. Students can learn to copy text, graphics, and sound from web pages that can later be used in multimedia authoring projects. When planning an online activity, I suggest you review Bard Williams' suggestions[7]:

- What are your goals for the lesson? What do you want to accomplish? Is using the Internet the best way to accomplish your goals?
- Identify and analyze the Internet resources your students may use before hand.
- Before class begins, make sure all hardware, software, and connections are working.
- Make step-by-step procedures for your students.
- Set parameters for time.
- Build in opportunities for feedback.
- What should the final product be? How will you evaluate it?
- Identify how and when students should, can, or must use their fellow students, teachers, and parents as resources.
- Make sure you try everything yourself first.

WebQuests

WebQuests have become one of the most popular learning experiences using the Internet in all areas of education. There is a wealth of support information on the Internet and music teachers can use this medium to create interactive and exciting web lessons.

> **Teaching Strategy 159**
> Teachers design music-related WebQuest activities for students.

A WebQuest, as defined by Bernie Dodge of San Diego State University, is an inquiry-oriented activity in which some or all of the information that learners interact with comes from resources on the Internet. WebQuests are designed to bring together the most effective instructional practices into one integrated student activity. A WebQuest is a type of well-organized scavenger hunt using the World Wide Web as the medium. Some excellent sites to learn about WebQuests include:

San Diego State University . . . . .http://webquest.sdsu.edu/
Best WebQuests . . . . .www.bestwebquests.com/
Kathy Schrock . . . . .http://kathyschrock.net/webquests/

Some examples of music WebQuests that are posted on the Internet are:

Radio Days—A WebQuest . . .www.thematzats.com/radio/index.html
A Mozart WebQuest
http://www.spa3.k12.sc.us/WebQuests/mozart/Travel%20log.html

A WebQuest has five distinct areas. These include introduction, task, process, resources, evaluation, and conclusion. The introduction should include an engaging first statement that draws the reader in while setting the stage for the WebQuest. It is the guiding or central question around which the WebQuest revolves.

The second part is the task. This should include a description of the end result of the students' work: the culminating performance or product that drives all the activities in the WebQuest. This can be in the form of a series of questions that must be answered or a problem to be solved.

The third part is the process and this should include a step-by-step description of how the learners will accomplish the tasks. It typically includes online and offline resources and guidance on individual steps in the process.

The resources section includes a detailed description of any physical resources needed to implement the lesson. The list should include some web addresses of pages to be used in the WebQuest.

The fifth section is the evaluation. Here a specific way to evaluate the final task is defined. The evaluation may include rubrics or tests to measure competencies and accomplishment:

The last section of the WebQuest is the conclusion. This typically would include reflections and a summary of the lesson and/or ideas for further exploration.

You can create your own WebQuests, or go out to the Web and search for ones that have been authored by other music teachers. Sometimes these can be used as-is and can be a very time saving technique.

Check out some of the sample music webquests on Bill Bauer's site devoted to this area: http://homepage.mac.com/wbauer/atmi2000/.

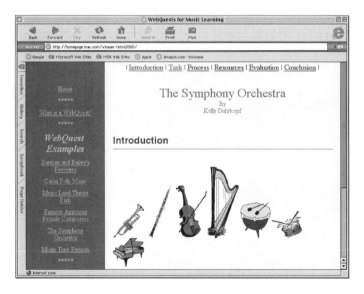

Figure 11.9: Bill Bauer's music WebQuest page
(http://homepage.mac.com/wbauer/atmi2000/)

Capturing Web Sites on Your Computer's Hard Drive

If you don't have access to the web in your classroom or music studio, but would like to display information from a particular site, capturing web sites is an option. You can capture portions or entire web sites on your computer's hard drive to use in class.

When you are connected to the Internet, you can capture the text, graphics, and media files to your hard drive. After the information is copied, the web site is available on the computer's hard drive and can be accessed offline. This is referred to as an offline copy of a web site. Using Microsoft Internet Explorer, it is as simple as choosing Save As from the File menu. Then select Web Archive.

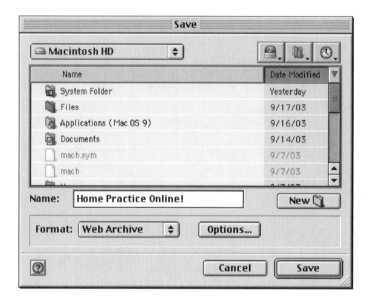

Figure 11.10: Saving a web archive using Internet Explorer

When copying web sites to your hard drive, it is important to click on the Options button and check the media types to download. Typically, I would check all of the media types to download to the computers hard drive.

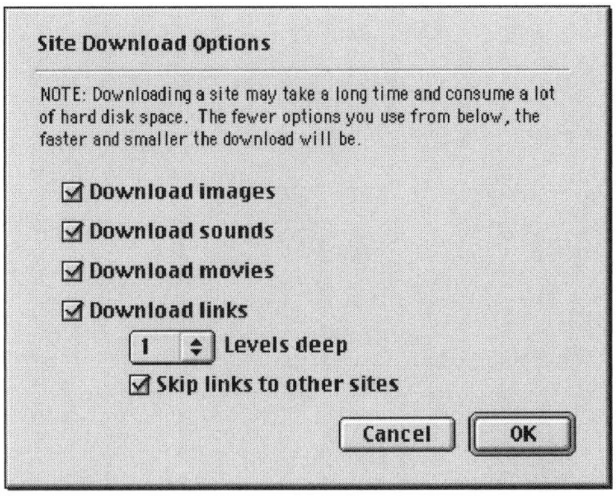

Site Download Options

NOTE: Downloading a site may take a long time and consume a lot of hard disk space. The fewer options you use from below, the faster and smaller the download will be.

☑ **Download images**
☑ **Download sounds**
☑ **Download movies**
☑ **Download links**
    [1] [▲▼] Levels deep
    ☑ Skip links to other sites

[Cancel] [OK]

Figure 11.11: Selecting the Site Download Options in Internet Explorer

If you have an active web connection in your classroom, this option is not necessary, but it is a good way to archive information for later use. One advantage to capturing web sites on your hard drive and accessing them offline is that you can control the content students can access.

Authoring Web Pages

School web pages are now the norm and music department web pages are becoming more and more common. Web pages can be created by teachers to provide information to students and parents. Students can author web pages to create multimedia projects and post them on the World Wide Web.

> **Teaching Strategy 160**
> Develop a music department web page as an information source for students and parents.

Jeff Waggoner lists the many advantages to creating a music department web site. His site is "...designed as a communications tool for students, parents, the community, and the world."[8] Teachers can post information that relates to the curriculum being studied.

Students can learn to create web pages using HTML (Hyper-Text Markup Language) and software designed to make the web page creation process easier. These programs are called HTML editors and will be described later in this chapter.

323

Creating Web Pages the Quick and Easy Way

The fastest and easiest way to create a web page is to use word processing or presentation software that has the capability to save a project or presentation in HTML format or saved as a web page. This is an option if you or your students want to convert a project to post on the school web site and there is no time to learn how to create a web page using HTML code or an HTML editor. Microsoft Word, AppleWorks, and other software programs have this built-in capability.

HTML Code and HTML Editors

Primarily, there are two ways to generate the code that is used to display text, graphics, movies, and sound on Internet web pages. This code is called HTML (hypertext markup language). You can learn to type HTML code or you can use an HTML editor to create the code.

Serious web authors recommend that students learn the commands of HTML and enter the code themselves. However, for teachers and students there is an alternative that is easier to learn. Use an HTML editor that acts more like a word processor.

HTML Editors

Most HTML editors cost from $100 on up. However, there is a free HTML editor called Netscape Communicator from www.netscape.com. This program is a free HTML editor and it works on Macintosh and Windows computers. Students and teachers can use this free program to create multimedia rich web pages.

HTML editors also are sold commercially. I recommend Microsoft FrontPage for Windows and Macintosh. FrontPage is used by many schools and includes a lot of multimedia applications. Another excellent HTML editor is DreamWeaver by Macromedia for Macintosh and Windows. This is a powerful HTML editor. There is a special education version of the program and lots of educational materials that can be downloaded from Macromedia's web site.

Which HTML editor to choose? Check with your school technology department and see what they recommend. Often, the school already has web design software that the music department can use for teacher and student use.

Teacher Web Sites

If creating your own web site using an HTML editor is not in your future, there are several companies who offer teacher web site hosting, usually for a small annual fee. An example of this type of site is www.teacherweb.com. Teachers can use online tools to post text and references to web sites. Typically, these sites do not support a lot of multimedia elements, but it is a good way to get a site up and running for information and communication with students and parents.

Instructional Applications via the Web

On school web pages, many teachers include instructional materials for students in addition to information and performance calendars. The Technology Institute for Music Educators (TI:ME) web site has a wealth of projects. Check them out at www.ti-me.org/projects.htm. One of my favorites is Scott Watson's practice online web page, where he includes sound files of the pieces being rehearsed by his elementary band.

Teachers are using the web to enhance music learning. Review the list of instructional web sites on the companion CD-ROM to explore more of these innovative applications of the World Wide Web.

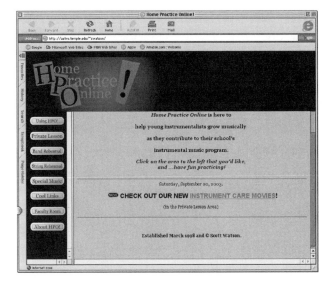

Figure 11.12: Scott Watson's Home Practice Online
(http://astro.temple.edu/~swatson)

Web and Copyright

Items that display on a web site are usually covered by international copyright. Refer to Chapter 16 for an in-depth review of this important issue.

Summary

There are many advantages to multimedia applications. Both students and teachers can use multimedia as a tool to create a variety of materials. There are many ways to integrate multimedia into the music curriculum. Multimedia can be a teacher's tool and a productive application that can be used by students. There are different levels of multimedia authoring tools that can be used including word processors, presentation software, and multimedia authoring tools. An understanding of file formats is necessary when working with this medium. No matter what area of multimedia is selected, both students and teachers will find it to be a most useful tool for a wide range of educational applications.

Review Questions

1. Define multimedia.
2. List several advantages and disadvantages of multimedia for teachers and students.
3. What are the three main uses of multimedia?
4. List the three types of multimedia tools.
5. Define the term file type and list three different examples.
6. What are the common formats of graphic files?
7. Describe the various ways to capture graphics that are displayed on a computer screen (referred to as screen capture).
8. List the most common formats for digital video.
9. What is the most common program for creating computer animations?
10. What is file compression? Why is it useful when working with digital video and digital audio?
11. What is needed to convert MIDI files to audio for burning to a CD?
12. List two or more student multimedia projects using a word processor.
13. List two or more student multimedia applications using presentation software.

14. What is Kid Pix? Describe how it might be used for music learning.
15. What is HyperStudio? Describe how it might be used for music learning.
16. What is a WebQuest? Describe how it might be used for music learning.
17. Where can a teacher find information about creating a WebQuest?
18. What is HTML?
19. What is the advantage to using an HTML editor?
20. How are Internet web pages being used for instructional purposes? Give two examples of web sites appropriate for elementary or secondary music students.

CD-ROM activities

- Project 11.1 Go to one of the web links listed in this project and download the picture to your computer's drive. Next, place it in a word processing program or other multimedia software program of your choice.
- Project 11.2 Use a scanner or digital camera to capture a picture. Open it and edit it in a drawing or picture editing software program. Edit the picture to include cropping, resizing, and changing the brightness and contrast.
- Project 11.3 Using one of the graphic and sound files on the CD-ROM, create a multimedia project by combining text, sound, and graphics. Use any multimedia capable multimedia software such as Microsoft Word, AppleWorks, PowerPoint, and other appropriate programs.
- Project 11.4. Create a presentation using Microsoft PowerPoint, Apple Keynote, or other presentation software. The presentation should include text, graphics, and sound.
- Project 11.5: Using a word processor such as Microsoft Word or AppleWorks create a file that includes text and graphics. Save it as a web page. Open the saved web page in a web browser. Brainstorm ways this could be used in the music classroom.

CD-ROM Tutorials and Lesson Plans

- Tutorial 11.1 How to convert a MIDI/audio file to QuickTime
- Tutorial 11.2 Creating a web page using HTML
- Tutorial 11.3 Creating a web page using Macromedia Dreamweaver
- Tutorial 11.4 How to crop and resize a picture using Microsoft Word
- Tutorial 11.5 How to capture music notation in graphic format

Reference

Dodge, Bernie. *Some thoughts about WebQuests*. San Diego State University http://edweb.sdsu.edu/courses/edtec596/about_webquests.html.

Bauer, William (2000) *WebQuests for music learning*. Association for Technology in Music Instruction Conference. November 2-5, 2000 Toronto.

Robinette, Michelle. (1995) *Mac multimedia for teachers*. IDG Books Worldwide. Foster City, CA.

Langol, S. et al (1999) TI:ME 2C: Integrating technology into the music curriculum. TI:ME, Wyncote, PA..

Pew Internet and American Life Project (2002, August 14) The digital disconnect: The widening gap between Internet-savvy students and their schools. Retrieved August 20, 2002 from http://www.pewinternet.org/reports/toc.asp?Report=67.

Mash, David S. (1998) *Musicians and multimedia*. Warner Bros. Publications. Miami.

Waleson, Heidi (1994) *Interactive Beethoven, digital Stravinsky*. The Wall Street Journal, April 12, pg. A16.

Bonaiuto, Susan et al (2003). Grant application to United States Department of Education, Office of Innovation and Improvement -- FY03 Arts in Education Model Development and Dissemination Grant Program. *Improved student achievement through multimedia teaching and learning*. TI:ME, Wyncote, PA.

Fenton, Kevin. (1998). Using multimedia to develop musicianship. *Music Educators Journal*, September, pages 27-32.

Kuzmich, John (2000). Building your own web page. *School Band and Orchestra Magazine*. January.

Kuzmich, John (2003). Web development series: guide to graphic editor software applications. *School Band and Orchestra Magazine*.

Sebald, David (1997). Web your program: an internet primer for music educators. *Choral Journal (37)* 9, 9-14

Simkins, Michael; Cole, Karen; and Tavalin, Fern. (2002) *Increasing student learning through multimedia projects*. Association for Supervision & Curriculum Development, Alexandria, VA.

Chapter 12

Electronic Keyboard Labs

Music Education National Standards 1, 3, 4, 5
NETS (National Educational Technology Standards): 1, 2, 3, 4

Chapter 4 dealt with selecting an electronic keyboard and basic applications of keyboards in the classroom and rehearsal hall. This chapter explores the concept of integrating an entire lab of electronic keyboards and computers into the music curriculum.

The Wurlitzer Design

Educational electronic keyboard labs are not new. School districts have been using electronic keyboard labs for more than 40 years. The Wurlitzer Company introduced the concept of an electronic keyboard lab to music education in the 1960s. Although the Wurlitzer Company no longer sells classroom keyboard labs, it was one of the first companies to recognize the power of a classroom of electronic keyboards. Many school districts and colleges purchased Wurlitzer keyboard labs and some are still in use today.

You may have experienced a Wurlitzer lab as a child. The Wurlitzer lab was designed so that each student had his or her own keyboard. Headphones were used to control the sound output and to permit each student to practice without disturbing others in the lab. The next key component of the Wurlitzer lab was the use of a teacher controller, a console that connected each station to the teacher. The teacher could listen to each student, communicate with individuals, small groups, or the entire class using a micro-phone and headset.

Figure 12.1: Teacher station with a classroom controller

Lab Applications

Today's keyboard labs are more powerful and far less expensive than the 1960s labs. Thanks to the emergence of inexpensive electronic keyboards, MIDI, and computers, keyboard labs can be configured to offer much more than group piano instruction. Applications include composition (notation), recording (sequencing and digital audio), practice, performance, computer-assisted instruction, and multimedia. Imagine being able to use and explore some or all of the options presented in Chapters 4-11 in a classroom MIDI keyboard lab and computer setting.

New Tools

If a single MIDI keyboard provides "crayons" for the music class, then a MIDI keyboard lab resembles the art room with a station for each child to paint, color, and create. Technology is used to involve students in the learning process and provide them with a medium to experience higher level thinking skills such as creativity and composition.

I view MIDI keyboards and especially the MIDI keyboard lab as the music student's primary creative tool. Students become active learners using this medium that, in their own words, is "cool" and offers unlimited musical experiences. Students become more enthusiastic about music class when they are actively involved in the learning process. I also have found that electronic keyboards provide the proper medium for exploring the areas of creativity and improvisation.

A MIDI keyboard lab can serve many different purposes. It can provide performance instruments in the classroom, allow teaching of piano pedagogy, and, with the appropriate hardware and software, provide students with a medium to compose, arrange, and create music.

Tools for Classroom Music

After a few years of teaching only instrumental music at the middle school level, I was asked to teach several sections of general classroom music. The curriculum at the time would best be described as lecture format: primarily the teacher talked and the students listened. I also found that overall students had negative feelings about music class. When asked, they frequently responded that, "music class is boring." It became obvious to me that I needed to find a way to transform general music into a more exciting place and to involve students more in the learning process. I also wanted to maintain the curriculum of teaching students about music history, music reading, and performance.

Figure 12.2: Student listening to the sounds of an electronic keyboard

The answer for me was to explore the possibility of a MIDI lab to provide hands-on learning for my students. After spending some time reviewing the options, I was able to raise the needed funds for my first MIDI lab. Chapter 17 presents a variety of strategies for procuring the necessary funding for a MIDI lab. After teaching middle school classroom music in a MIDI lab for more than 10 years, I can't imagine teaching without it. If I lost my MIDI keyboard lab for some reason I'd put a mortgage on my house or sell a car to get it back. Seriously!

Student-owned Instruments

Interestingly enough, when I was first exploring ideas for integrating MIDI keyboards into the curriculum, I found that many of my students had electronic keyboards at home. Because many of my students had keyboards of their own, I decided to try an experiment. I invited students to bring in their instruments to school for an after-school electronic keyboard class. A significant number of students volunteered. For the most part, we spent time learning how to use the features on each student's instrument. Having as many different brands of keyboards as there were students in the class certainly presented a challenge. I chose to teach them the basic operation of their instrument, since many only knew how to play the keyboard's "demo." Once students were familiar with their individual instrument's operation, I began to teach them to play simple melodies. I found that students enjoyed performing together as a group and learning to operate their keyboards.

This experience convinced me to pursue the addition of a keyboard lab in my middle school. It was relatively easy to convince school administrators of the benefits of a keyboard lab because they could see and hear the benefits for themselves before they committed any funds.

Setting the Goals

Before determining the configuration of your MIDI lab, be clear about how it will be used. Is it going to be for general music at the middle school or elementary level? Is it a high school lab that will be used by students of many ability levels? Is it a lab for a university setting primarily geared toward teaching functional piano? Is it a place where composition will be explored?

Once the goals are established, then the proper lab equipment can be selected. You may want to visit schools that are already using labs for some ideas. You can visit the web sites of companies who specialist in keyboard labs including www.soundtree.com, www.lentine.com, www.yamaha.com, and www.rolandus.com.

Selecting the Equipment (Hardware)

MIDI keyboard labs represent a significant investment, and you will want to be certain that the correct lab has been selected from the many options available. As reviewed in Chapter 4, there are many models and types of MIDI keyboards and they each have strong and weak points. Choose the keyboard model carefully. Start with a thorough reading of Chapter 4. Next, visit local stores and other school districts to get hands-on experience with several types of keyboards. Music educator state, regional, and national conferences are another excellent venue to evaluate MIDI keyboards.

Number of Keyboards to Purchase

To decide how many keyboards to purchase, first, determine the maximum number of student stations that are needed. Do you need one station per student or can students work in pairs? What is the maximum class size you will be required to teach in the lab? If students are grouped two per keyboard, it reduces by half the total number of keyboards needed for a lab. As a general rule, I recommend purchasing one station per student. The teacher will also require a station for demonstration and to communicate with students. For a maximum class size of thirty students, there will need to be a total of 31 stations, which includes one for the teacher.

Lab Options

With so many MIDI lab possibilities, I have organized them into three types:

- Option #1: MIDI keyboards only. The primary activity is playing the MIDI keyboard in a variety of activities. (Lowest cost: $15,000-$25,000.)

- Option #2: MIDI keyboards with built-in sequencers or digital pianos connected to an external MIDI sequencer. With the addition of the MIDI sequencer, students can play the keyboards and use the MIDI sequencer for practice and composition. (Moderate cost: $25,000-$40,000.)

- Option #3: A MIDI keyboard and a computer at every student station. This option offers the most options. Everything in options 1 and 2 is included. In addition, since each station contains a Macintosh or Windows computer connected to the MIDI keyboard software applications can be added such as music notation, computer-assisted instruction, MIDI sequencing, digital audio, and multimedia. In other words, all of the options described in Chapters 4-11 in this book can be included in a lab setting for an entire class of students. (Highest cost: $50,000-$70,000 or more depending upon features.)

Each of these options will serve some students better than others. They also each require different budget allocations.

The Lab Controller

At the beginning of this chapter, the original Wurlitzer electronic keyboard lab design was mentioned. One of the main components of this lab was a unit that connected all of the keyboards in the lab together and permitted the teacher to monitor and communicate with individual students. This unit is usually referred to as a group controller and is an essential part of any electronic keyboard lab.

> **Teaching Strategy 161**
> Include a classroom controller to interconnect all of the keyboards in the classroom.

Group controllers are designed to be used by the teacher to help facilitate instruction in the lab. The keyboards are connected to a central unit. Today's typical lab controller allows the teacher to communicate with individual students, groups, and the entire class. Other devices, like CD players, can be connected to the controller.

With a group controller in the lab, teachers can play examples for the class and listen in as each student practices on their instrument. Also, lab controllers permit teachers to group students together to practice and perform duets and quartets. Most manufacturers, including Korg, Roland, and Yamaha, offer group controllers for their labs. Lab controller units usually allow for 16 keyboards to be connected and some are expandable to 32 stations.

Be sure to include a controller in your lab planning. Without a controller, it is difficult to monitor student work and impossible to communicate with the entire class for lecture, performance, and sharing activities. There are several models from which to choose including the Yamaha MCL11, the Technics SX-ECSLC2, Lentine's Music MEDIA Lab Controller 16, and the Korg GEC3.

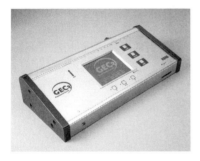

Figure 12.4: Korg's GEC3 Group Education Controller

Figure 12.5: Yamaha's MCL100 group piano controller

Lab Furniture

It is important to include the purchase of appropriate ergonomically designed furniture on which to place the keyboards. Simply putting them on cafeteria-style tables is not recommended. Companies such as Wenger and OmniRax offer customized tables that can be used in the MIDI lab. Be sure to purchase appropriate furniture that can be expanded should you decide to add additional instruments and/or equipment to the lab.

Figure 12.6: Wenger lab furniture

Figure 12.7: Omni-Rax music lab furniture

Vendor Assistance

Regardless of the lab option selected, I strongly recommend working with a company that specializes in the delivery, installation, and support of MIDI labs. You can piece together all of the parts of the lab yourself, but the installation and support required by a MIDI lab is significant. There are several companies who offer MIDI lab hardware including SoundTree, Yamaha, Roland, Brook Mays, Lentine's Music, and others. Check with other educators who have MIDI labs and get their advice. Maintaining a MIDI lab is no small task, and having assistance at the installation and during ongoing use is extremely important.

LAB OPTION #1:
MIDI Keyboards in a Lab Setting

The least expensive lab option is to purchase a lab of electronic keyboards and one controller. This lab can be used at the elementary, secondary, and college levels. The keyboards can be installed in the classroom using keyboard stands and/or using customized keyboard lab furniture.

Elementary/Middle School–MIDI Keyboards

When considering lab Option #1, MIDI keyboards at the elementary level, consider creating a lab using portable electronic keyboards (see Chapter 4). Portable keyboards are easy to use and offer some excellent options for younger students. You will need to select curriculum materials. Examples of curricular materials are reviewed later in this chapter.

A second option for the elementary/middle school level is Yamaha's Music in Education (MIE) lab, designed specifically to be used in the general music classroom. Yamaha introduced a new, upgraded version in 2000. MIE has the most complete curriculum of any electronic keyboard lab available today. The MIE lab comes as a complete package—16 keyboards, software, and curriculum. The school must supply one Macintosh computer to control the lab. The cost of the lab is $14,900 for 16 keyboards. However, because the keyboards are designed to be used by two students at a time, a class of up to 32 students can be easily accommodated. This lab has been in existence for years and the many schools that have purchased it have reported very positive results. The curriculum consists of several years worth of integrated lessons. If you choose the Yamaha Musician in Education (MIE) lab, the teacher station is already designed by Yamaha with complete software for the lab. All you need to supply is a Macintosh or Windows computer. MIE is geared toward teaching musical concepts. The goal is for students to visually and aurally identify concepts and then apply that concept to a creative endeavor.

> **Teaching Strategy 162**
>
> At the elementary and middle school levels, consider the Music In Education lab and curriculum from Yamaha. It is a complete, multi-year curriculum designed for elementary and middle school level students. For more information go to www.musicineducation.com.

Middle School/High School/ College – MIDI Keyboard Lab

The Option #1 lab at the secondary and college level can take two distinct paths. First, it can be centered on a programmable keyboard or synthesizer (see Chapter 4). Students can perform on the instruments and create and edit sound using the programmable functions of the keyboard. The primary function of this lab is playing and performing on the MIDI keyboard.

The second option is to focus on basic piano skills and choose a digital piano with weighted keys (see Chapter 4). These keyboards emulate the feel of an acoustic piano.

I have worked with some secondary schools and colleges who start with Option #1 with the goal of adding computers or other equipment to take it to the next level in later years. This can be an excellent way to get started at a lower cost to your institution. Keep this in mind if you find that funds are insufficient for the higher priced lab options.

Teacher Station

The teacher station for Option #1 should include the same keyboard model used by the students. In addition, I highly recommend that the teacher station include a Macintosh or Windows computer connected via MIDI. The computer should be equipped with MIDI sequencing and notation software. The computer can be used to generate accompaniments for student practice and performance. It also can serve as the teacher's tool for many activities such as keeping student records and printing notation.

LAB OPTION #2:
MIDI Keyboard Workstations with
Built-in Sequencers and Other Recording Capabilities

The key difference with Option #2 is that instead of just keyboards, workstations are used. A workstation is an electronic keyboard with recording capabilities via a MIDI sequencer. Typically, a keyboard workstation would also be the instrument of choice in Option #3 (see Chapter 4). Korg, Roland, and Yamaha offer a variety of workstations. With a workstation, students can load and save files, and use the built-in recording device as a practice and composition tool.

The workstation MIDI sequencer is a bit more difficult to use than software sequencers using a computer (see Chapter 8). The display screen on a keyboard workstation is smaller than a computer and using the built-in sequencing software takes some time to learn. The advantage is that students and teacher have access to MIDI sequencing without the cost of computers at every station.

Teacher Station

The teacher station should have the same keyboard model as the students. In addition, the teacher station should also be connected to a computer via MIDI. The computer should be loaded with sequencing software, accompaniment software such as Band-in-a-Box, and a notation program such as Finale or Sibelius. The software will enable the teacher to create demonstration and practice accompaniments and to print music notation examples.

Figure 12.7: Teacher station equipped with keyboard and computer

LAB OPTION #3:
MIDI Keyboards and Computers at Each Student Station

The significant difference with this option is the addition of a Macintosh or Windows computer connected to *every* keyboard in the lab. The advantage is being able to incorporate computer software applications in the lab in addition to piano performance. This can include any or all of the applications discussed throughout this book including computer-assisted instruction, sequencing, notation, and multimedia. The trade off is that this type of lab is expensive.

Figure 12.8: Student lab equipped with MIDI keyboards and computers

Lab Summary

Specific Keyboard Models

Regardless of lab configuration, choose the best keyboard for the applications that you plan to integrate into the lab. Especially consider portable keyboards at the elementary level, programmable synthesizers or, if the emphasis is on teaching piano skills, digital pianos at the secondary level. See Chapter 4 for references on specific models and keyboard options.

Teacher Station

The teacher station should have the same keyboard as each student station plus a computer. Ideally, the teacher station should also include a computer projector to display the computer image for the entire class.

Total Lab Cost

The major vendors, SoundTree, Yamaha, Roland, Brook Mayes, and Lentines, all offer a variety of lab and financing options. General price ranges for each of the lab options are listed below. The estimates include the group controller, cables, and headphones. Pricing will differ significantly depending on the model of keyboard, software, and other features. Contact two or more lab vendors for specific detailed estimates and be sure to include all of the recommended gear previously mentioned in this chapter. Although the price tags may seem very high, there are ways to procure the necessary funds which are discussed in Chapter 17.

> **Option #1**: 17 stations–MIDI keyboards (16 student and one teacher) with furniture, teacher's station also includes a computer. Cost range: $14,900 - $25,000.

> **Option #2**: 17 stations–MIDI keyboard workstations (16 student and one teacher) with furniture, teacher's station also includes a computer. Cost range: $25,000-$40,000.

> **Option #3**: 17 stations–MIDI keyboards and computers (16 student and one teacher) with furniture, teacher's station also includes a computer. Cost range: $50,000-$70,000.

Developing the Curriculum

The second area to consider when purchasing a MIDI lab is curriculum. You can develop your own or adopt a new one. In this section, I will review each lab option and list some possible curriculum applications. I recommend developing the curriculum activities by referencing the MENC National Standards.[1] These standards are:

MENC National Standards:

1. Singing, alone and with others, a varied repertoire of music
2. Performing on instruments, alone and with others, a varied repertoire of music
3. Improvising melodies, harmonies, and accompaniments
4. Composing and arranging music within specified guidelines
5. Reading and notating music
6. Listening to, analyzing, and describing music
7. Evaluating music and music performances
8. Understanding relationships between music, the other arts, and disciplines outside the arts
9. Understanding music in relation to history and culture

Curriculum Options for Lab Option #1:

Performing (Standards #1, #2), Reading (Standard #5), and Evaluating (Standard #7)

At the elementary level, keyboards can be used to perform single line melodies. As soon as students are able to play melodies on their electronic keyboards, musical notation can be introduced. Students can learn to read and play simple five-note diatonic patterns and melodies such as Mary Had a Little Lamb and Lightly Row.

There are also keyboard methods available for the electronic keyboard. Alfred's Electronic Keyboards course is one method that could be used.

Teaching Strategy 163

Use a beginning keyboard method designed for use with portable electronic keyboards.

Most electronic keyboards are capable of producing percussion sounds. Each key on the instrument takes on the sound a different percussion instrument. Students enjoy playing percussion sounds. Many activities can be included in the curriculum that employ percussion performance on the electronic keyboard.

> ### Teaching Strategy 164
> Use the electronic keyboard's capability of generating percussion sounds to help students perform rhythmically (i.e. steady beat).

The keyboard's percussion sounds can be used to help students play a steady beat, accompany each other while playing songs, and other rhythm-oriented activities. Students enjoy learning to play drum beats and patterns.

Listening/Analyzing (Standard #6) and History (Standard #9)

Because even the least expensive electronic keyboards offer a wide variety of sounds, usually 100 or more, students can experiment with different timbres.

> ### Teaching Strategy 165
> Encourage students to explore the many sounds their instrument is capable of producing to help them understand the concept of timbre.

Allow students to choose any timbre for a piece they are learning to play. Consider asking them to change timbres for different phrases or sections of a song to help them understand form. For example, students could select a brass sound for the A section and a string sound for the B section, then return to the brass sound for the A section. Students can also group sounds by instrument families and, in many cases, vary and alter the parameters of the sound. Most keyboards have some ethnic instrument sounds such as steel drums and bag pipes. These instrument sounds can be used as a vehicle for discussing different cultures and their indigenous instruments.

Improvising (Standard #3) and Composing Music (Standard #4)

Many electronic keyboards can create automatic rhythms and chordal accompaniments. After learning to play a melody, students can program their instrument to play an accompaniment.

Teaching Strategy 166

Use the auto bass/chord/rhythm function of the keyboard to create accompaniments for improvisations.

Teach students some basic chord functions such as tonic and dominant, and then ask them to improvise a melody. Initially, it is helpful to limit their compositions to the first five notes of the scale.

Teaching Strategy 167

Have students compose simple melodies based on the first five notes of the scale and then record them using their own keyboard.

After composing a song, students can record it using the keyboard record function and share their piece with other members of the class.

These are just a sampling of ideas for building an Option #1 lab in the curriculum. As you begin to incorporate electronic keyboards, you will find more and more ways to use them.

Performing (Standards #1, #2), Reading (Standard #5), and Evaluating (Standard #7)

In an Option #1 lab at the secondary level, performing and reading activities can be expanded.

> ### Teaching Strategy 168
> When teaching a general music unit, such as the Baroque era, students can learn to play melodies from the period.

In sixth grade general music class, I teach a Baroque music unit. Students spend time in the keyboard lab learning to play the opening theme to Bach's Toccata in D Minor and the melody from Handel's "Hail the Conquering Hero." I try to chose appealing melodies that suit the ability level of the students. Students are usually more willing to listen to and learn about compositions that they have experienced on the keyboard. Classical themes can also be introduced such as the "Ode to Joy" from Beethoven's 9th Symphony and the theme from Dvorak's *New World Symphony*. In this way a wide variety of repertoire can be introduced. Students also enjoy learning to play simple pop melodies such as Led Zeppelin's "Stairway to Heaven" and "With a Little Help from My Friends" by the Beatles.

> ### Teaching Strategy 169
> Use electronic keyboards to teach basic piano skills. Consider using an electronic keyboard method book.

There are several electronic keyboard courses on the market designed for the beginning piano student. Publishers such as Alfred, Belwin, Neil Kjos, and others offer materials designed for group piano instruction.

> ### Teaching Strategy 170
> Use the teacher-station computer to generate a recorded accompaniment for students practice and performance.

From the teacher station, generate an accompaniment with which the students can perform. Students can practice and perform while listening to the recorded accompaniment part. Using an accompaniment not only makes the simple melodies more interesting, it also helps the kids learn to play in tempo. The teacher can slow the tempo down at first and increase it as the class becomes more adept at playing the melody.

> **Teaching Strategy 171**
> When the lab has a teacher controller, students can be grouped in pairs and quartets to practice and perform in chamber groups.

After learning to play melodies alone and with a recorded accompaniment, students can then begin to play in small ensembles. Most lab controllers allow for student stations to be grouped together in duets or quartets. Bach chorales or other pieces can be rehearsed and performed in chamber groups.

Improvising (Standard #3) and Composing Music (Standard #4)

As student's knowledge and skills improve, they can create more complex improvisations. As students learn left hand chords, they can improvise harmony parts. Some educators feel it is better for students to play and perform chords of various qualities rather than drilling students on the spelling and identification of triads.[2] In the keyboard lab, composition and improvisation can be encouraged.

Curriculum Ideas for Lab Option #2 (Electronic Keyboards with MIDI Sequencers)

Option #2 labs support all of the previously mentioned activities. The enhancement is that each student station has its own MIDI sequencer (see Chapter 8). This means that students can load MIDI files with which to play along and they can use the sequencer to create even complex compositions and arrangements. Since many keyboards now include a built-in sequencer, students can use their sequences as a performance and composition tool.

Performing (Standards #1, #2), Reading (Standard #5), and Evaluating (Standard #7)

There are many piano method books that are written with older beginners in mind.

Teaching Strategy 172

Use an older beginner piano method to teach basic piano to secondary and college level students.

Using an adult piano method such as Sandy Feldstein's *Adult Piano Method*, published by Belwin, or the *Adult All-in-One Course* by Alfred, can be successful in the secondary and college level keyboard lab. Using an adult keyboard method, students can begin to learn basic piano in the keyboard lab.

Teaching Strategy 173

Use Standard MIDI files to act as an accompanist for students when they practice pieces on the keyboard.

Many publishers offer Standard MIDI files that can be used by students for practice and composition. For example, Hal Leonard publishes a selection of Standard MIDI files including Fantasia—a selection of pieces from the movies, Broadway Hits, and the Best of the Beatles. Each collection of songs in Standard MIDI format can be purchased for $29.95. If a copy is purchased for each student station, students can load the disk into their sequencer and play along and practice individually. Using these pre-recorded songs students can learn to play with a steady tempo.

Listening/Analyzing (Standard #6) and History (Standard #9)

Sequencers can be used to analyze music from various time periods.

> **Teaching Strategy 174**
>
> Using Standard MIDI files, allow students to manipulate the parts, i.e.
> re-orchestrate the piece, add new introductions and endings, etc.

For example, if you purchase Hal Leonard's Fantasia Standard MIDI files, students can listen to Bach's *Toccata* and *Fugue in D Minor* and analyze the form, tonality, orchestration, and other aspects of the piece. In addition, students can re-orchestrate the composition, including adding ritards and crescendos to the piece. Remember how exciting it was when you first listened to the recording Switched on Bach by W. Carlos? This recording was an updated re-orchestration of Bach's music. Students can create their own unique versions of music in a Switched on Bach manner, re-orchestrating and arranging music with the sequencer.

If the lab contains a programmable keyboard or a sound module, students can experiment with all the properties of sound.

> **Teaching Strategy 175**
>
> Use programmable keyboards, workstations, or sound modules to help
> students discover and alter the properties of sound.

Don Muro[4] describes several ways to use a workstation and computer lab to experience the properties of sound. Muro suggests taking each property of sound, beginning with pitch, timbre, and loudness, and asking students to find an extremely high and an extremely low sound on their keyboard. The lab gives every student a place to select and create their own low and high sound. Timbre can be demonstrated using the many sounds on every keyboard. Students can alter the sound to change the timbre in original ways.

In the area of sound and sound properties, an excellent resource is the text *Fundamentals of Music Technology* by Mauricio and Adams. This text helps students understand the basic concepts of music synthesis. It can be particularly useful in the secondary classroom.

Improvising (Standard #3) and Composing Music (Standard #4)

Using the built-in sequencer, students can manipulate compositions in a way that is not possible with any other medium. In the SoundTree *General Music Curriculum*, I wrote 11 units that use the sequencer to give students control over the musical elements and to let students experience music in creative, unique ways. The lessons require that all stations have access to a sequencer or computer running sequencing software. I wrote the curriculum with the MENC National Standards in mind and they are organized into the areas of performing, arranging/creating, and composing. The curriculum is published by SoundTree.

Lessons number one and two center around Bach's D Minor two-part invention. The students load a MIDI file into their sequencers. First, students learn to start and stop the sequencer. The lesson then requires them to interact with the music.

> ### Teaching Strategy 176
> Load a MIDI file into each student's sequencer and allow them to become the conductor by changing the tempo and creating ritards and accelerandos.

Students are asked to alter the tempo. They also enter a ritard at the end and a slight accelerando at the beginning. The teacher can then share each person's piece using the group controller.

After experimenting with tempo, students change the timbre of their keyboard but are asked to include each of the instrument families. For example, one student group may choose to change the timbre of the invention every phrase. In this manner, students make the orchestration their own and actually manipulate the musical elements.

> ### Teaching Strategy 177
> Students compose their own original improvisations and compositions using a sequencer.

With a sequencer, students can create improvisations and save their performances to disk. Lesson 10 in the SoundTree *General Music Curriculum* involves playing a jazz 12-bar blues progression and learning to improvise using the blues scale. Students can improvise and practice along with the recorded sequence. Then, when they are ready, they save a performance to disk and play it back for themselves and others. After improvising patterns, chords, and melodies, students can begin to compose their own compositions. The sequencer is their own personal recording studio where they can experiment and adapt their composition to suit their own personal taste.

Curriculum Ideas for Lab Option #3: A MIDI Keyboard and a Computer at Every Station

With lab Option #3, a computer is connected to the keyboard at each student station. All of the above applications can be realized in this lab, plus there are several significant new possibilities using the computers.

Listening/Analyzing (Standard #6) and History (Standard #9)

First, each student can use CAI packages at their own station.

Teaching Strategy 178

Now that computers are connected to each student station in the lab, consider adding one or more CAI programs for each station.

Students can be assigned different programs according to their ability levels. For example, a beginning student might be working with software to improve knowledge of note names while an advanced student is concentrating on intervals or chord recognition. Other software can be selected to address specific student needs.

Improvising (Standard #3)
and Composing Music (Standard #4)

Music composition is enhanced when a computer is added to the electronic keyboard. A software sequencer, as explained in Chapter 5, is quick and clear so students can more easily make changes in timbre, tempi, and just about any parameter of an arrangement.

Teaching Strategy 179

Consider adopting a curriculum designed to be used with computers and keyboards. An example is the SoundTree *General Music Curriculum*.

In the SoundTree *General Music Curriculum*, students are asked to copy and paste the melody Are You Sleeping to create a round. Then they are asked to add chords and other notes to embellish the arrangement, thus creating an original version of the song.

Figure 12.9: The SoundTree *General Music Curriculum*

With computers, students can use a notation program to write and print out music notation.

> **Teaching Strategy 180**
>
> Consider adding a notation program to the lab curriculum when computers are in place at each student station.

A notation program lets students notate and print out songs, arrangements, and complete orchestral compositions. All of the notation options mentioned in Chapter 7 can be applied in the lab with computers connected to each keyboard. High school and college level students could use a notation program to print out scores and parts. Elementary and middle school students can use a program to print out melodies, simple compositions, and arrangements of existing pieces.

A computer adds a significant enhancement to the keyboard lab. From middle school to college level this is recommended as budget permits.

Performance Options

Throughout this chapter, several performance-related applications have been mentioned, including playing one- and two-hand melodies on the electronic keyboard and performing with a recorded accompaniment. In addition to these activities, the electronic keyboard lab provides another unique option: an electronic keyboard ensemble.

> **Teaching Strategy 181**
>
> Use the keyboard lab to rehearse an electronic ensemble.

In the electronic keyboard ensemble, students become part of a performing group following a conductor and playing individual parts. Further, a keyboard ensemble will provide you with an excellent way to showcase your lab to the school and/or public in concert performances.[3]

Electro-Acoustic Ensemble

Because band and orchestra contain a blend of different instrument families, consider including some acoustic instruments with the electronic keyboards. Any instrument can be added to the ensemble.

> **Teaching Strategy 182**
>
> Consider adding acoustic instruments to augment the electronic keyboard ensemble and create an electro-acoustic ensemble.

Blending electronic and acoustic instruments together creates an electro-acoustic ensemble.[8] Some of the most popular and successful instruments to add to the ensemble are percussion and wind instruments. Electronic controllers (see Chapter 5) also add a new dimension to the group. Offering a special elective to students who are interested in pursuing their keyboard experience is a good way to begin a keyboard ensemble. After school hours is the usual time for this ensemble to meet and rehearse.

The Guitar Lab

MIDI keyboards are not the only instrument that can be included in the lab. Instead of electronic keyboards as the lab instrument, electric guitars can be used. Students use headphones and the instructor can communicate with the class using the same teacher controller discussed earlier in this chapter. A guitar lab is especially helpful in schools that teach classroom guitar. Of course, it is possible to combine electronic pianos and electric guitars in the same lab.

Keyboard Lab Courses and Scheduling

The keyboard lab can be scheduled in a variety of ways, depending upon the option chosen and the grade level that uses the lab. Many applications can be incorporated into the existing general music curriculum. At the college level, many new electives can be offered.[9] The following table lists some of the options for the various labs.

LAB OPTIONS	DESCRIPTION
Option #1	Instruments used in general music to play melodies
	Keyboard ensemble perform classical and/or jazz
	Piano instruction in the general music class: beginning, intermediate, advanced
Option #2	All of option #1 plus....
	Composing and practicing music with sequencers
Option #3	All of option #2 plus...
	Introduction to music technology
	Compose and print music notation using computer
	Computer-assisted instruction (CAI)
	Sound design
	Techniques of digital audio
	Any software-based activity

Lab Set-up

There are three basic ways to set up a keyboard lab in the classroom: classroom style, facing rows, and around the perimeter of the classroom. Each has its strengths and weaknesses.

> **Teaching Strategy 183**
> Carefully select the best set-up of your lab: classroom style, facing rows, or around the perimeter of the classroom.

In classroom style, the keyboards are set in rows with the students facing the instructor. The advantage is that all the students are facing the instructor and can view blackboards and projection screens. The negative is that keyboards are facing away from the teacher so it is difficult to see each student's hand position.

Facing rows is one of the most popular ways to set up keyboard labs. Students are facing each other which facilitates playing in small groups and in performance ensembles. This is the best set-up for all-around lab applications.

Figure 12.10: Students in lab facing rows

A third option is to place the keyboards around the perimeter of the classroom with the students facing the walls. This requires a large room but it leaves space in the middle of the room for other activities. The teacher can easily see all of the computer screens while students are working. The down side of this set-up is that students must turn around to see the front of the room. Use this lab set-up if you have a very large room and you want to maintain a space in the center of the room for other classes or class activities.

Lab Management and Teacher Training

Once the MIDI lab equipment has been chosen and ordered, a new set of challenges arises; namely, installation, training, and support. The simplest way to meet these challenges is to head them off early, and set aside funds for installation and training in your initial proposal. When you write up the specifications for the MIDI lab, be sure to include installation of the equipment by the company or manufacturer. Installation of the hardware and configuring the software can be an enormous task.

It is also very important to get staff training on the operation of the MIDI lab. One week of staff training is recommended for teachers who will be teaching in the lab. On-site training is best.

A final important consideration is on-going technical support. Be sure that the company or music store that you choose has excellent after-the-sale support. Good tech support is a key component for managing a successful MIDI lab.

Summary

MIDI keyboard labs are making a significant impact on music education. The number of MIDI lab has increased significantly over the past several years. There are several different types of MIDI labs. These include labs with MIDI keyboards, MIDI workstations, and MIDI keyboards connected to computers. The MIDI lab can be used to enhance the national standards. A MIDI lab provides educators with a medium that can be used to teach a variety of courses and electives to students at every level.

Review Questions

1. What company first introduced the concept of a classroom of electronic keyboards? When was this first introduced to music education?
2. In what ways does a MIDI lab resemble an art room and how does it improve music learning for students?
3. What is the primary application of MIDI keyboard lab Option #1?
4. What is the primary application of MIDI keyboard lab Option #2?
5. What is the primary application of MIDI keyboard lab Option #3?
6. What is a lab controller and why is it important to include in the MIDI lab?
7. Lab furniture is another important part of the lab. List several options for appropriate lab furniture selection.
8. What are the advantages to working with a vendor who has experience selling and servicing MIDI labs?
9. What is MIE? What applications does it have for the elementary/middle school classroom? How does learning in an MIE lab differ from traditional general music settings?
10. What applications can be realized using MIDI keyboard lab Option #1 at the elementary level? The secondary/college level?
11. What applications can be realized using MIDI keyboard lab Option #2 at the elementary level? The secondary/college level?

12. What applications can be realized using MIDI keyboard lab Option #3 at the elementary level? The secondary/college level?

13. List 3-5 strategies that you think are especially helpful for integrating the MIDI lab with the music national standards.

14. What is an electro-acoustic ensemble?

15. What other instruments can be used in a MIDI lab other than piano keyboards?

16. List several courses and electives that could be offered in the MIDI lab.

17. What are the basic room set-up options for the MIDI lab? Why is it important to include teacher training as part of the MIDI lab purchase?

18. Review the planning process for purchasing a MIDI lab. Include the sequence of things to consider with emphasis on curriculum and learning goals.

CD-ROM Activities

- Project 12.1: Select one of the 3 keyboard lab options listed in this chapter and write up a proposal.
- Project 12.2: Prepare a budget for a music technology lab. Contact companies and/or their web sites for prices and recommendations.
- Project 12.3. Prepare a list of activities that you will include in the MIDI lab. Be sure to address as many of the music education national standards as possible. Prepare one or more of the activities using a MIDI keyboard and be prepared to demonstrate the skills in class.

CD-ROM Lesson Plans

- 12.1 Yamaha MIE curriculum sample lesson: Module 1: Steady Beat
- 12.2 Alfred Play Piano Now: Unit 2 White Keys, pages 30 and 31
- 12.3 Exploring General Music in the Keyboard Lab: Lesson 4: Playing Chords
- 12.4 SoundTree General Music Curriculum : Lesson 5 – 1812 Overture
- 12.5 SoundTree Elementary Curriculum : Lesson 1

Reference

Appell, Claudia, J. (1993). Keyboard instruction in the music classroom. *Music Educators Journal*, May pp 21-24.

Booty, C. Editor (1990). *TIPS: Technology for music educators.* Music Educators National Conference, Reston,VA.

Blakeslee, Michael, Editor (1994). *National Standards for Arts Education.* Music Educators National Conference, Reston, VA.

Chamberlain, L. et al (1993). Success with keyboard in middle school. *Music Educators Journal*, March.

Hilley, Martha and Pardue, Tommie (1996). *Strategies for teaching: Middle-level and high school keyboard.* MENC, Reston, VA.

Kuzmich, John (2003). Music technology labs: Getting their classes wired. *School Band and Orchestra Magazine.* April.

Mauricio, D & Adams, S. (1994). *Fundamentals of music technology.* ConsultantHelp Software, Agoura, CA.

Mauricio, D. (2003) *Music Mentor Series Volume one, An easy method for teaching music technology.* Roland US.

Muro, Don (1995). Music workstation applications for the classroom and the lab. *SoundTree Educational News*, Vol. 2 Issue 1. June.

Purse, Lynn (1991) Creating an electronic keyboard ensemble. *Roland Keyboard Educator*, Spring/Summer, 1991.

Rudolph, Thomas (1995). *The SoundTree general music curriculum.* SoundTree, Westbury, N.Y.

Rudolph, Thomas. (1995) developing performance outcomes with electronic keyboards. *PMEA News*, March.

Chapter 13

Setting Up a
Computer Studio

Music Education National Standards: 8
NETS (National Education Technology Standards): 1

This chapter explains single station computer studio. It includes an overview
of the best hardware for classrooms and rehearsal rooms.

How Will I Use It?

The initial step in selecting appropriate hardware for a computer studio is to
determine your goals for the system. Is a stand-alone computer sufficient, or
do you need a computer and MIDI keyboard? Will it be a practice room or
a studio where students compose and record music? Are you going to record
digital audio as well as MIDI data? Will you be synchronizing music to video
or film? What kind of budget do you have? Depending on the purpose, different equipment must be purchased. There are four main areas to consider:

- computer model
- MIDI equipment: interface, keyboards, and sound modules
- audio recording equipment
- amplification

Because there is a wide range of needs, I have divided computer studio configurations into three areas:

1. A single MIDI keyboard and computer
2. A MIDI studio with a computer and two or more MIDI devices for student and/or teacher use
3. An advanced studio including a computer and two or more MIDI devices with digital audio recording capabilities

Selecting the Computer

As mentioned in Chapter 3, there are two computer platforms to consider: the Apple Macintosh and computers running Microsoft Windows. Most of the applications discussed throughout this book can be realized on either platform. My advice is to purchase the same type of computer that is already in your educational institution unless you have a personal preference. If your school has Macintosh computers, then go with the Macintosh; if your school has Windows PCs, then Windows is the best choice. If you purchase the same computer model that is already elsewhere in your school or institution, you should be able to find technical assistance when you run into trouble.

MIDI Set-ups

MIDI set-up possibilities are organized into three categories: the single MIDI keyboard system, the MIDI studio with multiple MIDI devices, and the digital audio MIDI studio. Each of these set-ups fulfills a different purpose. A single MIDI keyboard system is most common, as it is the simplest and the least expensive. A MIDI studio with multiple MIDI devices has more sound producing capabilities and costs more. A digital audio MIDI studio includes several MIDI devices, has digital recording and acoustic sound editing capabilities; and, not coincidentally, the highest cost of the three.

The Single MIDI Keyboard Music System

The single MIDI keyboard system is the least expensive. Several components are required; a computer, MIDI keyboard, MIDI interface and cables, amplification, and audio recording device.

After selecting the computer and printer, the next two items to address are the MIDI interface and the MIDI keyboard. In most instances connecting a MIDI keyboard to a computer requires a MIDI interface. With a single MIDI keyboard system, the MIDI interface can be of the simplest type.

Macintosh computers and Windows laptop models must use an external MIDI interface. An interface that can connect to one MIDI keyboard will cost in the $50 range such as the Midisport UNO MIDI.

Figure 13.1: Midisport Uno interface by M-Audio

Most Windows desktop models come with a built-in SoundCard. If the SoundCard is a Sound Blaster 64 or a Turtle Beach compatible sound card, the MIDI interface is already built-in. All you will need is a special MIDI cable that connects to the back of the SoundCard via the game port. These cables typically cost from $15–$20 and they are available at most computer stores and music technology vendors.

A complete on-line tutorial on how to connect a MIDI keyboard to a soundcard is available on the Turtle Beach web site at:

http://www.turtlebeach.com/site/kb_ftp/8953004.asp.

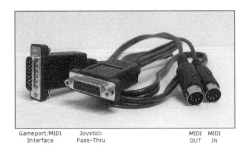

Gameport/MIDI   Joystick   MIDI   MIDI
Interface   Pass-Thru   OUT   IN

Figure 13.2: Windows MIDI cables that connect to a SoundCard

MIDI Cables

The basic MIDI connection requires two separate MIDI cables. Midisport Uno and SoundCard MIDI cable both come with two MIDI cables. However, some MIDI interfaces do not include the MIDI cables and they must be purchased separately. MIDI cables can be purchased in a variety of colors. It is a good idea to purchase two different colored cables so that it will be easier to check the connection between your MIDI gear and computer. Usually 4-6 foot length MIDI cables will suffice. If your keyboard is a long way from your computer, you might want to consider 8-10 foot long cables.

Making the Connection

Once the MIDI connection method has been determined, the next challenge is connecting the interface to the MIDI keyboard. First, take one MIDI cable and connect it to the IN port of the interface. There is a right and wrong way to insert the plug. Be careful when connecting the cables—they can be inserted upside down and damaged. Line up the five pins so that they exactly match the interface socket. Second, connect the other end of that same cable to the OUT port on the back of the keyboard. Third, connect the second cable to the OUT port on the interface and connect the other end to the IN port on the back of the keyboard. After connecting the MIDI interface to the computer and keyboard, connect the audio cable from the keyboard to the amplifier. A standard guitar chord with a male 1/4-inch phono plug on each end is usually all that is required to connect to the amplifier. If another type of cord is needed, purchase an adapter.

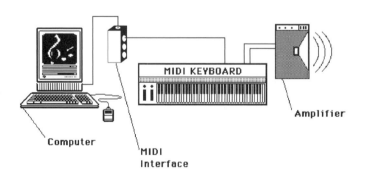

Figure 13.3: Single MIDI keyboard set-up

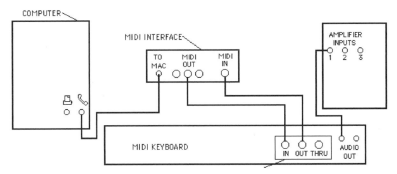

Figure 13.4: Single MIDI keyboard connections

The Studio with Multiple MIDI Devices

For more options in the MIDI studio, consider adding two or more MIDI devices. The advantage is that using multiple MIDI devices allows you to access a wide variety of sounds for your sequences. In addition to multiple MIDI sound sources, you should include an audio mixer and audio tape recorder.

Adding MIDI Modules

Why add another MIDI module? Primarily because there is no single MIDI keyboard that has every sound you will need. Each keyboard has both good and bad sounds. For example, if you want to reproduce classical instruments such as the bass clarinet, double reeds, and the like, you should consider a sound module specifically designed to reproduce orchestral sounds. The Proteus Orchestral module is one example of a sound module designed to play back traditional acoustic instruments. Also, there are MIDI modules that only produce a variety of excellent piano samples and MIDI modules dedicated to producing just percussion sounds. Just about any sound you can imagine can be found on a specific MIDI module. Thanks to MIDI sound modules, you can add additional sound sources as the need arises and budget permits.

The MIDI Interface for Multiple MIDI Devices

A MIDI interface with one input and two or three outputs will suffice for a MIDI setup with multiple MIDI devices. If you are adding more than one key-board, or if you have more than *three* sound modules, consider purchasing a more expensive MIDI interface. Several companies produce more powerful MIDI interfaces that allow for the connection of multiple MIDI devices. For example, M-Audio (www.m-audio.com) produces a wide range of MIDI interfaces. For multiple MIDI sound sources, consider the M-Audio 8X8 USB interface. These MIDI interfaces cost several hundred dollars more than the basic interface. However, they give you control over many more MIDI input and output ports. In addition, these more expensive interfaces also allow for you to send and receive SMPTE time code, which is essential when working with MIDI and film scoring.

Figure 13.5: M-Audio 8 X 8 MIDI interface

Connecting Multiple MIDI Devices

When you have two or more MIDI devices, the connection becomes a bit more complicated. Take one MIDI cable and connect it to the MIDI OUT of the keyboard and insert the other end of the same cable to the MIDI IN of the MIDI interface. Next, connect the second MIDI Cable to the MIDI IN of the sound module and the other end of the MIDI cable to the MIDI OUT of the MIDI interface.

The set-up below will also work if you have a MIDI controller keyboard, which is a keyboard that does not produce sound, and a MIDI module or MIDI capable sound card. This is a good option for someone who has a Windows computer with a MIDI compatible sound card and only needs a piano keyboard to input data.

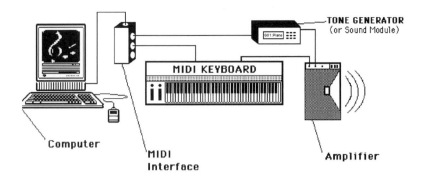

Figure 13.6: Connecting two or more MIDI sound sources

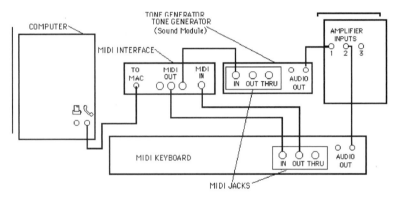

Figure 13.7: Connecting two or more MIDI sound sources: a close-up view

Software Synthesis

If you buy a Macintosh or Windows computer today, it will come equipped with at least rudimentary sound-synthesis capability. A Windows PC running Windows 95 or later comes equipped with a soundcard that can generate multitimbral sound output. Apple includes QuickTime with all G3, G4, and G5 models. Therefore, most computers can play back MIDI through the computer's internal sound synthesis capabilities.

It is also possible to purchase software synthesizers, referred to as software synths that provide a higher-quality sound output than the built-in options. A software synthesizer is a program with much the same function as a piece of MIDI hardware, except that it uses the memory and storage capability of the computer. With a software synth, a computer can generate high-quality sound and thereby eliminate the need for additional pieces of MIDI hardware.

The computer's sound-producing capability can be added to the existing pieces of hardware in the studio.

Some MIDI software comes with built-in software synths and others can be purchased and added as needed. Companies including Edirol (www.edirol.com), and BitHeadz (www.bitheadz.com) offer a range of software synths. Their software synths can emulate analog and digital synths and samplers. Software synths can be purchased for less than the cost of their hardware counterparts and can be used in conjunction with hardware units.

The MIDI Studio with Digital Audio Recording Capability

For a bigger financial investment, it is possible to purchase an interface that has both MIDI and digital audio built-in. This is the best choice for users who want a MIDI interface as well as digital audio inputs and outputs (see Chapter 9). Expect to pay in the $500 range and up for these interfaces. They typically connect to the computer via USB or Firewire cables.

Figure 13.9: The UA-700 USB audio and MIDI interface by Edirol

Microphones

If recording digital audio is included in your computer studio plan, good quality microphones will also be needed. See Chapter 9 for specific recommendations.

Recording Audio CDs

One additional piece of very helpful hardware is a CD recorder for making CDs. For example, suppose you have created a sequence accompaniment for a performing group and would like to make a CD to give students for practice, or to use during rehearsal. You can use a standard CD recording deck to make the recording (see Chapter 9).

To record a sequence, you need to connect the CD recording deck to the output of the keyboard. Check the ports on the back of your keyboard, but typically you will need male 1/4-inch phono plugs on one end to connect to the keyboard and male RCA plugs on the other end for the CD recorder. If your keyboard only has one MONO output, then purchase a Y-adapter with a male 1/4-inch plug on one end and two male RCA plugs on the other. Once the connection is made, simply press record and start the sequencer. Be sure to check the recording levels on the CD recorder since the keyboard may send a very strong signal and cause distortion. You can listen to the recording as it is made by plugging headphones into the headphone jack of the CD recorder deck.

Amplification

A computer studio needs a way for music to be heard. If the studio is in an office or practice room, stereo headphones may suffice. Headphones can be connected to the computer's output or the MIDI keyboard's output.

If the computer station is going to be in a classroom or rehearsal hall, amplification is needed. The best option is to purchase powered monitors. These devices look like speakers, but they also have a built-in power source. This eliminates the need for an amplifier and speakers because they both are included in one compact unit. Simply connect the output of the computer or MIDI keyboard to the input of the powered monitors.

Figure 13.10: Fostex powered monitors

Mixer

A mixer is a unit that can combine a variety of audio signals. A mixer is very helpful when you need to connect several audio output sources such as a computer, MIDI keyboard, CD player, and other devices. The mixer allows independent control of the volume of each device. Mixers come in different sizes and configurations. The key factor is the maximum number of inputs available. To determine the number of inputs you need, add up all of the separate devices that you have in your studio. Remember to count both the left and right channel for stereo devises. A good quality mixer is an important part of the computer studio.

Figure 13.11: Eight-input mixer by Mackie

Projection Systems

Many times it is helpful for an entire class or ensemble to see what is on the computer screen. Perhaps you want to share a multimedia presentation with a class or display music created on a notation program. For classroom demonstrations, the image must be displayed large enough for everyone to see. There are several computer projection options: displaying the computer image on a large screen TV, using a computer projector, and using a SmartBoard.

Teaching Strategy 184

Add a projection system to your set-up and display screen images for an entire classes and performing ensembles.

Consider connecting a computer to a large screen television, computer monitor, or video display. Often schools and school libraries have large screen televisions that can be viewed by an entire class. Getting connected to a television or large screen monitor may be as simple as connecting the computer output to the large screen monitor. In some cases, an interface or connector is needed. Focus Enhancements (www.focusinfo.com) makes a device for Macintosh and Windows computers that allows the computer to connect to most televisions. The cost of the connecting device runs from $200-$300 depending upon the computer model you use. This does not include the cost of the television.

If you have the budget, consider purchasing a dedicated computer projection unit to display the screen images of the computer. The advantage of using a projector is that the image can be made quite large and can be displayed on any screen. In a rehearsal room, consider having the computer projector installed permanently into the ceiling of the room. With a computer projector, you can display any image from the computer. Expect to pay from $1,000-$2,000 for a computer projector.

Figure 13.12: Computer data projector by inFocus

SmartBoards

The most expensive option is to purchase a SmartBoard (www.smartboard.com) to display the computer screen for a classroom. These devices cost around $5,000. Think of a SmartBoard as a computer-controlled touch sensitive screen. Students and teachers can touch the SmartBoard to manipulate the program or image being displayed. Students get physically involved by touching the SmartBoard. A SmartBoard can help enhance student interest. A SmartBoard connects to the computer and is touch sensitive so that simply touching the SmartBoard performs commands or mouse clicks. Other features of the SmartBoard include the ability to write and erase electronically on the board using a touch-sensitive pen. The images written on the board can also be saved as computer files to be used later.

> **Teaching Strategy 185**
> Use SmartBoard technology to provide a large interactive display for teachers and students.

Figure 13.13: SmartBoard by Smart Technologies, Inc.
(www.smarttech.com)

Any music software program can be displayed on the SmartBoard and students can interact with it during a lesson. For example, consider displaying music notation software (see Chapter 7). Students can interact with the software using the touch sensitive SmartBoard to enter and alter notation.

A SmartBoard can also be used with instructional software (see Chapter 6). Students can answer questions by simply touching the SmartBoard surface. Then, save all their work to one file that you can print, e-mail, or post on a web site. More information on SmartBoard technology can be viewed at http://www.smarttech.com/.

Equipment Security

Once you have invested in a MIDI studio, it needs to be protected. There are three steps that should be taken to insure that the electronic equipment in the school is properly maintained. [7]

- Make sure the equipment is secure.
- Find the best environment for the equipment.
- Establish policies regarding the equipment's use.

Try to place equipment in rooms that can be secured and locked at the end of each day. If possible, it is a good idea to put the technology lab in a room by itself. An additional option is to provide locking cabinets in the music room so units can be stored and locked away at the end of the day.

Take some time to investigate the electrical service at your institution. It is always a good precaution to buy a good surge protector for your room or office. These are available from any computer store and will protect the equipment from electrical surges that can ruin electronic equipment.

To protect from theft, the equipment in your room should be clearly labeled in indelible ink. Also, be sure that the equipment is covered by your personal or school insurance plan so that, if stolen, the equipment will be replaced.

The final step is to have clear, established policies regarding use of the equipment. Students need to be trained and must understand how to properly treat the equipment.

Furniture and Ergonomics

It is important to have the correct physical set-up for any MIDI studio. This means selecting hardware that will best suit your lab's physical requirements and design. Most keyboard manufactures sell customized furniture for MIDI set-ups.

Figure 13.14: Custom furniture for the MIDI lab set-up

In addition to lab furniture, Wenger Corporation also sells a well-designed mobile cart for computers and related technology, making this an excellent choice for music teachers who move from classroom to classroom. Be sure to spend time selecting furniture since the proper set-up is important for a well-organized and productive studio.

The Checklist

Following is a checklist of the hardware devices listed in this chapter. You will first need to select the studio that you intent to develop and then select the various items.

ITEM DESCRIPTION	SINGLE MIDI KEYBOARD	MULTIPLE MIDI DEVICES	DIGITAL AUDIO
Computer:			
Standard computer	X	X	
Computer with additional storage capacity			X
Printer:			
Injet	(select one that fits your needs and budget)		
Laser			
Display Unit:			
Television connector			
Computer projector	(select one that fits your needs and budget)		
SmartBoard			
MIDI interface:			
Standard MIDI interface	X		
MIDI interface with multiple IN's and OUT's		X	
MIDI interface with SMPTE capability			X
MIDI cables	X	X	X
Digital Audio Recording Unit:			
Stand-alone CD recorder	X		
Multi-track CD recorder			X
Mixer:			
4–8 input mixer	X	X	X
MIDI devices:			
MIDI keyboard	X	X	X
MIDI module		X	X
Microphones:			
1–2 Dynamic Microphones			X
Pair of condenser microphones			
Furniture			
Custom music furniture	X	X	X

Figure 13.15: Computer hardware checklist

Review Questions:

1. What are the four main areas to consider when constructing a single computer studio for the classroom or rehearsal room?
2. What are the three types of MIDI configurations?
3. What are powered monitors?
4. What is the function of a mixer?
5. List the three options for projecting a computer image to an entire class.
6. What is needed to connect the computer's video output to a large screen television?
7. What makes a SmartBoard different from the other types of computer projection?
8. What is a recommended MIDI interface for one MIDI keyboard and a computer?
9. What is a recommended MIDI interface for multiple MIDI devices?
10. What is needed to connect a MIDI keyboard to a Windows SoundCard?
11. What is a MIDI module?
12. What is a software synth?
13. What device is needed to connect both MIDI and digital audio to a computer?
14. What security measures should be considered?

CD-ROM Activities

- Project 13.1 Design a MIDI studio for a classroom or office. Make a list of all the equipment and software you will need and the types of required connections. Then draw a diagram showing each of the components and indicate how to connect MIDI, audio, video, and power among the devices.
- Project 13.2 Select a software application that would be enhanced by displaying the computer image to an entire class or performing group. Choose the type of display unit you plan to use and describe a lesson using the device.

- Project 13.3 Refer to the checklist at the end of this chapter. First select the type of MIDI set-up you require and then list the specific components you will need for the system.

Reference

Bloom, Michael (1987). *Music through MIDI*. Microsoft Press, Redmond, WA.

Freeman, Peter (1994). All for one. *Electronic Musician*, April 1994. pp. 31-52.

Gibson, Bill. (1996). *The audio pro home recording course*. MIX Books, Vallegio, CA.

Hoffman, B. (1994) Managing technological resources. *Teaching Music*, August. pp. 36-37.

Kassner, Kirk (2000). One computer can deliver whole class instruction. *Music Educators Journal*, May, 2000, Vol. 86 Issue 6, p 34.

Keating, C. and Anderton, C, Editors. (1998). *Digital home recording–Tips, techniques, and tools for home studio production*. Backbeat Books, San Francisco.

Klinger, Michael (1995). The one computer classroom. *Music Educators Journal*. December. pp. 34-35.

Milstead, Bill. (2001) *Home recording power!* Muska & Lipman Publishing, Boston.

Reese, S., & Davis, A. (1998). The systems approach to music technology. *Music Educators Journal*, 85(1), 24-28.

Rudolph, Thomas and Leonard, Vincent. (2001). *Recording in the digital world*. Berklee Press, Boston.

Chapter 14

Productivity Applications: Administrative and Database

Music Education National Standards: 8
NETS (National Education Technology Standards): 1, 2, 3

The same computer used to run music instructional software, notation programs, and sequencing software can also be used for administrative applications. The classroom computer can be a music learning station one period and an information manager the next. The use of computer software can significantly reduce the time teachers need to complete administrative duties.

With the appropriate software your classroom computer can perform specialized tasks. It can serve as a word processor and file keeper. Special software can assist in a wide variety of areas including writing a marching band drill, maintaining fund raising records, computing grades, and printing letters.

Essential Hardware

For any administrative task, a computer and printer are needed. If there is a computer on the teacher's desk, it should be connected to a printer. The printer that produces music notation will also print correspondence, instrument inventory, and library listings. See Chapter 3 for a description of the basic types of printers.

The other component to consider for administrative applications is selecting the proper software. This chapter will review the main types of administrative and database software that are especially helpful to music teachers.

Administrative programs fall into two main categories: those written for general use and those written with a specific purpose in mind. A wide range of individuals can use general use programs. For example, professionals, regardless of their profession, can use the same software for typing letters, creating forms, lists, and calculating figures. General use programs include word processors for typing letters and documents, database programs for managing lists of information, and spreadsheets for calculating columns of numbers.

Specific purpose programs are written with one specific application in mind. For example, a program designed to create monthly calendars has one specific purpose: to produce a customized printed calendar. Other specific purpose programs include those for creating signs and posters and marching band charting software to help create and print marching band drills.

General Purpose Application: Word Processing

One of the most beneficial general purpose computer applications is word processing. Word processing is using the computer as an electronic typewriter. A word processor is capable of rearranging and editing text, correcting mistakes, checking for misspelled words, instantly moving margins, boldfacing or italicizing words, and more—all at the touch of a keystroke and without wasting paper.

Teaching Strategy 186

Use word processing software to save time preparing letters and forms.

Word processors temporarily store characters in the computer's memory and display the text on the computer's screen. Using the computer's memory for temporary storage facilitates correcting mistakes. Letters, words, and paragraphs may be erased, moved, or replaced by a few mouse movements or keystrokes. When work on a document is complete it is saved to disk and can be recalled, revised, and reused at a later date.

Thesaurus, Spelling, and Grammar Checkers

Today's word processors include a variety of helpful features including spelling and grammar checkers.

> ### Teaching Strategy 187
> Take advantage of the many add-on features of today's word processing programs including spelling and grammar checkers and thesaurus to improve the quality and content of letters and documents.

All word processors are not the same nor do they all have the same features. However, the more powerful programs such as Microsoft Word, WordPerfect, and AppleWorks contain a wide range of options.

A grammar checker is also a most helpful tool. When the grammar checker is selected, the document is scanned for grammatical errors. For example, I selected the following sentence and asked the computer, running Microsoft Word, to check it for grammar. The sentence I typed was "The computer can be a excellent typing tool for a music teacher."

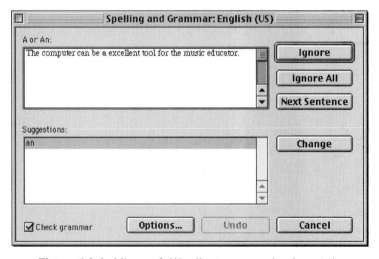

Figure 14.1: Microsoft Word's grammar checker option

Note that the grammar checker not only found and identified an error but also suggested a possible correction. For most music teachers who function as their own secretary, a built-in electronic grammar checker can be handy tool.

A built-in thesaurus is also a nice feature to have at your fingertips. While typing a letter or document, simply highlight or select a word and choose the thesaurus. I typed the word "musical" into the word processor and selected the thesaurus from the tools menu. The following list of words was displayed:

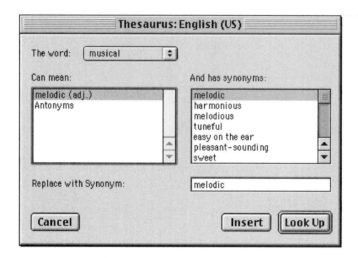

Figure 14.2: Microsoft Word's thesaurus options for the word "musical"

These built-in options: spelling, grammar checkers, and thesaurus, can not only save proofing time but also improve the overall quality of the letters and documents that a music teacher creates.

Saving and Reusing Files

After typing a document on a word processor, always save the information to disk. When a letter is saved to disk it is referred to as a file. Every computer sold today comes equipped with a built-in disk drive that stores documents and other files. Saving the file to disk means that it can be recalled at a later time for viewing, editing, or printing.

Over the past few years I have developed a folder of letters saved on my computer hard drive that I use during the school year. Each year I recall a particular letter, change the dates and other information and reprint it. This saves a tremendous amount of time preparing letters and forms, especially those that are used from year to year.

> ### Teaching Strategy 188
> Save letters, forms, lesson plans, and other documents to disk to save time typing materials that are reused every year.

For example, if you host a band, chorus, or jazz festival, consider using the word processor to enter all the forms and letters. The next time you host a festival, all you need to do is change the dates, times, and any other relevant information and reprint the letters. This not only saves time, but will also help to prevent forgetting important categories such as sending thank you letters to the music parent group!

Letters for Sale

Tim Lautzenheiser has created a series of publications that contain letters and forms specifically written for music teachers. All of his products are published by Hal Leonard and include letters that can be opened by any word processor, edited, and printed out. There are sample letters, brochures, and vital data for parents and administrators on computer disk! Edit, personalize, and mail merge while saving valuable time. His publications include:

- Choir Director's Communication Kit
- Director's Communication Kit
- Essential Elements 2000 Band Directors Communication Kit
- High School Director's Communication Kit
- Creative Communication (Classroom Resource for classroom teachers)

When you purchase any of the above kits (versions available for Macintosh or Windows) you receive a printout of the letters as well as a CD containing all the files. Each letter is designed to be used for a particular audience and/or time of year. The letters are professionally written and designed to be used throughout the school year.

> ### Teaching Strategy 189
> Don't reinvent the wheel. Whenever possible look for appropriate published materials that can help you save time and improve your results, for example, the Director's Communication Kit.

Thanks to the power of word processors these letters can be altered to fit any school's needs. The files come in text format, so they can be opened by any word processor. Simply open the letter using your word processor, make the necessary changes to salutation, institution, and signature names, and print the letter. An excerpt from one of the letters designed to be sent to a school administrator follows:

> Pro-Active Letter for Administrator
>
> Dear (Correct title/name),
>
> This letter comes to you as a personal thank you for your continued support of our band program. So much of our success is directly tied to administrative encouragement and help we receive in our ongoing efforts to create a quality band experience for our students. Although busy agendas often seem to get in the way of expressing our appreciation, we do not take for granted your genuine efforts on our behalf.
>
> Every committed educator sees his/her discipline as vital to the growth and development of the child. Likewise, I feel the same about MUSIC and how it relates to the fundamental value system we should be bringing to every young girl and boy who walks through our school doors. Recently I came across a quote by Illinois Senator Paul Simon. It is not a political statement, but rather a viewpoint of education expressing a unique logic and different position concerning the benefits of music in our schools.
>
> "Very few days go by that the media does not compare our economy, educational system, business endeavors and productivity to those of the Japanese. Ironically, the Japanese consider Western music as a basic part of their children's education..."

Figure 14.3: An excerpt from one of the letters in the Director's Communication Kit

As you can tell by the above example, Tim Lautzenheiser has created extremely well written letters that can be used by band directors and music educators.

Database

Database programs are related to word processors in that they both primarily deal with text. However, databases are used to manipulate specific pieces of information. A database can be thought of as a collection of specific lists of information. A checking account, telephone directory, or recipe file is usually stored in databases.

I use a database to help me manage student information. I enter the information about each student in my classes and performing groups into my database. I include the instrument, last name, first name, address, telephone number, email address, and any other information I may need throughout the school year. A database program can also organize a list of performing dates, instrument inventory, uniforms, and choir robes, thus acting as a sophisticated card file for your music library.

> ### Teaching Strategy 190
> Use a database program to organize student information, inventory, uniforms, and any other list of information you need to manage.

I frequently use the database that contains the information for my classes and performing groups. I create separate database files for each of my classes and performing ensembles. With my performing groups, I enter the first and last name and instrument.

name last	name first	instru
ABBOTT	DAN	TRUMPET
ANDERSON	JESSE	TRBN
ANDREW	JASMINE	FLUTE
ANTENDA	NICOLE	FLUTE
ASHLINE	DWIGHT	SAX
BAGELMEN	ADAM	SAX
BENNENT	JESSICA	SAX
BETTER	JEANNETTE	CLARINET
BLIGHTLY	JACOB	TRUMPET
BLAIRING	JAKE	FLUTE
CANNING	TERRY	
CATELDA	MARC	SAX
CHARLESON	MIGUEL	SAX
CHANG	CATHY	FLUTE
COHAR	DANA	CLARINET

Figure 14.4: Database sorted by last name

Database programs refer to the general areas of information as fields. In this case there are three fields: first name, last name, and instrument. A record is all the information about one particular item or person, one horizontal row in Figure 14.4. There are 15 records displayed in the example. When several records are combined into one group of information it is referred to as a file. The above example of a file shows three fields—first name, last name, and instrument—and 15 records or sets of information about one individual. Databases can contain dozens of fields and hundreds of records. Once the information is entered it can be edited, sorted, and printed. A database can sort any field. For example, when I want to print a list of my students in alphabetical order I select the last name column and choose sort. In an instant, the entire class or ensemble information is alphabetized. Students can be organized by instrument, last name, grade, or any other field that you create in the database file.

The flexibility of a database allows for sorting the information by instrument. This is helpful when preparing a seating listing or for taking attendance. An example of a portion of my band class database sorted by instrument is:

Band Data Base (DB)

name last	name first	instru
REANLDI	BRIAN	BARITONE
BETTER	JEANNETTE	CLARINET
COLLAR	DANA	CLARINET
GLINGER	MATTHEW	CLARINET
GRAMINSKY	KIM	CLARINET
HOLLINGTON	EMILY	CLARINET
LEVERING	MEGAN	CLARINET
MICKY	LAURIE	CLARINET
MILLER	JOANNE	CLARINET
NATALIE	KRISTEN	CLARINET
O'RORKE	KATE	CLARINET
PROPER	LARISSA	CLARINET
ROTH	SARAH	CLARINET
SMYTH	NICOLE	CLARINET
VALLOR	MERYL	CLARINET

Figure 14.5: Class list database sorted by instrument

Numbers can also be entered and sorted in a database. When I am seating the band by their audition score, I enter their total audition score into one field, or column. Then I ask the computer to sort from the highest to the lowest score and by individual instruments. Viola! In a second I have a list of the new seating assignments based on audition scores. In seconds, the computer completes a task that used to take me hours to compute by hand. A database is a terrific tool when you are planning to take a trip with an ensemble. Typically when taking a music trip, a host of lists needs to be printed, including a telephone chain list, alphabetical list by homeroom, bus lists, etc.

Another excellent use for a database is to enter your music library titles. Once the pieces are entered by title, composer, arranger, and difficulty level, it takes but a minute to search for a particular piece or composer. I also keep my musical instrument inventory on a database. A musical instrument database can be organized by instrument, school, serial number, student, or any other area that needs to be tracked.

Teaching Strategy 191

Students can create a database of information being studied such as composers. Database fields can include date of birth, country, and other information.

A database can be used by students. They can be instructed to create a database of the composers they have studied. They can create database fields such as date of birth, country, style, representative compositions, and other information.

There are different levels of database programs. AppleWorks has a simple database. Microsoft Access (Windows) and Filemaker Pro (Windows and Macintosh) are more advanced database programs. If you want to have more control over you files, then consider purchasing a high-end database such as Access or Filmaker Pro.

Mailmerge

Suppose you want to send a letter to all of the members of your performing ensemble. If you have a word processor that supports mail merge, such as Microsoft Word, the software can automatically insert the names and addresses of each person in the database on an individualized printout. You first create a document that has everything but the name and address of the recipients. Then you enter a special text string into the letter. When you run the mailmerge, it replaces the text strings with the actual names and address information from the database. Check your software for specific instructions on how to accomplish a mailmerge.

Spreadsheets

When mathematical formulas and calculations are needed use a spreadsheet. Spreadsheets are the best choice when managing numbers.

Teaching Strategy 192

Use a spreadsheet to manage an ensemble or music department budget.

A spreadsheet looks like columns of numbers. Spreadsheets can contain up to several hundred rows and columns where information and formulas can be stored. The following screen is from a spreadsheet. Notice the numbers representing rows and the letters as columns. The computer's screen displays only a portion of the spreadsheet at any one time. The remainder of the spreadsheet can be seen by scrolling horizontally and vertically.

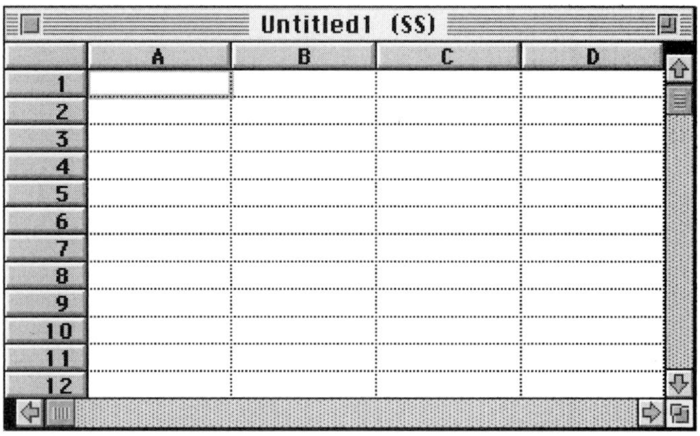

Figure 14.6: A sample spreadsheet

A school music budget can be calculated using a spreadsheet. Below is an example of a music department budget that has been projected and calculated with the spreadsheet.

	A	B	C	D	E
1	MONTH	SUPPLIES	REPAIRS	INSTRUMENTS	SHEET MUSIC
2	September	$150.00	$25.00	$500.00	$125.00
3	October	$50.00	$0.00	$0.00	$0.00
4	November	$0.00	$0.00	$0.00	$0.00
5	December	$100.00	$75.00	$0.00	$50.00
6	January	$50.00	$150.00	$0.00	$0.00
7					
8	TOTAL	$350.00	$250.00	$500.00	$175.00
9					
10	BUDGET AMT.	$500.00	$300.00	$1000.00	$300.00
11					
12	AVAILABLE BAL.	$150.00	$50.00	$500.00	$125.00
13					

Figure 14.7: Spreadsheet of a sample budget

The computation occurs in rows 8 and 12: "TOTAL BUDGET AMT." and "AVAILABLE BAL." These rows use formulas that I entered to automatically calculate the totals based on the amounts in the rows above. Any time an amount is entered or changed in rows 2 through 6, the total is automatically calculated. These formulas are entered by the user. Any mathematical formula can be entered into the spreadsheet for instant calculation. Think of a spreadsheet as a visual calculator.

Other areas that can be aided by using a spreadsheet include tracking student fund raising efforts and computing lists of grades. In the world outside of education, spreadsheets are used to compute tax returns, calculate amortization schedules, and balance checking accounts. Microsoft Excel and AppleWorks Spreadsheet are two popular applications in this category.

Integrated Software

Word processing, database, and spreadsheet applications can be purchased as separate, individual programs. However, most publishers combine several programs into one package, referred to as integrated software. A typical integrated package contains a word processor, database, spreadsheet, and other applications such as presentation software. Examples of integrated software are Microsoft Office for Macintosh and Windows and AppleWorks for the Macintosh. These excellent all-purpose programs can supply most of the administrative computing needs a music teacher requires.

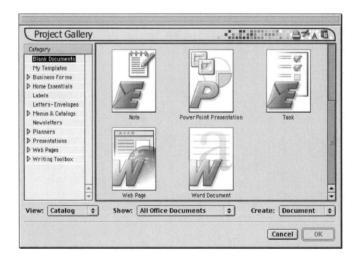

Figure 14.8: Microsoft Office Project Gallery

There are administrative programs designed specifically for music teachers. Pyware's Music Administrator for Macintosh and Windows is an example of a program that is designed specifically for music teachers.

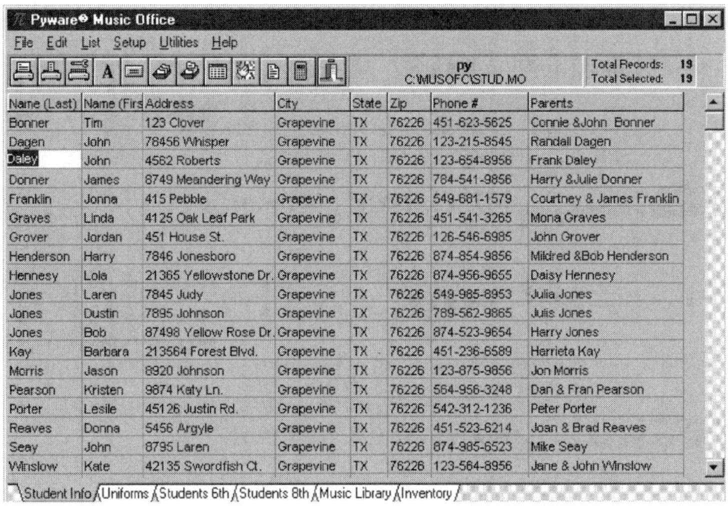

Name (Last)	Name (Firs	Address	City	State	Zip	Phone #	Parents
Bonner	Tim	123 Clover	Grapevine	TX	76226	451-623-5625	Connie &John Bonner
Dagen	John	78456 Whisper	Grapevine	TX	76226	123-215-8545	Randall Dagen
Daley	John	4562 Roberts	Grapevine	TX	76226	123-654-8956	Frank Daley
Donner	James	8749 Meandering Way	Grapevine	TX	76226	784-541-9856	Harry &Julie Donner
Franklin	Jonna	415 Pebble	Grapevine	TX	76226	549-681-1579	Courtney & James Franklin
Graves	Linda	4125 Oak Leaf Park	Grapevine	TX	76226	451-541-3265	Mona Graves
Grover	Jordan	451 House St.	Grapevine	TX	76226	126-546-6985	John Grover
Henderson	Harry	7846 Jonesboro	Grapevine	TX	76226	874-854-9856	Mildred &Bob Henderson
Hennesy	Lola	21365 Yellowstone Dr.	Grapevine	TX	76226	874-956-9655	Daisy Hennesy
Jones	Laren	7845 Judy	Grapevine	TX	76226	549-985-8953	Julia Jones
Jones	Dustin	7895 Johnson	Grapevine	TX	76226	789-562-9865	Julis Jones
Jones	Bob	87498 Yellow Rose Dr.	Grapevine	TX	76226	874-523-9654	Harry Jones
Kay	Barbara	213564 Forest Blvd.	Grapevine	TX	76226	451-236-6589	Harrieta Kay
Morris	Jason	8920 Johnson	Grapevine	TX	76226	123-875-9856	Jon Morris
Pearson	Kristen	9874 Katy Ln.	Grapevine	TX	76226	564-956-3248	Dan & Fran Pearson
Porter	Lesile	45126 Justin Rd.	Grapevine	TX	76226	542-312-1236	Peter Porter
Reaves	Donna	5456 Argyle	Grapevine	TX	76226	451-523-6214	Joan & Brad Reaves
Seay	John	8795 Laren	Grapevine	TX	76226	874-985-6523	Mike Seay
Winslow	Kate	42135 Swordfish Ct.	Grapevine	TX	76226	123-564-8956	Jane & John Winslow

Figure 14.9: Music Administrator by Pyware

Music Administrator has database and spreadsheet functions prepared specifically for music including grades, inventory, and mailing lists/labels. All of these different functions could be designed using a general use program such as Microsoft Office and AppleWorks. However, Music Administrator saves time by providing the templates. There are some additional programs such as instrumentation forecasting and uniform control that are beneficial to the music teacher. If you do not have experience with a general use program such as Microsoft Office or AppleWorks, consider a pre-designed program such as Music Administrator.

Desktop Publishing

Most word processors can manipulate text and graphics. With a word processor you can import pictures, draw, and manipulate text size and style to some extent.

> **Teaching Strategy 193**
>
> Save time and money using an integrated software package to prepare concert programs in-house.

Concert programs can be prepared in-house using a word processor, which can save money on printing costs. Many band, orchestra, and choral directors produce newsletters to distribute to their students and parents. With the many advanced features of today's word processors, columns can be created to make a document look like a newsletter and graphics can be imported and pasted into a document. Students can become involved in the production of a music department newsletter and use the computer in the classroom to produce it. For more advanced applications, special page layout programs such as Aldus PageMaker or QuarkXpress can be used. However, in most cases, a word processor is all that's needed to create professional looking concert programs and newsletters.

Specific Purpose Programs

In addition to the general-purpose programs such as word processing, database, and spreadsheet, there are other administrative applications that have been specifically written for one particular purpose. These include programs that are made specifically for teachers. Some of the more popular programs include electronic grade book programs such as Gradekeeper for Macintosh and Windows (www.gradekeeper.com), and Grade Machine by Misty City Software (www.mistycity.com). Check with your school tech support staff and other teachers to see what grading programs they are using. Grading programs are very popular with all teachers.

Unlike a spreadsheet, where each file must be designed by the user, a grade manager comes ready to go. Simply type in the names of your students and enter the grades. There is no need to enter formulas, because they are built into the program.

An indispensable program for music teachers is The Print Shop by Broderbund software for Macintosh and Windows. The Print Shop is designed for computer novices and creates signs, posters, and cards. The Print Shop can be used to design a concert program cover or promotional literature. The Print Shop can automatically create custom calendars that can be printed for students. Simply type in the events for the month and create a custom printed calendar for your students and parents.

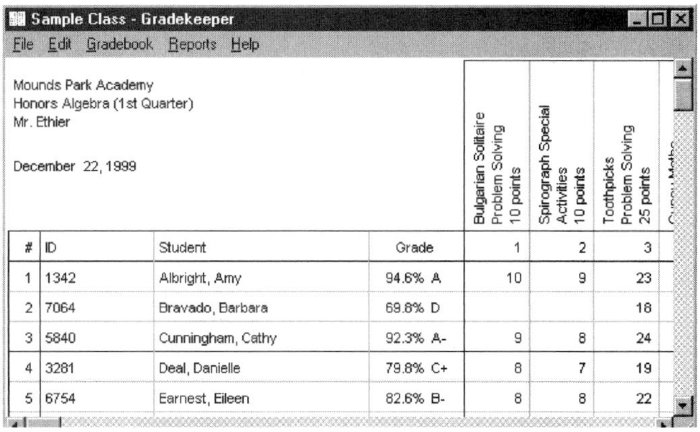

Figure 14.10: Gradekeeper for Macintosh and Windows (www.gradekeeper.com)

Marching Band Charting Software

Several publishers produce software to assist the band director in creating drills for a marching band half time shows. A marching band design program is to the show designer what a word processor is to the author. Drill charting software is used to plot various formations in a half-time show and print outs. By assisting with the tedious job of drawing marching band formations, the time to create a drill can be reduced once the software is mastered.

Pyware 3D by Pyware (www.pyware.com) for Macintosh and Windows can change perspective to show the drill from different angles, simulating the effect of looking at the formation from various parts of the field. The spacing selection option instructs the computer to draw a formation at a given interval and number of places that quickly shows how movement of members will effect the overall formation.

The "identification mode" codes symbols to represent different sections of a marching unit: flags, percussion, brass, and woodwinds. Pyware 3D can record music for the half-time show using a MIDI keyboard and sequencer and then play the music while the computer animates the accompanying show.

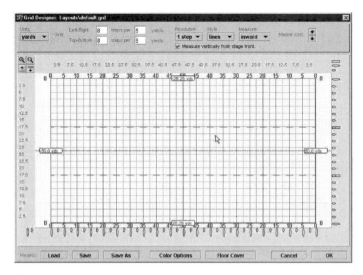

Figure 14.11: Pyware 3D marching band charting software

Teaching Strategy 194

Use marching band charting software to save time writing drill charts and to animate the show with sound.

As with any powerful piece of software, it will take time to master a drill writing program. However, charting software can help band directors reduce the time needed to plot and adjust the formations and graphs. It also offers a tool students can use to better understand and learn marching band half-time shows.

Multimedia and Presentation Software

Chapter 11 covered a variety of multimedia applications that can be used by teachers and students to enhance productivity. Review this chapter for a description of presentation software and multimedia applications of word processors and other software.

Finding a Training Source

One of the most beneficial aspects common to all administrative software is special purpose programs are used by teachers in many subject areas. With this in mind, there are many local public school, continuing education, and college courses designed to teach the basics of most programs. I recommend finding out which word processor other teachers in your school use and then taking a course on how to operate this particular package.

Taking a course with an instructor who knows the software is absolutely the best way to learn a program. However, training videos and DVDs can also assist and save time when learning software on your own. A good video or DVD is a notch better than reading the manual. Check out a recent copy of a computer magazine available at most news stands or search the Internet to find advertisements for training videos by a variety of companies.

Another tip is to look for books written by a third party about a particular program. There are third party books designed to help learn the common administrative software programs such as word processors, databases, and spreadsheet programs. I usually do a search on www.amazon.com when I am looking for a book on a new program I want to learn.

Ergonomic Consideration

Ergonomic considerations are important, especially if you use your computer on a regular basis. Many repetitive motion syndromes plague computer users. These real problems are much easier to prevent than remedy. It is important to have an appropriate area for the computer with the screen and computer typing keyboard at the appropriate height. I recommend consulting with someone at a computer store to ensure that the appropriate furniture is purchased with your system.

Consideration also needs to be given to preventing eye strain when using computers. Some people experience severe eye strain. There are filters available for screens that can reduce eye fatigue. Find these in computer stores and mail order houses.

You may want to purchase a workstation that is designed to be used with computers and MIDI keyboards. Wenger Corporation and some other companies offer specially designed workstations for music and computer hardware.

You will be using your computer for many applications, so don't overlook the importance of an ergonomic setting.

Handheld Devices

Handheld devices, also know as handheld computers or PDAs (personal digital assistants), are made by several companies including Palm and Sony. They are much less expensive than personal computers as they sell in the $150-$450 range. Educators and students are taking advantage of handheld technology to enhance productivity in general and administrative tasks in particular.

> **Teaching Strategy 195**
> Students and teachers use PDAs to enhance productivity.

Studies have shown that handheld devices can have a positive impact on education. They can help in collecting data, writing papers, checking facts, synching data with desktops and laptops, and collaborating on projects.

Figure 14.12: Palm IIIe and portable keyboard

Just about all of the administrative applications mentioned earlier in this chapter can be accomplished with a handheld. Programs including word processors, spreadsheets, and database can be run on these devices. The advantage is portability, because these devices can fit in your pocket.

I use my handheld to keep track of my appointments and calendar. In addition, I also have purchased music software that turns the device into a metronome and tuner. See Chapter 6, page 118 for a description of PDA instructional software. Grades can be entered into a PDA and then transferred to a computer. Teachers who move from room to room can take advantage of PDAs in the classroom.

Summary

The administrative use of computers can be a very powerful application for music teachers. A computer and a printer can become an indispensable aid for creating documents, lists and other printed materials. Word processors, databases, specialized software, and handheld devices can help the music teacher be more productive.

Review Questions

1. What is the essential hardware needed for productivity applications?
2. What are the two categories of administrative software?
3. What is the advantage of using a word processor?
4. What is the advantage of using a spelling and grammar checker?
5. Several communication kits are mentioned in this chapter. How can this type of package be helpful to the music specialist?
6. What is a database program? Give an example of how it can be used by a music specialist.
7. What is a spreadsheet? What is the primary function of a spreadsheet program?
8. What is integrated productivity software?
9. Give an example of a specific purpose program and explain how it differs from a general purpose program.
10. List a popular grading program for Macintosh or Windows.
11. What software is available to marching band show writers?
12. List two or more ways to get training on the use of administrative software.

13. What are ergonomic considerations and why should they be considered?
14. What is a PDA? Give an example listing the make and model.
15. List several ways a PDA can be used by teachers and/or students.

CD-ROM Activities

Project 14.1 In this chapter it was suggested that teachers create a disk of letters and forms needed for a school year. Make a list of the documents that should be included. Examples would include a welcome letter to parents at the beginning of the school year, letters to students announcing the performance calendar, and so forth. Create at least one letter, run a spelling check, and print the document.

Project 14.2 Do an investigation and find the name of a general purpose program such as a word processor or database program that is in use in your school by teachers. List at least two ways to apply the software in the music curriculum.

Project 14.3 Create a printed program for a performance. Include text and graphics. Print a copy of the program.

Project 14.4 Prepare a proposal to purchase one computer and printer for the music office. Address the proposal to the school principal. Review this chapter and list as many advantages as you can for using the computer and appropriate software.

Project 14.5 This chapter reviewed word processing software and how the teacher can use it. Many schools use computer labs for students to type reports and papers. Suppose that a music class could also use this facility. Brainstorm two or three ways that word processing software could be used with students as part of a general music curriculum unit or lesson.

CD-ROM Lesson Plans

None for this Chapter

Reference

Dean, Katie (2003). PDAs good for education. *Wired News* (www.wired.com).

Kuzmich, John. (2001). Music office software: Getting organized. *School Band & Orchestra Magazine*, (May).

Lautzenheiser, Tim (1993). *Director's communication kit.* Hal Leonard Corporation, Milwaukee, WI.

Shields, J. & Poftak, A. (2002) A report card on handheld computing. *Technology & Learning*, Volume 22, Number 7, 24-36.

Tam, Pui-Wing. (2000) The new teacher's pet: Handheld. *The Wall Street Journal Online*, August 1, 200.

Taylor, C. (2001) Music in the palm of your hand. *Electronic Musician*, December, 42-58.

Chapter 15

Implementing Technology: Curriculum Considerations

This chapter will explore ways computers and/or electronic instruments can be used in music education with an emphasis on how to integrate technology into the music curriculum. Throughout this text many applications of technology have been presented. The ideas presented in this chapter should help provide a plan for integrating technology into the music classroom.

The first section of this chapter deals with the hierarchy of technology applications beginning with one electronic keyboard in the class or rehearsal room and advancing to an installed music technology lab. This hierarchy of applications can be used as a plan to integrate technology at various stages dependent upon the teacher's expertise and school budget considerations.

The second portion of this chapter presents a list of the areas of technology that may be used by teachers and students. This skill-oriented section can also be helpful when selecting the best application for a particular class.

The national standards for music have been addressed in several chapters throughout the text. The final section of this chapter more completely deals with these standards and explores ways they can be enhanced with the use of technology.

Hierarchy of Technology Applications

The applications shared here are listed from the most simple to the most complex. There is a logical, step-by-step progression for integrating technology in music education. However, it is possible to pick and choose the applications that best fit one's own teaching situation.

The hierarchy of applications is as follows:

1. Electronic keyboards/instruments in the classroom and ensemble
2. A computer for teacher use
3. A computer and electronic keyboard for teacher use
4. One computer in the music classroom
5. Several (1-3) computers in the classroom for student use
6. Using the school computer lab
7. An electronic keyboard lab in the music room with one computer for the teacher's station
8. A computer and keyboard lab in the music room

Electronic Keyboards in the Classroom and Ensemble

One of the easiest ways to begin to use technology is to purchase one or more electronic keyboards for use in the classroom and performing ensembles such as chorus, jazz band, concert band, and orchestra. Today's keyboards (see Chapter 4) offer a wide range of advantages to music teachers. Using an electronic keyboard is an easy and effective way to begin to implement technology in the music curriculum.

Computer on the Teacher's Desk

Many teachers state that they are not comfortable using a computer in their classroom because they do not have experience using the technology. This is a valid point. I recommend that all teachers become familiar with the computer first, before attempting to use it in the classroom. The initial step is to procure a computer to be used as a teacher's tool for word processing. Beginning applications include using the computer for administrative tasks to create letters, lesson plans, concert programs, and to pursue the many more time saving applications described in Chapter 14.

   If the computer has Internet access (Chapter 2), the teacher can begin to do research for lessons, search for information, and share ideas with music teachers around the world.

   The emphasis here is using the computer as a tool to assist the teacher with the many administrative tasks that he/she faces from day to day. After gaining some experience the computer will be of invaluable assistance in helping reduce the time spent on administrative items.

Computer and Electronic Keyboard on the Teacher's Desk

After becoming familiar with operating a computer by using administrative software such as a word processor, the music teacher can add a MIDI keyboard and purchase MIDI software. For example, with a MIDI keyboard and computer, teachers can purchase and create sequences and recordings. These can be used for class demonstration or for accompaniments for classroom and rehearsals. Also, many teachers find using notation software extremely helpful when creating custom parts for students (see Chapter 7).

Connecting the Computer to a Large Screen Display

Assuming a computer and MIDI keyboard are available, the computer can be connected to a large screen television or other display device to show computer images to an entire class or performing group (Chapter 13). Once the large display has been added to the classroom, the teacher can use instructional software as a demonstration medium for students. Now the entire class or ensemble benefits from the technology, yet the only investment is in one system and a display unit.

Computer music games (Chapter 6) can be fun and educational, both as classroom activities and for individual student use. Also, notation programs can be displayed for students, and teachers and/or students can perform live or in real time and watch the computer create the notation.

Several Computer Stations (1-3) for Student Use

Many music teachers take advantage of the computer as a drill and practice device to help students reinforce concepts being learned in the classroom or to challenge students in new areas (Chapter 6). One popular way to accomplish this is to install one, two, or three computers in the music classroom. Stereo headphones will allow students to work quietly and independently. The most common application is to use one or more computer-assisted instruction programs and allow students to use the computer during music class, or before and after school. Students can use instructional software to learn and reinforce music concepts.

If a practice room is available in the rehearsal area, installing a computer and keyboard there can be a terrific enhancement to student learning. With a sequencer, students can practice with an accompaniment. Using specialized practice devices (Chapter 8), a practice room can be transformed into a music studio.

Using the School Computer Lab

Most schools have one or more computer labs located within the school. Traditionally, the major subject teachers in math, science, and English use school computer labs. It is possible to use the school computer lab with an entire music class provided software is made available and if the music teacher can gain access to the lab. Since the computers in the school computer lab are not usually connected to MIDI keyboards, students are limited primarily to CAI applications. Students can drill and practice music theory, aural skills, and use computer games.

The advantage of using a computer lab is that many students can work independently at their own rate. Another activity that can be explored in the computer lab is composing music using music notation software. Every notation program allows the user to input music using the computer's type-writer keyboard, arrow keys, and mouse. Music can be entered in the lab and then performed on a MIDI set-up back in the music room.

Electronic Keyboard Lab in the Music Room

The next option is to purchase a complete electronic keyboard lab for the music classroom. Every student in the class can work hands-on. This is an expensive proposition and requires sufficient space to house keyboards. Chapter 12 deals with the specifics of adding a keyboard lab to the music curriculum. Students can use the electronic keyboards to learn basic piano skills, experiment with the many timbres available on today's keyboards, and, if a workstation is purchased, begin to practice with a sequencer and record their own original music.

Once a keyboard lab is installed, a single computer connected to the teacher's station can be a tool for the instructor to create accompaniments for the songs and compositions being learned in the lab. Developing a lab takes quite a bit of planning and preparation, but the effort will pay off when the MIDI keyboard lab is installed in the music room. Chapter 16 explores ways to fund the purchase of technology.

Installing a Computer and Keyboard Lab in the Music Room

The most powerful option is to install a lab with computers and MIDI keyboards at each student station. Obviously, this is the most expensive choice. Often this is left for the secondary school or college/university, although schools at all levels are adding this type of a lab for student use.

Once the lab is in place in the high school or college, many courses and electives can be offered. These courses can be offered to those students who are enrolled in performing groups such as band, orchestra, and chorus. Also, a technology lab can be the ideal place to excite the non-performer about music. Ken Raessler[1] states that students can be thought of as both performers and consumers. The performers are those students who participate in the school performing groups such as band, orchestra, and chorus. The consumers are those students not enrolled in performing groups. Raessler points out that we need to address the performers *and* the consumers of music in our curricular offerings. Also, the national percentage of students enrolled in high school performing groups is approximately 10% nationally. That leaves quite a few students who are potential customers for the music technology lab. These students can experience technology by taking electives at the secondary level. A computer and keyboard lab can be the ideal place to encourage all students to participate in music. Some high schools find that sharing the lab with other subjects can be successful. For example, music and art could share a central lab. This is possible by adding digitizing boards and appropriate software for the art curriculum.

Once the keyboard lab is installed, a wide range of courses can be offered.[2] Some possible courses include the following:

1. Performance
   - Piano instruction: beginning, intermediate, advanced, and adult classes can be offered. These can be separate courses in the lab.
   - Performance classes that emphasize a specific style such as classical or jazz. This course would be for those with some piano performance capability.

2. Music technology
   - Introduction to music technology: an overview of all the possible applications with a focus on CAI, sequencing, and notation.
   - Sound design: classes where students will learn to create, edit, and design sounds.
   - Techniques of digital audio: this course requires an advanced MIDI studio with digital audio capability. The concepts of mixing, using effects devices, and other aspects of recording can be addressed.
   - Creating multimedia projects: With multimedia applications, students can create presentations and other projects using the computer and keyboard.

3. Music composition
   - Students can produce original compositions using MIDI sequencers and print out scores and parts using notation software.
   - Music composition: Using intelligent software applications, students can create and manipulate sound and create original compositions.

4. Music theory, ear-training, and music history
   - Using instructional software, students can drill music theory and ear training concepts.
   - Music history and music appreciation can be enhanced using appropriate materials in the lab.

The computer lab could be scheduled all day with a variety of the above courses in the high school and college. Many high schools and colleges are exploring the many options of a computer and keyboard lab. The biggest hurdle in many instances is the procurement of equipment. Unless the lab is used exclusively with existing classes, such as general music, additional staff must also be considered.

The National Standards and Technology

Another important strategy to explore when considering technology is embracing the National Standards for Arts Education developed by Music Educators National Conference.[3] The MENC National Standards provide an excellent set of benchmarks for music instruction. Music teachers should evaluate their own curriculum in relation to the nine national standards. The use of technology, specifically computers, software, and electronic keyboards, can help teachers meet the national standards in a wide variety of ways. When applying technology to the national standards, every type of technology should be used: electronic instruments, sequencing, notation, instructional software, multimedia, and administrative applications.

The national standards are organized into nine distinct areas developed by a team of music educators in conjunction with MENC. Following are some ways to integrate technology with each standard.

1. Singing, alone and with others, a varied repertoire of music

With a computer connected to a MIDI keyboard, sequencing software can provide choral directors and classroom music specialists with a sophisticated tool to create, record, and playback accompaniments. A single computer and keyboard on the teacher's desk can be used here to create appropriate accompaniments for performing groups. Computer software can be used to generate practice tapes students can take home.

Students can use instructional software that is designed to help vocalists improve their aural skills. Some instructional software is designed to help students practice singing and pitch matching. The student sings into a microphone and the computer then analyzes the performance and provides the vocalist with aural feedback.

2. Performing on instruments, alone and with others, a varied repertoire of music

Students can use electronic instruments in bands, orchestras, and choruses as accompaniment instruments and to replace instruments not present in ensembles. Electronic instruments continue to drop in price, making them an affordable addition to performing groups.

An electronic keyboard lab can provide a performance and creativity medium for students. Students in general music can learn to perform using electronic keyboards. Curriculum materials for teaching general music with an electronic keyboard lab are available from a variety of publishers (Chapter 12).

3. Improvising melodies, harmonies, and accompaniments

Teachers can also use notation software to print out exercises and materials for students to use as they improvise. The printing of scales, patterns, and other helpful exercises can be accomplished using a notation program.

Teaching students to improvise can be a challenge. A computer and a MIDI sequencing program can provide students with a practice accompanist. Standard MIDI files, available from a wide variety of publishers, give the teacher instant access to MIDI files of all styles. A sequencer can be used as an accompanist for students as they explore the world of improvisation. Creative software (Chapter 10) can be used by students as a practice tool. Using a program such as Band-in-a-Box students can experiment with harmonies and accompaniments. Students can then improvise on the keyboard or an acoustic instrument using Band-in-a-Box as the accompanist.

4. Composing and arranging music within specified guidelines

It is often challenging to find traditional ways for students to compose and arrange music. Notation software (Chapter 7) turns the computer into a music processor. Many programs are available for students from the elementary to the university level. Using notation software such as Finale or Sibelius, students can compose music and listen to it played back on a MIDI keyboard. Students can then print out their compositions. Technology becomes the music student's crayons.

5. Reading and notating music

Many teachers find using notation software to be an excellent tool for creating printed musical examples for use in rehearsal hall and classes. Additionally, original music, warm-ups, and technical exercises can be composed and printed. Custom printed materials can help students learn to read music.

Instructional software can help students drill note reading and recognize rhythm and tonal patterns. Instructional software can be used to reinforce note reading skills.

6. *Listening to, analyzing, and describing music*

Instructional software offers dozens of programs that can be used to reinforce the student's ability to analyze and describe music. There are programs designed to help students learn music theory, ear-training programs to drill chord types, intervals, and more.

7. *Evaluating music and music performances*

The Internet provides students and teachers with a limitless amount of sound files that can be used to evaluate music and music performances (see Chapters 2 and 11).

Another helpful application is to have students record performances using MIDI keyboard and notation software. The notation software then translates the performance into printed music that is displayed on the computer screen. The notation can be viewed and printed out for evaluation by students and teachers. Student performances can also be recorded into a sequencer and digital audio software and played back for analysis.

8. *Understanding relationships between music, the other arts,*
   and disciplines outside the arts

Any time students create projects using multimedia applications they are delving into areas outside of the arts. When students use the Internet to search for information or to complete a WebQuest (see Chapter 11), they are dabbling in other disciplines.

Because computers and electronic instruments can be programmed by students, they provide a medium to make connections with the other arts and disciplines outside the arts. For example, in a keyboard lab, students can learn to create and modify sounds. In order to make changes to a sound, the physical properties must be understood, thus linking music with science and mathematics.

9. *Understanding music in relation to history and culture*

There are instructional programs about classical, jazz, and contemporary music available to help students understand the relationship between music, history, and culture. Using the Internet, students can study virtually any topic in music history and related cultures.

Opportunity-to-Learn Standards for Music Technology

Immediately following the release of the National Standards for Music Education in 1994, MENC (www.menc.org) released the Opportunity-to-Learn Standards for Music Education as a guide to what schools should provide to help students achieve the National Standards for Music Education. MENC recommends that states adopt these Opportunity-to-Learn standards or use them as a basis for developing their own.[4] The Opportunity-to-Learn Standards for Music Technology are organized into four distinct areas:

- Curriculum and scheduling
- Staffing, equipment
- Materials/software
- Facilities

Each of the above areas are divided into lists that include minimal and desirable recommendations. For example, under the heading staffing for grades 1-5 or 1-6 includes six minimal recommendations and an additional three that are desirable:

1. A planned program of ongoing staff development to provide teachers with training in applying technology in the curriculum is in place. Training is available on a variety of levels to match the varying backgrounds and proficiency of teachers.

There are additional recommendations listed numbers 2-6. Under desirable, there are three additional recommendations. One of which is:

8. Music teachers have ready access to Internet-based professional development opportunities.

A copy of the Opportunity-to-Learn Standards for Music Technology can be viewed and printed online. The complete version of the document can be viewed and printed from the web location:

www.menc.org/publication/books/techstan.htm.

MENC allows educators to print the standards from the web site and asks for a contribution of $5.00 for the publication.

The Opportunity-to-Learn Standards for Music Technology contain helpful recommendations for teachers and administrators. I suggest you purchase or download a copy and review your program against it. The document can be helpful when budgeting for technology.

Summary

Technology offers a wide variety of applications for both teachers and students. This chapter outlined eight ways to bring technology into the music curriculum. These are: electronic instruments in the classroom and ensemble; a computer on the teacher's desk; a computer and electronic keyboard on the teacher's desk; one computer in the music classroom (at the teacher's station); several (1-3) computers in the classroom for student use; using the school computer lab; installing an electronic keyboard lab in the music room; and installing a computer and keyboard lab in the music room. These eight approaches can be used in any order or combination. There are several areas of music technology including administrative, electronic keyboards, sequencing, notation, and instructional software.

Technology can be used to support the nine National Standards for Music Education developed by Music Educators National Conference. The Opportunity-to-Learn Standards for Music Technology can be used to review your present technology offerings and to plan for future use of technology.

Review Questions

1. List the hierarchy of applications for implementing technology into the music curriculum.
2. Name one application for a computer on the teacher's desk.
3. What applications can be realized with a computer and MIDI keyboard in the classroom?
4. What student use can be realized with 1-3 computers in the classroom?
5. List ways that the school computer lab can be used in the music curriculum?
6. Once a keyboard lab is installed in a classroom, list the four areas of courses that could be offered.
7. List an application for music technology for each of the nine national standards.

8. Who produced the Opportunity-to-Learn standards? How can these be used by music specialists?

CD-ROM Activities

Project 15.1 Interview two teachers who use computers in their teaching. Find out how they use the computer and categorize their uses as either teacher or student use.

Project 15.2 Select one or more of the national standards and brainstorm three additional ways technology can be used to support these standards; name specific applications and computer programs that could be used.

CD-ROM Lesson Plans

None for this chapter

Reference

Carpenter, Robert A. (MCMXCI) *Technology in the music classroom.* Alfred Publishing, Van Nuys, CA

Raessler, Kenneth (2003). *Aspiring to excel.* GIA Publications, Inc. Chicago.

Rudolph, T.; Richmond, F.; Mash. D.; and Williams D. (2002) *Technology strategies for music education.* Hal Leonard Publishing Corp. Second Edition. Milwaukee, WI

Taylor, Robert, P. Editor (1980) *The computer in the school: Tutor, tool, tutee.* Teachers College Press, New York.

Williams, David, Chair. (1999) *Opportunity-to-Learn Standards for Music Technology.* MENC, The National Association for Music Education. Reston, VA.

Chapter 16

Copyright Law

Music Education National Standards: 8
NETS (National Education Technology Standards): 2, 6

This chapter provides an overview of the copyright law and its applications in music education. It is important for music teachers to have an understanding and awareness of copyright law in general and the fair use allowances in particular. There are three areas to be considered. First, music teachers must be aware of the restrictions and rights regarding printed music, especially when making copies, arrangements, using notation software, and creating MIDI sequences. Second, teachers need to understand the legal issues regarding software duplication and use. And third, educators need to know how to get permission for reproducing copyrighted works on CD and DVD recordings.

The United States Copyright Law is a very complex document. Music educators can find assistance in understanding this complex law in two excellent publications. The first is a free resource designed for music educators: *The United States Copyright Law: A Guide for Music Educators* (see Figure 16.1). This publication is a joint effort by several organizations including MENC, Music Publishers' Association of The United States, Music Teachers National Association, National Association of Schools of Music, and the National Music Publishers' Association. There is no copyright claimed by this document. Music educators are encouraged to reproduce it to assure its widest possible circulation.

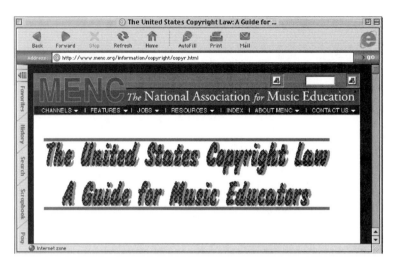

Figure 16.1: MENC copyright law web site
www.menc.org/information/copyright/copyr.html

Another helpful publication is the book *Copyright: The Complete Guide for Music Educators, 2nd edition*.[1] Jay Althouse, the author, is a composer and music educator and has written an easy to read, practical book covering the impact and ramifications of the copyright law for music teachers as it relates to printed music and performance rights.

Why a Copyright Law?

The copyright law is designed to protect the rights of composers and authors. Musical compositions, arrangements, and computer music software are all subject to copyright protection. The music business, indeed the entire entertainment industry as we currently know it, would cease to exist without the copyright law.

The copyright law benefits music education in many ways. Without a copyright law there would be no financial incentive to write and publish music or to create music software. Commercial computer programs such as notation and sequencing software would not likely be created if the copyright law did not protect the authors from unauthorized duplication and distribution.

Over the years, the arts have flourished in societies where copyright laws were strongly enforced.[2] We, as music educators, need first to recognize that we benefit from the copyright law and second understand that if we abide by its restrictions we are insuring that quality music and music software will continue to be made available to us.

What Does the Copyright Law Cover?

The copyright law gives the owner the right to reproduce their own works in all media including printed music and recordings of any kind. Also protected are what is referred to as derivative works, or works that have been derived from the original such as arrangements for chorus, band, and other ensembles, MIDI files, and the like. The copyright owner also retains the right to distribute their work in print or any other form.[3]

The copyright law can be traced back more than 200 years. It has been updated several times responding to new technologies as they have been introduced. The copyright law was amended in 1909 to address the production of piano rolls. Prior to 1909, music was produced in only one form—printed sheet music. Under the 1909 revision of the copyright law, composers were to be compensated for mechanical production of their works in the form of piano rolls.

The next major revision came via the Copyright Act of 1976, which went into effect in 1978. It was designed to address the new technologies introduced after 1909, including radio and television broadcasts. The Copyright Renewal Act of 1992 made copyright renewal automatic and addressed audio home recording. In 1995, the Digital Performance Right in Sound Recordings Act defined audio digitized transmissions as public performances. The Copyright Act of 1999 extended the copyright of works after 1978 to the life of author plus 70 years and works prior to 1978 increased to 95 years of copyright protection.

Public Domain

If a work is in the public domain, it is no longer covered by the copyright law. Here is a simple way to determine if a piece of music is in the public domain: was the composition written prior to 1923? If so, the music is in public domain. This includes Scott Joplin and other composers who composed music prior to 1923. The copyright law changed in 1999 and granted works a 20-

year copyright extension. This means that there will be no more new music that will enter public domain until 2018.

If a work is in public domain, arrangements and adaptations may be made of the work without obtaining permission from the copyright owner. In other words, if you want to compose a band arrangement of the theme from Beethoven's Ninth Symphony, you may do so without infringing on copyright law because it was composed more than 75 years ago. The best way to keep track of new material entering public domain is via web sites that are listed later in this chapter.

If someone writes an arrangement of a public domain composition, the arrangement itself is subject to the copyright law. So, for example, if you purchase an arrangement of Beethoven's "Ode to Joy", the specific arrangement is protected by copyright. Public domain refers to the original composition the way it was originally scored by the composer.

Fair Use of Copyrighted Material

The Copyright Act of 1976 specifically addressed the issue of fair use of copyrighted materials for educational purposes. There are two areas of fair use:

- Emergency copying
- Academic use, other than performance

Educators are allowed to reproduce or reprint a copyrighted piece of music as long as an order is placed with a music dealer or the publisher. For example, let's suppose the first trumpet player in your jazz ensemble loses his or her folder the night of the jazz festival. You may enter the first trumpet parts using your notation program and print it out, as long as you replace the part by ordering it from the publisher and destroy the copy you made.

The second area of fair use is designed for classroom use. A teacher may make a copy of a portion of a work or enter it into a sequencer or notation program for use in the classroom for analysis or study. The musical example may not exceed 10% of the total work for class study as long as that 10% does not constitute a performable unit. Note that this fair use is restricted to non-performance uses. If you intend to create a workbook or a complete anthology of copyrighted works, then permission must be obtained from the copyright holder.

The following are expressly prohibited by the copyright law:

- Copying to avoid purchase
- Copying music for any kind of performance (note emergency exception above)
- Copying to create anthologies or compilations
- Reproducing material designed to be consumable such as workbooks, standardized tests, and answer sheets
- Charging students beyond the actual cost involved in making copies as permitted above

Notation Software to Edit and Simplify

Printed copies that have been purchased may be edited or simplified for educational purposes, so teachers who are using notation software (see Chapter 7) and have purchased copies of the music can use this software to save time preparing edited and simplified parts for students. The "fair use" options when using a notation program to print music include:

- Printing out warm-up exercises, scale exercises, and the like. So long as you don't copy exercises from a published method book, a notation program may be used to print out warm-ups and exercises.

- Printing readiness exercises for a particular piece. Suppose you have purchased an arrangement that you wish to perform with your band, orchestra, chorus, or other performing group. In most cases it would not be a violation of copyright to prepare exercises to help the students learn a particular work. For example, you may print out isolated rhythmic or melodic figures provided you have already purchased the arrangement or composition.

- The fair use guidelines allow for parts to be edited or simplified to suit your ensemble. For example, in my middle school concert band I have two trombones and 17 alto saxes. After I purchase an arrangement, I use a notation program to enter the third trombone part and print it for several of my alto saxophones. This is permitted under fair use guidelines. However, it is important not to change the nature of the work when editing or simplifying parts.

The best way to determine if you are violating the copyright law is to ask yourself if you are using technology (copy machine, computer, etc.) to "avoid purchase." If the answer is yes, you are most likely in violation of the copyright law with the exception of the fair use provided to music education as mentioned above.

> **Teaching Strategy 196**
>
> Follow this general rule: do not use technology to avoid purchasing a piece of music, recording, or other product.

Derivative Works (Arrangements)

Making arrangements of a copyrighted piece of music is an exclusive right of the copyright owner. However, under the music guidelines amplifying the fair use section of the law, educators may edit or simplify printed copies that have been purchased, provided that the fundamental character of the work is not distorted or the lyrics, if any, altered (or lyrics added if none exist). Therefore, in certain circumstances, music software can be used to edit or simplify arrangements for students.

If you use a notation program to create an arrangement or adaptation of a copyrighted work without written permission from the copyright owner, you may be in violation of the copyright law. Anyone wishing to arrange a copyrighted work with the exceptions noted above, must obtain permission from the copyright owner.

Scanning Software

Using a scanner to capture printed music for use in a notation program may be a fair or unfair use of the copyright law depending on the situation. Be sure to refer to copyright restrictions and fair use guidelines when using a notation scanning program. If you are entering music using the scanning program to avoid purchase, you are most likely in the wrong. However, if you are editing or simplifying parts, a scanner can be a quick way to capture music into your notation software program.

Sequencing and MIDI Files

The copyright owner has the sole right to create derivative works, and this includes creating sequences and MIDI files. If a composition is in the public domain, you may create an accompaniment or MIDI file. Folk songs such as "Hot Cross Buns" and "Lightly Row" are in the public domain. However, if you are using a copyrighted song written after 1923 that has not yet entered public domain, you must obtain permission to create a MIDI sequencer file of the work.

If you want to create or use a MIDI file of a piece of copyrighted music for practice or performance, you have several options. First check to see if a MIDI version of the song is available. The copyright owner can usually furnish this information. For example, many basal series such as Silver Burdett, McGraw-Hill, and others offer MIDI files that can be used for accompaniment and in performance. A growing number of publishers sell MIDI versions of copyrighted songs. These publishers have obtained the right to create the MIDI files and when you purchase them, you license the right to use the files for accompaniments and educational performances. If a published MIDI version of a composition is not available, contact the publisher to get permission to create a MIDI file.

Accompaniment Software

There are copyright considerations when using accompaniment software (Chapter 10) such as Band-in-a-Box to create files for students. If the song is copyrighted, then permission must be granted to create an arrangement for practice or performance. However, chord changes are not subject to copyright. The 12-bar blues progression is used for many songs. Creating a 12-bar blues progression for students would not be a violation of copyright unless it was directly used with a performance of a copyrighted song.

Recording an accompaniment part for rehearsal may be fair use, especially if the MIDI recording is being used for rehearsal purposes only. However, if the publisher offers a MIDI version of the composition, as some do, creating a MIDI sequence is in violation of copyright. It is always best to ask permission before making an arrangement, accompaniment, MIDI file, or other adaptation of a copyrighted work.

Downloading MIDI Files

Uploading and downloading MIDI files from the Internet or on-line services has the same copyright restrictions as other forms of music. Downloading and using a copyrighted MIDI file is an infringement of the law. CompuServe was sued by the National Music Publishers' Association in 1990 for allowing individuals to download the song "Unchained Melody". This was a class action suit on behalf of more than 140 publishers who owned compositions allegedly available on CompuServe at the time.[4] Individuals uploaded the file to CompuServe's computers and then other users were able to download a copy for their own use. This was a violation of the composer's rights and therefore a violation of copyright.

The Internet (Chapter 11) is a tremendous source of public domain music. There are literally thousands of files available that may be used by music educators for playback, printing, arranging, and other uses. When you are browsing the Web, search the words "MIDI files" and you will receive many locations that offer MIDI files. Once a MIDI file has been downloaded into your computer, you can import the file to your notation program and create an arrangement for your ensemble. See Chapter 2, page 36, for specific instructions for downloading and saving to disk.

Classical MIDI Archives

There are some web sites that feature only MIDI files of music in public domain. The most notable of these is the Classical MIDI Archives, a site that offers more than 28,000 MIDI files of pieces in the public domain. There are some restrictions on these files. Even though the arrangements on this site and similar sites are of music in the public domain, the arrangements themselves are the property of those who created them.

Check with each web site to determine what their restrictions are. For example, the Classical MIDI Archives lists its guidelines as a maximum of 20 files can be used for a commercial web site, a CD-ROM, DVD, or film/video and that individual contributors to the site must be contacted for permission to use their MIDI sequences.

Locating Public Domain Music and Public Domain Services

Earlier in this chapter public domain music was defined. There are sites on the Internet that can be of assistance. Some offer listings of public domain music. Others offer free and fee-based downloading of both MIDI files and sheet music versions of public domain songs.

If you are interested in looking for public domain music to arrange for your performing groups, then check out the free site Public Domain Info at www.pdinfo.com. This site has an extensive listing of public domain music and also offers sheet music and books for sale. Another helpful site to use when searching for public domain music is www.pubdomain.com. It charges a monthly fee to access its extensive library of public domain music. For choral music, the Choral Public Domain Library is located at www.cpdl.org. This is a free sheet music archive with many public domain choral works.

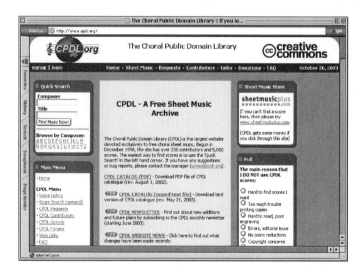

Figure 16.8: Choral Public Domain Library (www.cpdl.org)

Another excellent site is My Sheet Music www.mysheetmusic.com. It offers some sheet music downloads for free. It also offers a subscription service that provides access to thousands of files in sheet music format. There are other sites that offer similar services on the web.

Figure 16.9: www.sheetmusic.com

All of these sites can be very helpful to music teachers. For example, I was looking for some music for some MIDI lab students who asked for a particular piece by Beethoven, *Für Elise*. I did not have a copy in the piano book, so I found it online and printed a copy for free! The fact that Beethoven's music was written prior to 1923 means it is in the public domain.

Downloading Audio Files

Over the past few years, downloading and sharing of audio files has become commonplace. Millions of users share files including music, movies, software, images, and other digital files. Music files are usually swapped in MP3 format. MP3 is a form of file compression that reduces the size of a music file to approximately one tenth of its original size, making it faster to download. The audio quality is slightly reduced from the original. MP3 files have approximately the same audio quality of FM radio.

Many file sharing services are free. However, if the files are protected by copyright, then swapping files is a violation. Napster was the first file-sharing service. It was deemed illegal and was shut down in July of 2001. Other similar file-sharing sites have sprung up such as Kazaa and Morpheus. These sites allow users to share copyrighted material, which is a violation of copyright law.

I spoke with a class of seventh grade students and asked if they used Kazaa and other web sites to download music. The vast majority did. When I asked if it was a violation of the law, they responded that if it was illegal, they would not be able to copy the files. There is a general feeling that copying and swapping copyrighted music is OK. Music educators need to let students know that this is a violation of copyright.

Teaching Strategy 197

Educate your students regarding the copyright law. For example, sharing copies of copyrighted music such as MP3 files is a violation of copyright.

There are sites that offer downloaded music for a fee. These sites do not violate copyright because users are paying for the right to own the music, just as if you purchased music on disc from a store. Apple's iTunes is an example of a fee-based site to download music and other media without violating the copyright restrictions. Songs may be downloaded for a fee of $.99 per song for both Macintosh and Windows users. See figure 16.2.

There are other fee-based download sites. America Online's MusicNet has pricing and CD burning policies. A membership to America Online is required. RealOne Rhapsody charges a monthly fee ($9.95), then 79 cents per song. FullAudio's MusicNow charges $9.95 a month, then $.99 cents per song. MusicMatch's MX service starts at $4.95 per month for unlimited streaming. Streaming means you can listen to music on your computer for free, but you can't burn the songs to a CD or disc. If you are looking for independent artists, consider Emusic. Emusic does not feature big-label artists, but it does allow unlimited streaming and burning for $9.95 per month.

Figure 16.2: Apple's iTunes downloading site
www.apple.com/itunes/store/shop.html

If you are looking for classical music in MP3 format, then consider a subscription to the Classical MIDI Archives. Currently, the subscription price is $25.00 per year. Subscribers can access a wide variety of classical MP3 recordings that can be downloaded.

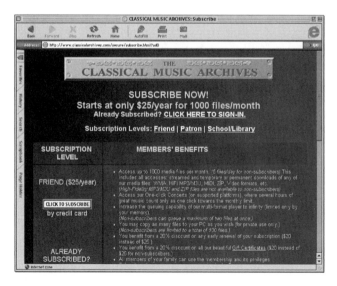

Figure 16.3: Classical MIDI Archives Subscription Service
www.classicalarchives.com/secure/subscribe.html

The fee-based download services are relatively new as of this writing, so be sure to do some research before selecting a service. Check with friends and colleagues and ask for their advice. Fee-based download services are the best way to accomplish all of your audio downloading needs.

Multimedia

Many people use authoring software such as Microsoft PowerPoint, Apple Keynote, and Hyperstudio to create multimedia presentations and projects (see Chapter 11). It is important to be aware of the copyright restrictions for using music and graphics in these applications. Purchasing an audio recording does not give you permission to use it in a multimedia presentation or application. Of course, you could create your own original compositions or make an arrangement of a piece of music in the public domain and import it into your presentation without violating the copyright law.

It is possible to obtain permission to use a copyrighted work in a multimedia presentation. If you are planning to use a graphic or sound file that you are downloading from an Internet site, contact the web master and request permission.

Another excellent source of sounds and graphics is to locate those that are royalty free and can be purchased and downloaded from many sites (Fig. 16.4 and Fig. 16.5, p. 426). Sounds and graphics can be purchased on CD or downloaded from the Internet. In some cases these are free or there can be a charge to purchase a CD or subscription. These images and sound files can then be used royalty-free in teacher and student presentations.

Figure 16.4: Royalty free sounds from Sounddogs.com

Figure 16.5: Royalty free clipart and sounds from www.clipart.com

Recordings and the Copyright Law

The copyright law allows music educators to make a single recording of a student performance for study and for the archives. Therefore, if you want to record your spring concert and archive it for the future or use it for study with your students, you may do so without violating the copyright law. However, if you want to make multiple copies of the performance and sell them to the students and/or community, you must pay a royalty for each copyrighted selection.

Many music educators use digital audio recording equipment to record student performances and distribute them to the students and community. I have done this as a fund raiser for our music program. We record our performing groups and then duplicate several hundred copies and sell them to the students, parents and community for $15.00 per CD. In order to comply with the copyright law, permission must be received and a royalty paid on all copyrighted songs.

The term for licensing any type of audio recording is a mechanical license. This term comes from the early days of recording when piano rolls were made and sold. Because they were mechanically produced, the term mechanical license was used. Today, mechanical license refers to all recordings made electronically or digitally and distributed in any form.

Teaching Strategy 198

Be sure to get the proper mechanical license before you record and distribute sound recordings to students, parents, and members of the community.

Obtaining the necessary license is not difficult. Many music publishers use agents for licensing this right rather than doing it themselves. The Harry Fox Agency, Inc., is the non-exclusive agent for most publishers (see Figure 16.6 on page 428). For the last CD project I completed, I went to the Harry Fox Agency web site and searched for the songs I wanted to include on the CD. I then completed the forms and paid the licensing fee. The average cost was $35 per selection. The Harry Fox Agency facilitates obtaining a license to record and distribute recordings for a profit. Music educators can then use this as a way to make money for the music program and to provide students and parents with a professional sounding and looking audio recording.

The Harry Fox web site includes a link for those distributing fewer than 2,500 copies of a recording (see Figure 16.7 on page 429). It is possible to search for specific selections on line. The www.songfile.com web site (which is linked on the main Harry Fox Agency site) is designed for those who wish to distribute less than 2,500 copies of a recording. The cost of the mechanical license is reduced for people who are producing less than 2,500 copies.

Of course you and/or your students can record music in the public domain or your original compositions without a license. Ken Simpson, a teacher in Atlanta, Georgia, produces a Christmas CD every year. The students write arrangements of songs in public domain so no license is needed. Simpson then sells the CD to the community and gives the proceeds to a local charity.

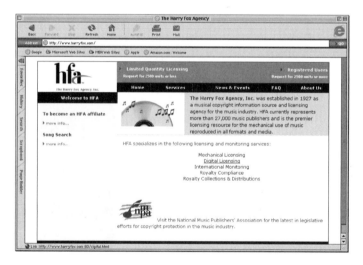

Figure 16.6: The Harry Fox Agency for licensing sound recordings

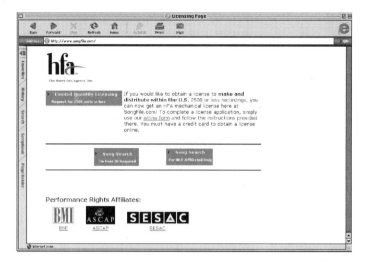

Figure 16.7: Songfile.com web site for licensing 2,500
or fewer copies of sound recordings

Computer Software and the Copyright Law

Computer software is almost always protected by copyright. Essentially, there are three types of computer software. They are:

1. Commercial software—The majority of programs sold today are copyrighted and protected from unauthorized duplication and distribution and are sold through retail stores or outlets. Usually, the copyright notice is placed right on the disk and looks like:

   © 2003, NAME OF COMPANY. All rights reserved.

   When a computer program starts-up, a copyright notice is usually displayed. If a piece of software is copyrighted, it is not lawful to make and/or distribute copies. Unauthorized copies are referred to as pirated copies. The copyright law permits the owner to make one archival copy of a piece of software. This means that you can make one copy and store it in a file cabinet to be used if the original disk becomes damaged or is lost or stolen. The archival copy should not be used unless the original is no longer functional.

2. Shareware—This is software that is copyrighted but not published. An individual writes a program and distributes it personally, usually via an online service or computer bulletin board. Typically, the author offers the software to users and allows them to try out the software without charge. If the user decides to keep it, they are asked to register the copy and send a nominal fee to the author, usually $10–$50. Shareware is a good place to go when budget is the main concern. Shareware is typically much less expensive than commercially produced titles.

   When I am looking for shareware, I use the web site www.downloads.com. Most shareware programs are listed here and can be downloaded from the site.

3. Freeware—These are programs that may be copied without charge. The authors of these programs have voluntarily released these programs for free and they are in the public domain.

   Typically, freeware is free for personal use. Often freeware programs are still covered by copyright in regard to distribution. It is unlawful to obtain a copy of a freeware program and then sell it to others for a profit.

   When searching for freeware, I also use www.download.com (see Figure 16.10). There are other sites that list freeware for specific areas such as music. An excellent site to search for free software titles is the Shareware Music Machine (see Figure 16.11).

Figure 16.10: Download site for shareware: www.download.com

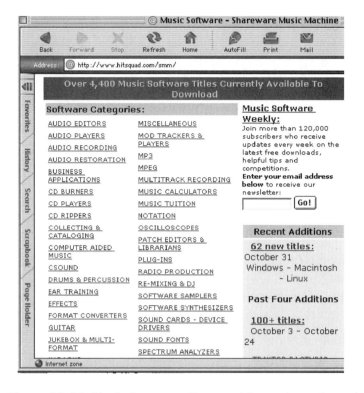

Figure 16.11: Music freeware site: www.hitsquad.com/smm/

It is important to understand that when you buy a piece of commercial software or you obtain a copy of a freeware or shareware program, you have obtained the right to use the software, *not* the right to duplicate or distribute it to others.

Site License and Lab Use

If you purchase a piece of commercial software, such as a music notation program, and you install it on each computer in the school computer lab, you have most likely violated the copyright law. When you buy a piece of software, you have purchased the right to use it on one computer. It would be lawful to purchase a piece of notation software for the computer in your music room. Students could learn to use the software one at a time. Over the course of the year, your entire class can use the program. This is not a violation of the copyright law. A violation occurs when you make an unauthorized copy for other computers in your room or school.

It is possible to obtain permission or a license to use multiple copies of a piece of software. There are several ways to obtain this permission. You may purchase a lab pack if the publisher makes one available. A lab pack is usually a package of 3–5 copies of a piece of software sold at a reduced cost. Now you have the right to use the number of copies that you purchased in the lab pack. If you received three copies, you may load the software onto three separate computers. It is illegal to make more than the number of copies you received in the lab pack.

If you want to put the software on multiple computers, contact the publisher or software distributor and ask if they offer a site license. A site license is the right to use a piece of software at a site such as a school district. The cost of a site license can be 10 or more times the cost of one copy of the software. Site licenses differ from publisher to publisher, so be sure to ask about any restrictions. Some site licenses can be used in a computer lab and others permit the school to make copies for all computers in the building.

Also check with the publisher to see if they offer volume discounts on their software. For example, a company may reduce the price of the software if you buy 10 copies or more. Sometimes this can be a more cost effective way than a site license to purchase software for your lab.

If you plan to use computer software in a lab with multiple computers, be sure to include software in the budget. It can be quite expensive to purchase lab packs, a site license, or multiple copies of the software you plan to use.

Demo Disks

Because it is sometimes difficult to determine if a piece of software is right for a particular situation, many companies offer demo versions of software that can be used for free. This is an excellent way to preview software before purchasing. Contact the publishers directly to see if a demo version of a program is available. Many times these programs are quite complete. For example, music notation demo programs often have all of the features of the program but cannot save or print.

Benefits of Purchasing Software

It is important to understand that the copyright law helps us as educators. If copyright law did not exist and authors did not receive compensation for their work, we would not have the tremendous volume of music software available to us. Therefore, there are many benefits to purchasing computer software and avoiding the use of pirated or illegal copies. Some of the benefits of purchasing software are:

- Many software writers depend on royalties for their income. If royalties are not paid, new and better software will not be written.

- If we do not buy a software package or product it will no longer be upgraded and improved. An example is the intelligent software program Band-in-a-Box by PG Music. The product is in its 12th version and each revision has improved significantly. I remember purchasing a copy of the first version of the program and it was quite simple compared to the current version. Purchasing software contributes to the industry and improvement of the products we use.

- Another reason for purchasing a copy of a piece of software is to become a registered user. It is very important to complete and return the registration card after buying a piece of software or register online. After becoming a registered user, you will receive notices of upgrades from the publisher. For example, when a product makes a move from version 2.0 to 2.1, many publishers send the upgrade to registered users free or at a nominal cost. If you have not completed the registration card then you will not receive notices of upgrades.

- After you purchase a piece of software, it is quite common to have questions about the program. Many companies will not give advice over the telephone or via email to anyone other than a registered user.

Educating Students

It is important to educate our students on the proper use of the copyrighted materials by both discussion and example.

> **Teaching Strategy 199**
> Educate students on the do's and don'ts of the copyright law.

One excellent way to introduce the concept of fair use to students is to discuss the issue of sampling other people's music in recordings. Rap music has frequently used sampling, where a portion of someone else's song is sampled and then used in another recording. It is possible to obtain a license to use someone else's recording in a song. However, it is illegal if the user has not been granted permission by the copyright owner. Examples of sampling in the pop music scene include frequent use of James Brown's trademark scream. Dozens of artists have used his scream in their own recordings.[5] Students can relate to the issue of sampling and will develop an understanding of the law. The key issue is for you, the teacher, to model appropriate behavior with regard to the copyright law.

Summary

Proper use of copyrighted material will ensure that composers, arrangers, and software authors will continue to create and update materials for our use. Students should be educated on what is permissible and what is not. It is very important for music educators to understand the copyright law and its ramifications.

Review Questions

1. There is a free publication available to music educators that is located on the MENC web site. What is the title and web address of this publication?
2. Why is there a copyright law? Who does this law protect?
3. What is covered by the copyright law?
4. Define public domain.
5. What is fair use and what specific areas does it address?
6. List three examples of fair use by a music educator using a notation program.
7. What are derivative works?

8. How would an educator get permission to arrange a copyrighted work?
9. If a published MIDI file is not available for a copyrighted work, what options do you have?
10. List one or more web sites that offer MIDI files for download that are in public domain.
11. List one or more sites that offer fee-based downloading services for audio files.
12. List one or more sites that offer royalty free sound and graphics files that can be used in multimedia projects.
13. What is a mechanical license?
14. What is the name of the mechanical licensing agency that is used by most publishers?
15. What is the web address to search for mechanical licenses?
16. List one or more web sites that offer downloads of public domain software.
17. List the three types of computer software.
18. What web site is available to search for freeware and shareware software?
19. What is a site license?
20. List the four benefits of purchasing software.

CD-ROM Activities

Project 16.1 Music that was composed prior to 1923 is considered to be in the public domain. Make a list of several composers whose works are most likely to be in the public domain and therefore may be used for arrangements or other songs.

Project 16.2 Design a checklist of do's and don'ts regarding the copyright law. Be sure to include a mention of fair use of copyrighted material. An excellent web source is www.educationworld.com.

Project 16.3 It is possible to obtain permission or license from the copyright owner to create an arrangement or other adaptation of copyrighted music. List the steps that a teacher should take to obtain the permission to arrange and/or adapt copyrighted music.

CD-ROM Lesson Plans

Copyright guidelines for students. Have students answer the questions in this lesson plan by searching web sites. Have them create a list of do's and don'ts for their personal use.

Reference

Althouse, Jay (1990). *Copyright: The complete guide for music educators, 2nd edition.* Alfred Publishing, Van Nuys, CA.

Higgs, Simon (1993). MIDI files & copyrights. *The International MIDI Association Bulletin,* Spring, 1993.

Krasilovsky, William and Shemel, Sidney. (2000). *This business of music, 8th edition.* Billboard Books, NY.

MENC, The National Association for Music Education. (2000). *The United States copyright law: A guide for music educators.* www.menc.org/information/copyright/copyr.html

Tomsho, Robert (1990). As sampling revolutionizes recording, debate grows over aesthetics, copyrights. The Wall Street Journal. November 19, 1990. pg. B3.

Wacholtz, Larry. (1996). *Star Tracks: Principles for success in the Music & entertainment industry.* Thumbs Up Publishing. Nashville.

Woo, Junda. (1993) Publisher sues CompuServe over a song. The Wall Street Journal. December 16, 1993, pg. B16.

Chapter 17

Funding and Proposal Writing

The cost of purchasing computers, software, and electronic instruments can be a strain on the school music budget. Most music departments do not have sufficient funds to support the purchase of computers, software, and electronic keyboard labs. As a result of this, teachers often need to identify alternative sources and ideas for purchasing hardware and software. In some cases, a school district or music department must locate outside sources to fund technology. This chapter explores sources of funding and offers suggestions for developing a proposal for the purchase of equipment and software.

Develop the "Why"

When developing a plan for the use of technology in music education keep the following steps in mind. First, identify and address specific goals that support the existing music curriculum. Why do you need to use technology? The answer to this question may very well determine whether or not you receive the necessary funds from your institution.

Begin by listing the benefits of using computers, electronic keyboards, and other technologies that you select in your current curriculum. Review the teaching strategies shared throughout the previous chapters and select several that will most significantly enhance a specific class or ensemble. Some benefits might include:

- To provide the teacher with a tool to create printed music and recorded exercises for student practice and performance.

- To provide the teacher with a reference and research tool (i.e. multimedia and the Internet).
- To enable students to compose, print, and perform their own compositions.

These are just a few of the many possible uses of technology. The important point is to identify reasons that support the unique advantages technology brings to the music curriculum. This initial step will help insure success and persuade administrators to support the procurement of the necessary equipment and training.

Another excellent way to develop the "why" for music technology is to review your institution's educational mission statement and music department goals and objectives. Most schools have graduation outcomes that include technology. At my school district, I was successful in convincing the administration that electronic keyboards and computers would enhance the goal for graduating students to be able to "understand and use technology," one of our district's graduation outcomes for all students. My administrators agreed that students would certainly benefit from using technology in mathematics, science, English, AND music. I also looked at my school's goals and found objectives such as including cooperative learning strategies and teaching to individual differences that the music department could address using technology.

Writing a Proposal

Later in this chapter I will review some strategies for finding outside funds for the purchase of technology hardware and software. However, even if the funds are readily available to you, be sure to have a definite plan in mind as it will surely help ensure the success of your program.

Many districts require teachers to prepare a written proposal when requesting new equipment. If you are seeking outside funds, a proposal is a must. With every proposal there are some common areas to consider.

Needs Assessment

This is usually the first and certainly the most important part of any proposal. It is usually the first section of a proposal. Describing the need gives the reader an impression of you and your level of expertise. It is a good idea to use a somewhat scholarly tone at first. Perhaps cite a few statistics about technology in general and/or music instruction. Keep this initial section brief and to the point.

In your needs assessment, show why the proposed materials are needed compared with what is currently in use. For example, in a state technology grant, one school district asked for money to develop a technology lab at the high school. The music teacher identified that students did not, for the most part, compose and create music in the traditional instrumental groups at the high school level. The need, therefore, was to utilize technology to allow students to participate in higher level thinking skills such as composing and printing original music.

When formulating the need, make the proposal student centered rather than administration or teacher focused. Educational agencies tend to be more interested in materials that directly help students learn, rather than supplying computers and related equipment for administrative assistance such as preparing documents, writing the marching band show, and other administrative tasks. However, once the computer is purchased for educational applications, it can be used after school hours for administrative tasks.

The Objectives

Each proposal must contain specific, measurable objectives. Many proposals are turned down because the objectives are not clearly stated. Make the objectives S.M.A.R.T. (Specific, Measurable, Appropriate, Result-oriented, and Timely).

Specific: Who is going to benefit from the technology and what activities will they be doing? For example, you may choose to develop a MIDI lab using one of your practice rooms or to add a computer for the mainstreamed students in the class.

Measurable: Both the activities and student progress must be measured in some way. For example, students who are learning to compose and create music might be assigned to the computer for 30 minutes each week. They will create and compose a specific number of pieces that will be printed out and recorded on disk.

Appropriate: Activities need to address a specific need that is appropriate for your students. For example, elementary students can learn to compose a simple melody; middle school students might be asked to compose melodies with an accompaniment; high school students might be asked to compose a four part arrangement. Be sure the objectives are well suited to the grade level and teaching load.

Result-Oriented: The results that will occur from the use of technology must be predicted. Some music educators have proposed to use technology to increase achievement scores, aptitude scores, and interest in the subject area or to decrease the drop-rate, etc. Most funding agencies are searching for proposals that are likely to succeed and have a positive impact on learning.

Timely: Students need to use the equipment for a specified amount of time. For example, general music classes could sign up for computer time so that each student has 30 minutes of practice per week from October through May. Also, your project should have a 1-2 year time limit. The benefit is that after the project has ended you are permitted to keep the equipment and software.

Activities

This is the main body of the proposal, and it needs to provide the reader with an idea of the exact flow of activities that will take place. The activities section is an outgrowth of the preceding objectives portion. Be sure to describe exactly how you plan to accomplish your objectives, and how you will get the most benefit out of the equipment for the most students.

Cost

Although technology is expensive, it can be described in a relatively accessible way. Wide student involvement is a key. For example, a classroom music teacher requests a computer, computer data projector, and MIDI keyboard so that she can display computer software for classroom demonstrations and activities. Because she teaches approximately 500 students per week, the per-pupil cost of the equipment is relatively low. The total cost is approximately $4,000 for the equipment and software. That comes to a student cost of $8.00 ($4,000 divided by 500). This is a relatively small amount of money on a per pupil basis. At that rate the predicted outcomes are a relative bargain.

Evaluation

The last section of the proposal is the overall evaluation. Evaluation is a study unto itself. There are many approaches one can take to educational evaluation. If you have written your objectives in a S.M.A.R.T. manner, the project evaluation will be quite simple, describing how the measures will be completed and by whom is the thrust of this portion.

Once you receive the funding, be sure to find out what is required of you in terms of reporting to the agency or institution that granted the money. Periodic reports are usually required.

Preparing the Budget

Your proposal should include a detailed budget. This includes a complete list of the hardware and software and other related equipment for your project. Be sure to include all materials:

- Computer and other hardware: secure prices from an education distributor

- Music hardware such as the electronic keyboard and MIDI interface

- Music software

- Staff training

Finally, remember one of the most frequently neglected areas, teacher training in technology. To successfully implement your plan, I suggest including at least two to three days of in-service training. Many teachers fail to use technology simply because they don't have the time to learn to use the equipment.

Identify Sources of Funding

If you are in a position to simply request a purchase order for the materials you need, then skip this section. Occasionally, I hear from a music educator who tells me that their district has contacted them and requested a proposal to purchase computer hardware and software for the music department. Sometimes school districts have funds allocated for technology over and above the school music budget. However, more often than not, educational institutions do not have the funds to purchase hardware and software for the music department. If you institution falls into this category, there are some strategies to help find the necessary funding.

School and Community Sources

There are many sources within the school and community that can provide funding sources for technology. Consider the following:

- **Tap the school-wide technology budget.** Find out if there is a district-wide technology budget. For example, contact the technology administrator in your district and ask if you can purchase software and hardware for the music department. If these funds are available, they can often be used without negatively impacting the music department budget.

- **Contact your school library.** Instead of ordering textbooks and periodicals for purchase by the library, ask for software. Once the music software is purchased by the library, you and/or your students can sign out the program for use in the music room.

- **Use the existing music budget.** For example, if you need to purchase an electronic keyboard to be used with an instrumental group or choral ensemble, consider purchasing a MIDI-capable keyboard or MIDI workstation. When it is not being used in rehearsal or performance, it can be connected to a computer for music software applications.

- **Use the music budget to purchase software.** Major publishers and music dealers offer software in their catalogs. Consider using your budget to purchase music software. Once the software is purchased, it can be used year after year.

- **Ask the PTO (Parent-Teacher Organization), band, orchestra, or choral parents group to sponsor technology.** One school district band director shared an interesting story with me. He demonstrated to his band parent association how the computer could be used to manage and track student fund raising accounts.

  The organization purchased a computer that was housed in and utilized by the music department during the week. The band parents used the computer on weekends to manage fund raising records.

- **Contact local service clubs such as Rotary and Optimists.** Often community groups contribute funds to the school system. They are also constantly looking for weekly speakers at their dinner meetings. Volunteer to give a presentation on the benefits of technology in the music curriculum. Perhaps the group will be willing to sponsor or co-sponsor a project to procure technology equipment and/or software for your classroom.

- **Contact businesses and ask if they are replacing their computers and/or printers in the near future.** I know of one school music teacher who contacted a national computer firm that had an office in her community and asked if it was discarding any computers or printers. The company donated its old equipment free of charge! The equipment was not state-of-the-art, but it was powerful enough to run most music software applications. This is a win-win situation because the school receives free equipment and the company gets a tax write-off.

- **Contact music vendors for assistance.** Another way to fund technology is to request lease-purchase terms from a vendor over a specified number of years. This can spread the cost over multiple years making it possible to purchase the necessary equipment.

- **Hold a gala keyboard ensemble benefit concert.** If you have enough keyboards to put together an ensemble, stage a concert to show the community what can be accomplished with electronic instruments. Be sure to invite a member of the press and charge for admission to help fund the development of a complete keyboard lab in your school.

External Funding Sources

If you are not successful in procuring school or community sources to fund your technology goals, consider approaching foundations and/or writing grants for the necessary funds. Beware! Looking for funding via foundations and grants can be a very time consuming process. One Philadelphia school district music teacher successfully received $50,000 from a foundation to create a technology lab in his school. However, the successful grant was written after many, many hours of phone calls, letter writing, and completing the application.

State and Federal Funds

There are pools of funds given to public and private schools by the federal and state governments. In some cases these moneys can be accessed for use by music departments for technology related goals. Most school districts have one person who is in charge of this funding. Find out who this person is and speak to them about your needs. Some funds are pre-determined by the state according to the size and location of the school district. These are called formula funds. The most popular formula funds are:

Title I—Elementary and Secondary Education Act. This emphasizes supplementing what is already done in the district for disadvantaged students. If you teach students in a mainstreamed situation, then a proposal could be written to address specific disadvantaged students' needs.[1] For example:

(1) Instructional music instruction could be used to help students at the low and high ends of the spectrum.
(2) Sequencers could be purchased so that students could compose music using a computer.
(3) A resource area for disadvantaged students could be developed to help them keep pace with other students.

State Compensatory Education Programs: These programs are similar to the Title I funds above, but are controlled by each individual state. Some states offer technology grants to schools. To find out if your state offers any technology programs to which you can apply, contact your department of education.

Another formula fund area is **Title IV,** which is designated to assist private and public schools in purchasing instructional materials and library resources. Music teachers could order materials that are placed in the library and then signed out and used in the music room. Many schools house a computer lab in the library. Title IV funds may be used appropriately to purchase materials in this area. Title IV fund applications are also available from the state department of education.

The critical step is to educate your administrators in the area of music applications and technology. Once they are aware of your needs, they may make funds available for your use from the money they already receive from state and federal sources.

Competitive Funds

There are several sources of competitive funds available to educators. These funds include private foundations and funds sponsored by the United States Office of Education. Many competitive funding sources require a great deal of effort and may not be the best source to fund a relatively small project. Start with your school district administration and ask for assistance.

There are competitive funds from **Title IV C: Improvement in Local Education.** These funds are provided by the federal government and distributed through the state education agency to support practices that improve education in the district. Another area of consideration is **Title II of the Education Amendments of 1978,** designed for basic skills improvement. These grants must be used to try to improve basic skills through the use of technology. Basic skills include reading, mathematics, oral communication, and written communication. Music teachers can address the issues of developing basic oral and written communication through music.

Successfully completing the application is an important task. Read the application carefully! Many applications are turned down simply because the directions were not followed exactly. For example, when federal grant applications are received, the first thing that happens is the pages are counted—regardless of content. All applications that exceed the page limit are automatically rejected, and are never even read. So be extremely careful to read and follow the instructions precisely.

Getting Help

There are companies that will assist you in the proposal writing process. They do this in the hopes that they will get your business should the proposal be funded. Contact the companies listed in Appendix A and ask for assistance in writing a funding proposal. SoundTree, for example, offers a proposal writing service for music educators at www.soundtree.com.

The best place to look for funding sources is to contact your school district administrator in charge of funding. Also, consider contacting a university or large city library and ask them about educational funding sources for technology.

After you successfully identify one or more funding sources, write a letter describing your idea and ask if they are interested in supporting your effort. Be sure to get the permission of your administrator and ask him/her to sign the letter to show you have the necessary support.

Internet Sites for Funding

You can use the Internet to locate educational funding sources. Be prepared to spend some significant time surfing the Internet. The information is out there but it can take some time to find. Information on locations for funding and how to write a successful proposal are available on the web. There are many excellent sites. The grantwriters.com site is an example of an excellent source for information on grants and grant writing.

Figure 17.1: Grant writing help at www.grantwriters.com

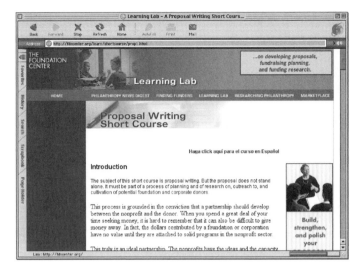

Figure 17.2: Proposal writing short course at:
http://fdncenter.org/learn/shortcourse/prop1.html

Summary

The benefits of trying to fund technology is that most schools are anxious to find ways to integrate technology into the school curriculum. Once administrators know of your interest, demonstrated by a well-written proposal, they may be more receptive to allocating or requesting funds for the music department. The Internet can be used as a resource for locating grant sources and tips for writing successful grant applications.

Review Questions

1. List three benefits of using technology in the music curriculum.
2. What is the first part of most proposals?
3. What is a S.M.A.R.T. objective?
4. What is the purpose of the activities section of the proposal?
5. How is the average cost of the proposal established?
6. What is the last part of a typical proposal?
7. What are the four main areas of the budget?
8. List several school and community sources for funding.
9. What are external funding sources?

10. What funding sources are available through state and federal sources?
11. What are competitive grants?
12. What web sites can be of assistance to educators?

CD-ROM activities

Project 17.1 Develop a proposal for music technology for your school or institution. Modify the proposal on the companion CD-ROM for your purposes.

Project 17.2 Meet with your school administrator in charge of federal funding. Find out what funding the district has applied for over the past five years with regard to technology.

Reference

Bauer, David. (2000). *Technology funding for schools*, Jossey-Bass, New York.

Bonaiuto, Susan. (2003) Proposal writing 101. *Music Education Technology Magazine*. Fall, 2003, Vol. 1 No. 1. Primedia. www.metmagazine.com

Norris, Dennis. (1998) *Get a grant: Yes you can!* Scholastic Professional Books, NY.

Rudolph, Thomas (1999). *Finding funds for music technology*. SoundTree, Melville, NY.

Ward, Deborah (1998). Grant writing do's and don'ts. *Technology and Learning Magazine*.

Appendix A

Publishers and Manufacturers

This appendix lists the companies who offer software, hardware, or services to music educators. These companies and their web sites are also on the companion CD-ROM.

Companies in **bold** offer music technology services, support and sales to music educators.

A

Aabaca, 5750 Shady Oak Rd., Minnetonka, MN 55343 • (952) 933-7307
www.aabaca.com or http://www.musicbarn.com

Ableton, Schönhauser Allee 6-7, D-10119 Berlin, Germany • www.ableton.com

Adobe Systems, Inc., 345 Park Ave., San Jose, CA 95110-2704 • (408) 536-6000
www.adobe.com

AKAI • www.akai.com

Alesis, 200 Scenic View Dr., Cumberland, RI 02864 • (401) 658-5760
www.alesis.com

Alfred Publishing, 16320 Roscoe Blvd. Suite 100, Van Nuys, CA 91406
(818) 891-5999 • www.alfred.com

Ambrosia Software, P.O. Box 23140, Rochester, NY 14692 • (585) 325-1910
www.ambrosiaSW

Apple Computer, 1 Infinite Loop, Cupertino, CA 95014 • (408) 996-1010
www.apple.com

Aquaminds • www.aquaminds.com

Ars Nova, P.O. Box 637, Kirkland, WA 98083 • (800) 445-4866
www.arsnova.com

Arturia, Rue de la Gare 38950, Saint Martin le Vinoux, France
www.arturia.com/en/studio.lasso

Audicity • http://audacity.sourceforge.net
Audio Technica • www.audio-technica.com

B

Bias, 1370 Industrial Ave., Suite A, Petaluma, CA 94952 • (800) 775-2427
www.bias-inc.com

Berklee Press and BerkleeMusic • www.berkleemusic.com

BerkleeShares, 1140 Boylston St., Boston, MA 02215 • (617) 747-2759
www.berkleeshares.com

BitHeadz, 2850 South County Trail, Suite 1, East Greenwich, RI 02818
(401) 886-7045 • www.bitheadz.com

Brook Mays Music Group, 8605 John W. Carpenter Fwy., Dallas, TX 75247
(800) 637-8966 • www.brookmays.com

C

Cakewalk, 51 Melcher St., Boston, MA 02210 • (888) 225-3925
www.cakewalk.com

Carl Fischer, Inc., 65 Bleecker St., New York, NY 10012 • (212) 777-0900
www.carlfischer.com

Casio, Chicago, IL 60601 • (800) 474-0903 or (800) 836-8580 • www.casio.com

CLEARVUE/eav, 6465 North Avondale Ave., Chicago, IL 60631
(800) 253-2788 • www.clearvue.com

D

Dancing Dots, 1754 Quarry Ln., P.O. Box 927, Valley Forge, PA 19482-0927
(610) 783-6692 • www.dancingdots.com

Digidesign, 2001 Junipero Serra Blvd., Daly City, CA 94014-3886
(650) 731-6300 • www.digidesign.com

Disklavier • www.yamahamusicsoft.com/disklavier

E

Edirol Corporation, 425 Sequoia Dr., Suite 114, Bellingham, WA 98226
(360) 594-4273 • www.edirol.com

Electronic Courseware Systems,1713 S. State St., Champaign, IL. 61820
(217) 359-7099 • www.ecsmedia.com

eMagic (a subsidiary of Apple Computer, Inc.) • www.emagic.de

eMedia, 664 NE Northlake Way, Seattle, WA • (888) 363-3424
www.emediamusic.com

F

Fatar • www.musicindustries.com

Focus Enhancements, 1370 Dell Ave., Campbell, CA 95008 • (408) 866-8300
www.focusinfo.com

G

GenieSoft, 113 Sommett Blvd., Summerville, SC 29483 • (843) 832-2365
www.geniesoft.com

Griffin Technology, 1619C Elm Hill Pike, Nashville, TN 37210
(615) 399-7000 • www.griffintechnology.com

GVOX, P.O. Box 2755, Westfield, NJ 07091-2755 • www.gvox.com

H

Hal Leonard Publishing, 7777 W. Bluemound Rd., Milwaukee, WI 53213-3439
(414) 774-3630 • www.halleonard.com

Harmonic Vision, 68 E. Wacker Place, 8th Floor, Chicago, IL 60601
(800) 474-0903 • www.harmonicvision.com

HyperStudio, Sunburst Technology, 1550 Executive Dr., Elgin, IL 60121
(800) 321-7511 • http://www.hyperstudio.com/

I

Intuem Companion Engineering and Design Corp., • www.intuem.com

J

J. D. Wall Publishing Co., P.O. Box 605, Merrick, NY 11566
www.jdwallpublishing.com

J.W. Pepper, PO Box 850, Valley Forge, PA • (800) 345-6296
www.jwpepper.com

K

Kelly's Music & Computers, P.O. Box 658, Pinawa, MB, ROE 1LO
(204) 753-5280 • www.KellysMusicAndComputers.com

Kid PiX, Riverdeep, Inc., 500 Redwood Blvd., Novato, CA 94947
(415) 763-4700 • www.kidpix.com

Korg USA, 316 S. Service Rd., Melville, NY 11747 • (516) 333-8737
www.korg.com

Kurzweil, P.O. Box 99995, Lakewood, WA 98499 • (253) 589-3200
www.kurzweilmusicsystems.com

L

Lemke Software, P.O. Box 6034, 31215 Peine, Germany • www.lemkesoft.de

Lentine's Music, 844 N. Main St., Akron, Ohio • (800) 822-6752
www.lentine.com

M

Mackie Designs, Inc., 16220 Wood-Red Rd. N.E., Woodinville, WA 98072
(800)-258-6883 • www.mackie.com

Macmillan/McGraw-Hill, 420 E. Danieldale Rd.. Desoto, TX 75115
(214) 695-6561 • www.mcgraw-hill.com

MakeMusic!, 6210 Bury Dr., Eden, MN 55346 • (952) 937-9611
www.makemusic.com

Making Music by Morton Subotnik • www.creatingmusic.com

M-Audio, 5795 Martin Rd., Irwindale, CA 91706 • (626) 633-9055
www.m-audio.com

McCormicks Enterprises, Inc., 216 W. Campus Dr., Arlington Heights, IL 60004
(800) 323-5201• www.mccormicksnet.com

MiBAC Music Software, P.O. Box 468, Northfield, MN 55057
(800) 645-3945 • www.mibac.com

Microsoft Inc., • www.microsoft.com

MIDI School House, P.O. Box 525, Greenland, NH 03840-0525
(603) 431 3033 • www.midischoolhouse.com

MIDI Workshop, P.O. Box 1277, 22 Bear Creek Lane, Carson, WA 98610
(509) 427-5655 • www.midiworkshop.com

Moog Music, (828) 251-0090 • http://www.moogmusic.com

MOTU, Mark of the Unicorn, 1280 Massachusetts Ave., Cambridge, MA 02138
(617) 576-2760 • www.motu.com

MusicMatch • www.musicmatch.com

Musitek, 410 Bryant Cir., Suite K, Ojai, CA 93023 • (800) 676-8055
www.musitek.com

Mysheetmusic.com, 1235 Fairview St., Suite 116, Burlington, Ontario
Canada L7S-2K9 • (877) 681-0703 • www.mysheetmusic.com

N

Notation Technologies • www.notationtechnologies.com

P

PGmusic, 266 Elmwood Ave., Suite 111, Buffalo, NY 14222 • (800) 268-6272
www.pgmusic.com

Photoscore, Neuratron Ltd., Lombard House, 12-17 Upper Bridge Street,
Canterbury, Kent CT1 2NF, United Kingdom
http://www.neuratron.com/photoscore.htm

PianoDisc Company, 4111 North Freeway Blvd., Sacramento, CA 95834
(800) 566-3472 • www.pianodisc.com

Pianomouse.com, 4120 Douglas Blvd., #306-224, Granite Bay, CA 95746
(888) 287-3380 • www.pianomouse.com

Propellorheads, Rosenlundsgatan 29c, S-118 63, Stockholm, Sweden
www.propellerheads.se

Pygraphics, P.O. Box 399, Argyle, TX 76226 • (800) 222-7536
www.pyware.com

R

Roland Corp. US, 5100 S. Eastern Ave., Los Angeles, CA 90040-2938
(323) 890-3700 • www.rolandus.com

S

Sharpeye, 21e Balnakeil, Durness Lairg, Sutherland IV27 4PT, Scotland, UK
www.visiv.co.uk/

Shure • www.shure.com

Sibelius, 1407 Oakland Blvd., Suite 103, Walnut Creek, CA 94596
(888) 474-2354 • www.sibelius.com

Silver Burdett/Scott Foresman • (800) 441-1438 • www.sbgmusic.com

SmartBoard, SMART Technologies Inc., Suite 600, 1177 – 11th Ave. SW,
Calgary, AB, CANADA T2R 1K9 • (888) 42-SMART • www.smarttech.com

Sonic Foundry, 222 W. Washington Ave., Suite 775, Madison, WI 53703
(608) 443-1600 • www.sonicfoundry.com

SoundTree, 316 S. Service Rd., Melville, NY 11747 • (800) 963-8733
www.soundtree.com

SoundTrek, 3695 Burnette Park Dr., Suite 3, Suwanee, GA 30024
(770) 831-8515 • www.soundtrek.com

Steinberg Media Technologies, GmbH Neuer, Hoeltigbaum 22-32, 22143
Hamburg, Germany • www.steinberg.net

Stick Enterprises, 6011 Woodlake Ave., Woodland Hills, CA 91367-3238
(818) 884-2001 • www.stick.com

Superscope Technologies, Inc., 2640 White Oak Circle, Aurora, IL 60504
(866) 371-4773 • www.superscopetechnologies.com

Suzuki Musical Instruments Corp., P.O. Box 261030, San Diego, CA 92196
(858) 566-9710 • www.suzukimusic.com

Sweetwater Music/ Technology Direct, 5335 Bass Rd., Fort Wayne, IN 46808
(800) 222-4700 • www.sweetwater.com

T

Tascam • www.tascam.com

W

Warner Bros. Publications, 15800 NW 48th Ave., Hialeah, FL 33014
(305) 521-1688 • www.warnerchappell.com

Wenger Corporation, 555 Park Dr., Owatonna, MN 55060 • (800) 733-0393
www.wengercorp.com

Y

Yamaha Corporation of America, 6600 Orangethorpe Ave.,
Buena Park, CA 90620 • (714) 522-9011 • www.yamaha.com

Yamaha Music in Education • www.musicineducation.com

Z

Zeta Music, 129 S. Rockford Dr., Tempe, AZ 85281 • (800) 622-6434
www.zetamusic.com

Appendix B

Magazines, Periodicals, and Organizations

Electronic Musician Magazine, 6400 Hollis St. #12, Emeryville, CA 94608
(510) 653-3307 • www.electronicmusician.com

Keyboard Magazine, 2800 Campus Dr., San Mateo, CA 94403 • (650) 513-4400
www.keyboardmag.com

Mix Magazine, 6400 Hollis St., #12, Emeryville, CA 94608 • www.mixmag.com

Music Education Technology Magazine , 6400 Hollis St., #12.
Emeryville, CA 94608 • (510) 653-3307 • www.metmagazine.com

Journal of Technology in Music Learning, Kim Walls, Editor, 1211 Brandt Dr.,
Tallahassee, FL 32308-5210
http://www.auburn.edu/outreach/dl/ctmu/jtml/page2.html

Roland Instruments of Change Newsletter/Roland Corporation U.S.
Debra Barbre , 5100 S. Eastern Ave., Los Angeles, CA 90040
www.rolandus.com/community/educator.asp

SoundTree Resource News, 316 S. Service Rd., Melville, NY 11747
(800) 963-8733 • www.soundtree.com

**Technology and Learning Magazine/Technology & Learning Subscription
Department,** P.O. Box 5052, Vandalia OH 45377 • (800) 607-4410
www.techlearning.com

Classroom Connect Newsletter, 8000 Marina Blvd., Suite 400,
Brisbane, CA 94005 • (800) 638-1639
http://corporate.classroom.com/newsletter.html

Music Education and Technology Organizations

ATMI: Association for Technology in Music Instruction • http://atmi.music.org

TDML: Technology Directions in Music Learning, David Sebald, The Division of Music, UTSA, 6900 N. Loop 1604 West, San Antonio, TX 78249 (210) 458-4355 • http://music.utsa.edu/tdml

TI-ME: Technology Institute for Music Educators, 305 Maple Ave. Wyncote, PA 19095 • (617) 747-2816 • www.ti-me.org

State Music Technology Organizations

CMEA California Music Educators Association Music and Technology Organization, Dr. Hal Peterson, Leland High School, 6677 Camden Ave., San Jose, CA 95120 • www.cmeabaysection.org/technology.html

META Music Education Technologist Association (serving Connecticut Music Educators) Walter Mamlok, 145 Strickland St., Glastonbury, CT 06033 • wmamlok@snet.net

Michigan Music Tech, Barton Polot, Editor, Michigan School Band & Orchestra Association, 2005 Baits Dr., Suite 104 Ann Arbor, MI 48109-2993 • (734) 764-8242 http://www.msboa.org/musictech/

Technology and Education Organizations

ISTE International Society for Technology in Education, 1710 Rhode Island Ave. NW, Suite 900, Washington, DC 20036 • (800) 336-5191 www.iste.org

ITEA International Technology Education Association, 1914 Association Dr., Suite 201, Reston, VA 20191 • (703) 860-2100 www.iteawww.org

George Lucus Educational Foundation, P.O. Box 3494, San Rafael, CA 94912 (415) 507-0399 • www.glef.org

Music Education Organizations

American Orff-Schulwerk Association, P.O. Box 391089, Cleveland, OH 44139-8089 • (440) 543-5366 • www.aosa.org

International Association of Jazz Educators, P.O. Box 724, Manhattan, KS 66502 www.iaje.org

International Society for Music Education, ISME International Office
P.O. Box 909, Nedlands 6909, WA • www.isme.org

MENC The National Association for Music Education National Conference
1902 Association Dr., Reston, VA 22091 • (800) 336-3768
www.menc.org

MTNA Music Teachers National Association, 441 Vine St., Ste. 505,
Cincinnati, OH 45202-2811 • (513) 421-1420 • www.mtna.org

Organization of American Kodaly Educators, 1612 - 29th, Ave. South,
Moorhead, MN 56560 • (218) 227-6253 • www.oake.org

Notes

Chapter 1

1. Dunn R. Learning—a matter of style. *Educational Leadership.* 1979; 36(6):430-432.
2. Gershenfeld Neil. *When Things Start to Think.* New York, NY: Henry Holt & Co Inc; 1999:43.
3. *A Nation at Risk.* archived at:
   http://www.ed.gov/pubs/NatAtRisk/risk.html
4. *National Standards for Arts Education.* Reston, VA: MENC The National Association for Music Education; 1994.
5. Facts About Technology Users. *New Ways in Music Education.* Grand Rapids, MI: Yamaha Corporation of America; Spring, 1994.
6. Nemiroff J. *Integrating computers into a reading readiness curriculum for preschoolers through teacher training and computer-based instruction.* ERIC Document Reproduction Service; 1988, ED 295 593 .
7. *National Standards for Arts Education.* Reston, VA: MENC The National Association for Music Education; 1994.
8. *National Standards for Arts Education.* Reston, VA: MENC The National Association for Music Education; 1994.
9. Rudolph TJ, Richmond F, Mash D, Williams D. *Technology Strategies for Music Education.* 2nd ed. Milwaukee, WI: Hal Leonard Publishing Co; 2002.
10. Chamberlin, et al. Success with keyboards in middle school. *Music Educators Journal.* May 1993;31-35.
11. Moore B. Technology—a resource providing new ways for music educators. *New Ways in Music Education.* Grand Rapids, MI: Yamaha Corporation of America; Fall, 1991.
12. Idea Bank. Does CAI really work? *Music Educators Journal.* December 1986.

13. Taylor R, ed. *The Computer in the School: Tutor, Tool, Tutee.* New York, NY: Teachers College Press; 1980.

14. Papert. Teaching children to think. In: Taylor R, ed. *The Computer in the School: Tutor, Tool, Tutee.* New York, NY: Teachers College Press; 1980;161.

15. Raessler K. *Aspiring to Excel.* Chicago, IL: GIA Publications Inc; 2003.

16. Rudolph TJ, Richmond F, Mash D, Williams D. *Technology Strategies for Music Education.* Milwaukee, WI: Hal Leonard Publishing Co; 1999:2.

17. Rudolph TJ, Richmond F, Mash D, Williams D. *Technology Strategies for Music Education.* Milwaukee, WI: Hal Leonard Publishing Co; 1999.

18: *National Standards for Arts Education.* Reston, VA: MENC The National Association for Music Education; 1994.

19. Webster P; Colwell R, Richardson C, eds. *The New Handbook of Research on Music Teaching and Learning.* New York, NY: Oxford University Press; 2002. (Taken from Computer-Based Technology and Music Teaching and Learning).

20. Argersinger C. Side-Effects of technology on music and musicians. *Jazz Educators Journal.* October 1993.

Chapter 2

1. Kongshem L. The executive educator's complete guide to the internet. *The Executive Educator.* April 1994;55-70.

2. Lichty T. *America Online for Macintosh: Membership Kit & Tour Guide.* 2nd ed. Chapel Hill, NC: Ventana Press Inc; 1994.

3. Griswold HE. Multiculturalism, music and the information highways. *Music Educators Journal.* November 1994;41-46.

Chapter 4

1. Idea Bank. Does CAI really work. *Music Educators Journal.* December 1986.

2. Moore B. Technology—a resource providing new ways for music educators. *New Ways in Music Education.* Grand Rapids, MI: Yamaha Corporation of America; Fall, 1991.

3. Appell CJ. Keyboard instruction in the music classroom. *Music Educators Journal.* May 1993;21-24.

4. Appell CJ. Keyboard instruction in the music classroom. *Music Educators Journal.* May 1993;21-24.

5. Wiggins J. Elementary music with synthesizers. *Music Educators Journal.* May 1993;25-30.

6. Wiggins J. Synthesizers in the elementary classroom. *MENC The National Association for Music Education.* Reston, VA: 1991.

7. Feldstein S, Cavalier D. *Keyboards in General Music.* Miami, FL: CPP/Belwin Inc.; 1991.

8. Muro D. *An Overview of Electronic Musical Instruments* [videotape]. Merreck, NY: JD Wall Publishing; 1991.

Chapter 5

1. Purse L, Rudolph TJ. *TI:ME 2A Electronic Instruments: Teacher's Guide.* TI-ME: Technology Institute for Music Educators, 305 Maple Avenue, Wyncote, PA 19095
(www.ti-me.org); 2000.

2. Purse L, Rudolph TJ. *TI:ME 2A Electronic Instruments: Teacher's Guide.* TI-ME: Technology Institute for Music Educators, 305 Maple Avenue, Wyncote, PA 19095
(www.ti-me.org); 2000.

3. Lehrman PD. NAMM Bits. *Mix Magazine.* California, PRIMEDIA Business Corp. May 2001. Available online at:
http://mixonline.com/ar/audio_namm_bits.

4. Mauricio D. Synth ensembles: a new source of energy for music performance. *Sound Tree Educational News*, 2000; Vol 7, Is 1.
Available online at:
http://hhs.suhsd.k12.ca.us/~musictech/pages/musictechensemble.html#star tinganensemblen.

5. Reuter R. The 21st century educational ensemble. *The TI:MES*, Fall, 2002. Wyncote, PA. Technology Institute for Music Educators.

6. Mauricio D. Synth ensembles: a new source of energy for music performance. *Sound Tree Educational News*, 2000; Vol 7, Is 1.
Available online at:
http://hhs.suhsd.k12.ca.us/~musictech/pages/musictechensemble.html#star tinganensemblen.

7. Purse L. Creating an Electronic Keyboard Ensemble. *Roland Keyboard Educator.* Spring/Summer, 1991.

Chapter 6

1. Taylor R, ed. *The Computer in the School: Tutor, Tool, Tutee.* New York, NY: Teachers College Press; 1980:3

2. Peters GD. Music software and emerging technology. *Music Educators Journal.* November 1992;22-25.

3. Peters GD. Music software and emerging technology. *Music Educators Journal*. November 1992;22-25.

4. Murphy B, ed. *Technology Directory*. Association for Technology in Music Instruction; 2002. http://www.music.org/atmi/Directory/Directory2002.html.

5. Brandon M, Pursell-Engler P. *A Guide for Using Software in the Music Classroom*. Flagstaff, AZ: PM Music; 1992.

Chapter 7

1. Nequist HP. *Music & Technology*. New York, NY: Billboard Books; 1989:12.

2. Ely MC. Software for classroom music making. *Music Educators Journal*. April 1993;41-43.

3. Litterst G. (1993). The EM guide to notation software. *Electronic Musician*. August 1993;31-46.

4. Kuzmich J. Music reading software--tomorrow's software today. *School Band and Orchestra Magazine*. November 2000.

5. Litterst G. (1993). The EM guide to notation software. *Electronic Musician*. August 1993;31-46.

6. Powell S. *Music Engraving Today*. New York, NY: Britchmark Music; 2002:198.

Chapter 8

1. Muro D. *The Art of Sequencing*. Miami, FL: CPP/Belwin Inc; 1993.

2. Deutsch H. *Synthesis: An Introduction to the History, Theory & Practice of Electronic Music*. Van Nuys, CA: Alfred Publishing; 1985.

3. Taylor R, ed. *The Computer in the School: Tutor, Tool, Tutee*. New York, NY: Teachers College Press; 1980.

Chapter 9

1. Hickey M, ed. Why and how to teach music composition. MENC *The National Association for Music Education*. Reston, VA; 2003.

2. Bonaiuto S, et al. Grant Application to United States Department of Education, Office of Innovation and Improvement--FY03 Arts in Education Model Development and Dissemination Grant Program. *Improved Student Achievement through Multimedia Teaching and Learning*. Wyncote, PA: TI:ME, 2003

Chapter 10

1. Murphy B, ed. *Technology Directory.* Association for Technology in Music Instruction; 2002.
   http://www.music.org/atmi/Directory/Directory2002.html.
2. Souvignier, Todd (2003). *Loops and grooves: The musician's guide to groove machines and loop sequencers.* Hal Leonard, Milwaukee. Page 1.
3. *National Standards for Arts Education.* Reston, VA: MENC The National Association for Music Education; 1994.

Chapter 11

1. Knorr E, ed. *The PC Bible.* 2nd ed. Peachpit Press: 1995. 2. Mash DS. *Musicians and Multimedia..* Miami, FL: Warner Bros Publications: 1998.
3. Williams D, Webster P. *Experiencing Music Technology.* 2nd ed. New York, NY: Schirmer Books: 1999:501.
4. Robinette M. *Mac Multimedia For Teachers.* Foster City, CA: IDG Books Worldwide; 1995:16.
5. Fenton K. Using multimedia to develop musicianship. *Music Educators Journal.* September 1998;27-32.
6. Robinette M. *Mac Multimedia For Teachers.* Foster City, CA: IDG Books Worldwide; 1995.
7. Williams B. *The Internet for Teachers.* 2nd ed. IDG Books; 3rd edition (July 14, 1999). pgs. 234-235.
8. Waggoner J. Creating a web presence. *School Band and Orchestra Magazine.* November 2001;13.

Chapter 12

1. Dunn R. Learning--a matter of style. *Educational Leadership.* 1979;36(6):430-432.
2. *National Standards for Arts Education.* Reston, VA: MENC The National Association for Music Education; 1994.
3. Booty C. *Tips: Technology.* Reston, VA: MENC The National Association for Music Education; 1994.
4. Muro D. Music workstation applications for the classroom. *Sound Tree Educational News.* 1995; Vol. 2, Is 1.
5. Mauricio D, Adams S. *Fundamentals of Music Technology.* Agoura, CA: Consultant Help Software; 1994.
6. Rudolph T. *The Sound Tree General Music Curriculum.* Westbury, NY: Sound Tree; 1995.
7. Purse L. Creating an electronic keyboard ensemble. *Roland Keyboard Educator.* Spring/Summer 1991.

8. Purse L. Creating an electronic keyboard ensemble. *Roland Keyboard Educator*. Spring/Summer 1991.
9. Mash D. *Computers and the Music Educator*. California: Digidesign; 1991.

Chapter 15

1. Raessler K. *Aspiring to Excel*. Chicago, IL: GIA Publications Inc; 2003.
2. Mash D. *Computers and the Music Educator*. California: Digidesign; 1991.
3. *National Standards for Arts Education*. Reston, VA: MENC The National Association for Music Education; 1994.
4. Williams D, ed. *Opportunity-to-Learn Standards for Music Technology*. Reston, VA: MENC The National Association for Music Education; 1999.

Chapter 16

1. Althouse J. *Copyright: The Complete Guide for Music Educators*. 2nd ed. Van Nuys, CA: Alfred Publishing; 1990.
2. Althouse J. *Copyright: The Complete Guide for Music Educators*. 2nd ed. Van Nuys, CA: Alfred Publishing; 1990.
3. Althouse J. *Copyright: The Complete Guide for Music Educators*. 2nd ed. Van Nuys, CA: Alfred Publishing; 1990.
4. Woo J. Publisher sues CompuServ over a song. *The Wall Street Journal*. December 16, 1993;B16.
5. Tomsho R. As sampling revolutionizes recording, debate grows over aesthetics, copyrights. *The Wall Street Journal*. November 19, 1990;B3.

Index

About the Author

Dr. Tom Rudolph is the Director of Music and middle school music instructor for Haverford Township School District, in Havertown, Pennsylvania. He is an adjunct Assistant Professor at The University of the Arts. Dr. Rudolph has authored seven books on music technology and his articles have appeared in the *Music Educators Journal*, *The Instrumentalist*, *Jazz Educator Journal* and *Music Education Technology* magazine. He was one of the founders of the Technology Institute for Music Educators (TI:ME) and currently serves as President of the organization. Rudolph has taught workshops in music technology at 17 institutions of higher learning and has trained over 3,500 music educators in his acclaimed workshops. He presented the music technology keynote address for Massachusetts State Conference in 1999, the MENC/TI:ME National Conference in 2002, and the Missouri State Conference in 2003.